THE
SHIELD
OF SILENCE

THE
SHIELD
OF SILENCE

HOW POWER PERPETUATES A CULTURE OF HARASSMENT AND BULLYING IN THE WORKPLACE

LAUREN STILLER RIKLEEN

ANKERWYCKE

Printed in the United States of America.

23 22 21 20 19   5 4 3 2 1

ISBN: 978-1-64105-407-2

Library of Congress Cataloging-in-Publication Data
Names: Rikleen, Lauren Stiller, author.
Title: The shield of silence : how power perpetuates a culture of harassment
    and bullying in the workplace / Lauren Stiller Rikleen.
Description: Chicago, Illinois : American Bar Association, [2019] | Includes
    index.
Identifiers: LCCN 2019006069 (print) | LCCN 2019008807 (ebook) | ISBN
    9781641054089 (epub) | ISBN 9781641054072 (hardcover)
Subjects: LCSH: Sexual harassment—United States. | Sexual harassment—Law
    and legislation—United States. | Bullying in the workplace—United States. |
    Discrimination in employment—United States.
Classification: LCC HD6060.5.U5 (ebook) | LCC HD6060.5.U5 R55 2019 (print) |
    DDC 302.3/5—dc23
LC record available at https://lccn.loc.gov/2019006069

Discounts are available for books ordered in bulk. Special consideration is given to state bars, CLE programs, and other bar-related organizations. Inquire at Book Publishing, ABA Publishing, American Bar Association, 321 N. Clark Street, Chicago, Illinois 60654-7598.

www.shopABA.org

This book is dedicated to those who, for far too long, have suffered in silence because they rightfully feared their reports of misconduct would not be believed or acted upon. I hope this book will contribute to a change in workplace culture, shifting power away from perpetrators and encouraging those who have experienced or witnessed workplace misconduct to end their silence.

Contents

Acknowledgments

This book has its roots in a study that was sponsored by the Women's Bar Association of Massachusetts (WBA). In early 2018, I had the special opportunity to be retained by the WBA to assist with a project to analyze the prevalence of harassment and other negative behaviors in Massachusetts law firms. The survey included a series of questions to determine whether the respondents had experienced certain behaviors. For each question answered affirmatively, the respondent was asked whether the incident had been reported. Those who did not report the behavior were asked why. The survey also provided an opportunity for the respondents to provide anecdotes.

In both analyzing the responses and writing the report, I was struck by the silence. For every question, the majority of the incidents went unreported. Yet so many of the anecdotes that were shared were haunting, demonstrating an overwhelming fear of retribution for speaking up, and a failure in so many of the firms to have an appropriate process in place to ensure misconduct could be reported without retaliation. Many of the respondents stated that the perpetrator was a senior person at the firm and the one to whom a report would have to be made.

Once the report for the WBA was completed, I continued to research other examples of workplace sexual harassment and misconduct, as well as the underlying reasons for silence in the face of such negative behaviors. Social science research provided a range of fascinating studies that helped shed light not only on the potential causes of the negative behaviors, but also on ways to bring about change. I also spoke with scores of individuals who shared stories about their own difficult experiences.

This book is an effort to bring together the research, the conversations, and proposed strategies for change in a way that is designed to be accessible and helpful to anyone who is committed to creating a safe, respectful, and inclusive workplace culture. Cultural change is required if we are ever to create the conditions that will end the misconduct as well as the silence.

I am grateful to the Women's Bar Association of Massachusetts for the opportunity to work with them on their groundbreaking survey, and for the support they have given me since. A special thanks is owed to the WBA president, and now friend, Meredith Ainbinder, and to the WBA's indomitable executive director, Margaret Talmers. Thanks, also, to the co-chairs of the WBA Law Firm Advancement Committee, who dedicated their time to ensuring this project's success: Jody Newman, Sarah Gagan, and Heather Gamache. Finally, a special thank you to the two initial cheerleaders for this project who helped move it forward from the days when it was an unstructured idea: former WBA president, Michele Liu Baillie, and the former WBA executive director, Pattye Comfort.

Two talented Boston College students supportive of this book helped obtain background research and provided a major assist with putting the endnotes into proper citation format—Sarah Mandelblatt and Meg Dolan. They are wonderful examples of BC women who will no doubt make a difference in the world. I am truly grateful for their help and their commitment to this project.

As the manuscript neared completion, I asked two people to review a draft and provide edits and comments. Both were extraordinarily helpful and I am so appreciative of their time. Mel Stiller went above and beyond the responsibilities of being my typically wonderful big brother by spending so much time and careful attention to detail. His edits were incredibly helpful. Rebecca Pontikes lent her skills as a lawyer specializing in this field to review the manuscript and made a number of thoughtful suggestions. I am grateful for her time and assistance.

I am also grateful to the publishing folks at the American Bar Association for their commitment to this book and their belief in its importance. A special thank you to Bryan Kay for going above and beyond, as well as to the editor, John Palmer, for his support.

Every project of mine bears the incredibly helpful fingerprints of my husband, Sander, whose support is far from abstract. His brilliant eye for detail provides the polish to all of my writing projects and his legendary flexibility has been the backbone of our family.

I am grateful as well to our children, Alex and Ilyse, for their special role in our lives, and feel so fortunate to now have in the family their respective spouses, Leslie and Sam. We are all fortunate for the legacy of love and support that has been passed down from my parents, Elaine and Joe Stiller, and Sander's parents, Rebecca and Alexander Rikleen.

Being part of a loving extended family makes the process of writing a book—and everything else—much easier. My thanks and love to each of you.

Learning to Be Quiet

Our Lips Are Sealed—Because They Must

Workplace culture dominates the lives of employees each day, setting the tone for how people treat one another. For those who work in difficult cultures, there is the hope that a seismic event will someday improve the workplace in a meaningful way.

When such a major event occurs, we seize on it for an indication that this time things will be different. Our hopes move us forward, betraying past lessons that continually remind us of the slow pace of progress, particularly when the possible change threatens a shift in existing power dynamics.

Certainly it was a seismic event when the *New York Times* and the *New Yorker* first published their allegations of sexual harassment and rape against Harvey Weinstein in October of 2017. In the months that followed this unmasking of one of Hollywood's most powerful men, allegations against other high-profile figures dominated the news and unleashed a torrent of questions, demands, accusations, debate, anger, sorrow, recriminations, and, in too many workplaces, continued silence.

There has hardly been an industry, business, professional services firm, or nonprofit sector untouched by the #MeToo movement that was reignited following those news stories. And, yes, it is important to emphasize that the movement was *reignited*, since it was founded by activist Tarana Burke. Burke launched MeToo in 2006 to help underprivileged women of color cope with sexual abuse, assault, and exploitation, connecting survivors to resources that can aid their healing, including through the power of knowing they are not alone.

As will be further described, harassment and other negative behaviors in the workplace are pervasive problems. The data points may vary somewhat, but they all basically tell a similar story of misconduct met with silence.

An ABC News/Washington Post poll revealed that 54 percent of American women have experienced unwanted and inappropriate sexual advances from men. Nearly a third reported unwanted advances from male coworkers and 25 percent stated it was from men who had influence over their work situation. Critically, only 42 percent of the women who experienced unwanted sexual advances at work reported the conduct to someone in a supervisory position, and 95 percent reported that male harassers usually go unpunished. In describing the emotional toll caused by the harassment, the respondents described feelings of anger, intimidation, humiliation, and shame.[1]

A survey conducted by Harris Poll on behalf of the nonprofit organization CARE (Cooperative for Assistance and Relief Everywhere) found that nearly 25 percent of men in eight countries—including the United States—said that it is sometimes or always acceptable for an employer to expect an employee to have "intimate interactions such as sex with them, a family member or a friend."[2]

For those hoping that the demographics of a younger population entering the workplace would bring about significant change, the results were sobering. In the United States, 44 percent of the male respondents between the ages of eighteen and thirty-four stated that it is sometimes or always acceptable to tell a sexual joke at work. In the United Kingdom, 35 percent of those between the ages of twenty-five and thirty-four thought it is sometimes or always acceptable "to pinch a colleague's bottom in jest."[3]

In another survey of men and women in businesses and law firms conducted by the *ABA Journal* and *Working Mother*, 68 percent of the female respondents indicated they experienced sexual harassment at work, but only 30 percent reported the behavior; 52 percent said the reason they did not report was because they feared negative impacts to their jobs. Only 27 percent said their complaints were taken seriously. For male respondents, the experiences were different. Of the 19 percent who reported they had experienced sexual harassment, 42 percent said they felt their complaints were taken seriously. The survey also showed how men and women see the workplace differently: "47 percent of the women said the behavior was tolerated in their organization (versus 30 percent of the men); and 45 percent of the women said they had no confidence their senior leadership would address the issue (versus 24 percent of the men)."[4]

Concerned about the continued high rates of harassment claims, the Equal Opportunity Employment Commission (EEOC) created the Task Force on the Study of Harassment in the Workplace to address the following:

> With legal liability long ago established, with reputational harm from harassment well known, with an entire cottage industry of workplace compliance and training adopted and encouraged for 30 years, why does so much harassment persist and take place in so many of our workplaces? And, most important of all, what can be done to prevent it? After 30 years—is there something we've been missing?[5]

To better understand the answer to these questions, the EEOC Task Force spent eighteen months undertaking an in-depth investigation that included nationwide hearings to collect testimony about people's workplace experiences, releasing its report in 2016.

Intriguingly, the EEOC Task Force found that as wide a range as 25 to 85 percent of women in various studies reported experiencing sexual harassment at work. In analyzing why there was such a wide variance in reported results, the EEOC identified that responses varied according to the survey methodology as well as the way in which the questions were phrased.

In particular, the Task Force found that when respondents were asked whether they experienced certain specific behaviors, the results were significantly higher than when respondents were asked a more general question of whether they had experienced sexual harassment: "Based on this consistent result, researchers have concluded that many individuals do not label certain forms of unwelcome sexually based behaviors—even if they view them as problematic or offensive—as 'sexual harassment.'"[6]

Another way to think about this data is that it provides victims with a way to rationalize their experiences—and their silence. After all, if it is not thought of as actual sexual harassment, then perhaps it's not so bad.

In a *Harvard Business Review* article about workplace sexual harassment, the authors offered several reasons why victims stay silent:

> *They wait to see whether the behavior will stop on its own, or they keep silent because they fear that reporting will be futile or that the harasser will retaliate. Rather than filing internal or external complaints, harassment targets tend to resort to informal and nonconfrontational remedies. They vent, cope, laugh it off, treat it as some kind of less threatening misunderstanding, or simply try to get on with their jobs (and lives). They may blame themselves, pretend it is not happening, or fall into self-destructive behaviors like eating disorders or drinking problems.*[7]

It has become evident that in addressing workplace misconduct, the focus must be broader than the commonly used, but more restrictive, term *sexual harassment*. The importance of using this broader lens is seen in many of the studies that will be described in subsequent chapters, as well as the important work of the EEOC Task Force.

The simple fact is that sexual harassment and other negative behaviors in the workplace will never be eliminated without first changing the circumstances that drive victims into silence—the overriding fear that reporting misconduct will risk their livelihood or result in their being ostracized in the workplace. As long as the organization's culture continues to reinforce a victim's fear of retaliation, the power dynamics will leave perpetrators confident that the system will shield their behavior.

Workplace cultures tolerant of misconduct impose enormous hardship on victims who try to survive the minefield. A group of scientists described the burden of coping with harassment as including:

> . . . reactions ranging from appeasing the harasser and minimizing the incidents, seeking social support from friends and family, professional therapy, strategizing on future responses, engaging in activities to improve mental and physical health, and simply trying to stay focused on the work. However, it does not typically include actually reporting the harassment to authorities.[8]

The silence is reinforced by another sad fact. Even when behaviors are reported, as will be explored in depth in this book, there is rarely a satisfactory result for the victim. The reasons are varied but exist across all work sectors. One young law student described her circumstances while working as a summer associate in a law firm:

> My mentor took me out for drinks and asked very invasive questions about my sex life. I reported this to my advisor and to the coordinator in charge of the summer associate program. It doesn't seem like anything happened and he remained my mentor for the rest of the summer.

Moreover, as will be described further, existing workplace structures and dynamics inherently thwart the very result that many policies claim to promote. For example, such structural impediments as the failure to hold people accountable are at the core of the historical inability of workplaces to eliminate harassment.

These deeply entrenched dynamics serve as a protective shield around perpetrators of negative behaviors. They also serve as a barrier that prevents victims from accessing the system that is supposed to protect them. As a group of leading academics noted:

> Existing structures that claim to address sexual harassment are inadequate and are built to protect institutions, not designed to bring justice to victims.[9]

Life Lessons in Silence as a Choice

It is not only the structures and norms within the workplace that protect those accused of misconduct. When ostensibly respectable people—particularly those in positions of power and privilege—are accused of behaviors that seem out of character, the instinct of their colleagues and advocates is often to protect and defend.

This dynamic was displayed in full force during the contentious nominations of Clarence Thomas in 1991 and Brett Kavanaugh in 2018 to the U.S. Supreme Court. More than a quarter of a century after his controversial appointment, *Boston Globe* columnist Margery Eagan questioned how Clarence Thomas has remained a justice of the U.S. Supreme Court, as the number of women who have come forward with allegations similar to Anita Hill's has grown to ten. Eagan wrote that four of these women were willing to testify when Anita Hill appeared before the Judiciary Committee, but they were not called. Another incident was reported by a young woman who stated he groped her after he began serving on the court.

In noting the research that has been done since Anita Hill first raised her concerns, Eagan questioned why no further action has been taken to impeach Justice Thomas over credible allegations that he lied to Congress. She stated that his role provides him with significant power over women's lives, as such matters come before the court:

> Here's a sampling of Thomas's votes impacting women. He voted to weaken women's pay protections . . . He voted to make it harder for a dining service worker—a woman and the department's only African-American—to sue a supervisor for racial and physical harassment. He voted to uphold a for-profit company's religious freedom over women's access to contraceptive coverage. . . .
>
> Twenty-seven years ago Anita Hill said Clarence Thomas spoke to her repeatedly about big breasts, kinky sex, his own prowess, and more. . . . Yet Thomas remains empowered to rule on the most intimate parts of your life, your sister's, daughter's, even granddaughter's.[10]

Eagan wrote this article approximately two months before Brett Kavanaugh was introduced to the world as a Supreme Court nominee. History, as well as the revelation of decades of silence, was soon repeated.

When Federal Circuit Court of Appeals Judge Kavanaugh was nominated to fill the open seat resulting from Justice Kennedy's retirement, Senate leadership set in motion an aggressive time frame for the review process and Judiciary Committee hearing. Shortly before the Judiciary Committee was to vote on sending the nomination to the floor of the Senate, an allegation emerged that, while he was a student at an elite private high school in Maryland, the nominee sexually assaulted fifteen-year-old Christine Blasey Ford at a party.

Dr. Ford had sent a confidential letter to Senator Dianne Feinstein, shortly after the nomination was announced, in which she shared information about her high school experience. Senator Feinstein did not publicly reveal the confidential information sent to her, but the story became the subject of a *Washington Post* article two months later, after the Judiciary Committee hearing on the nomination was concluded.

The public revelation of Dr. Ford's allegation resulted in explosive media attention and a concern about Judge Kavanaugh's fitness to serve on the highest court in the country. Amid this firestorm, people who knew the Supreme Court nominee during high school and others who attended Yale with him were coming forward, describing Brett Kavanaugh as a person who drank heavily and frequently. Other women alleged knowledge of incidents that raised further questions. Mark Judge, a high school classmate of Brett Kavanaugh, was identified by Dr. Ford as being in the room when she was assaulted. Mark Judge had previously authored a book about his battle with alcoholism that included discussion of his heavy drinking in high school and the school's social culture.[11]

In response to the significant public outcry, the House Judiciary Committee reopened its public hearing on the nomination, but only permitted testimony from Dr. Ford and Judge Kavanaugh. None of the others who had come forward or were otherwise identified as having key information were allowed to testify.

The all-male Republican members of the Judiciary Committee hired a female prosecutor from Arizona to ask their questions. By doing so, they hoped to avoid the scathing criticism endured by the then all-male Judiciary Committee when Anita Hill was interrogated about her sexual harassment allegations against nominee Clarence Thomas. Twenty-seven years after that hearing, there were still no Republican women serving on the Committee.[12]

The Judiciary Committee hearing and its aftermath painfully reinforced why Dr. Ford had chosen to keep her story secret for so long. Ford told her story quietly and carefully, answering each question posed by the prosecutor. Even as she could not remember extraneous details, she had a recall for the assault that any survivor would recognize. She described the pain of hearing the laughter of Brett Kavanaugh and Mark Judge while the assault was taking place and the fear of accidentally being murdered as a hand was placed over her mouth to keep her from screaming. She also recalled how she escaped from the room.

As victims of trauma well know, the fact that Dr. Ford could not recall the street address thirty-six years later or how she got home was irrelevant. It was the attack itself that was seared into her memory.

Judge Kavanaugh's testimony was fused with indignation. Beyond the anger he expressed for having to endure such public accusations, his testimony also demonstrated entitlement and belligerence toward some of the questioners. When asked about parties and drinking while attending prep school and college, he instead spoke about how hard he worked to get good grades and of his commitment to his athletics and his friends, avoiding direct questions about his drinking other than to stress that he liked beer.

When the female senators questioned Judge Kavanaugh, he responded dismissively, sometimes turning the questions back to them. When the prosecutor began asking Judge Kavanaugh questions on behalf of the male Republican senators, the senators instead dispensed with her role, as they actively joined the judge in his outrage. And in their angry defense of the judge against the accusations, the country was provided with insight into the way in which institutions weave protective webs to fend off potential smears on their image.

Dr. Ford's credible testimony was not simply dismissed. It was overrun by a freight train of power and privilege that crushed any weakness, whether in her telling of the assault or the circumstances in which her story was leaked to the media.

The hearing served to reinforce why victims of sexual assault have long endured silence over reporting: women do not tell their stories because they can't. Silence has long been the fuel that perpetuates bad conduct, but reporting that conduct has been weaponized against the victim in the form of character assassination, shaming, and disbelief.

During and in the aftermath of the hearing, nationwide protests, including in the Capitol, raised questions about the need for further investigation of other witnesses. Although the leadership of the Judiciary Committee was anxious to push the vote forward, a compromise was forged to allow a limited-scope FBI investigation.

The FBI, however, did not interview all of the potential witnesses who had come forward or were otherwise identified as having knowledge of Kavanaugh's behaviors in high school and college. Instead, the FBI only spoke with a small number of witnesses, as approved by the White House.

As the truncated investigation was taking place, President Trump aggressively mocked Dr. Ford's testimony at a campaign rally. He demeaned her experience and complained that men were being negatively impacted by the #MeToo movement.

A few days later, the Senate voted to confirm Judge Kavanaugh as an Associate Justice of the U.S. Supreme Court.

Professors Deborah Epstein and Lisa Goodman have described "how routinely women survivors face a Gaslight-style gauntlet of doubt, disbelief, and outright dismissal of their stories."[13] The data shows a pattern of disbelieving women victims in the justice system, revealing how courts both improperly and unfairly discount women's testimony and their trustworthiness. In an article describing the harms caused by a "pervasive pattern of credibility discounting and experiential dismissal," the scholars provided scientific theory that foreshadowed what was observed throughout the Brett Kavanaugh hearing and its aftermath:

> *First, the discrediting of survivors constitutes its own psychic injury—an institutional betrayal that echoes the psychological abuse women suffer at the hands of individual perpetrators. Second, the pronounced, nearly instinctive penchant for devaluing women's testimony is so deeply embedded within survivors' experience that it becomes a potent, independent obstacle to their efforts to obtain safety and justice.*
>
> *The reflexive discounting of women's stories of domestic violence finds analogs among the kindred diminutions and dismissals that harm so many other women who resist the abusive exercise of male power, from survivors of workplace harassment to victims of sexual assault on and off campus. For these women, too, credibility discounts both deepen the harm they experience and create yet another impediment to healing and justice.*[14]

In 2015, then Federal Circuit Court of Appeals Judge Kavanaugh began a speech by observing: "What happens at Georgetown Prep, stays at Georgetown Prep. That's been a good thing for all of us, I think." Certainly for Brett Kavanaugh, the shield of protection that began at an elite prep school continued through his Ivy League education and beyond. It is a shield of protection that has long stood the test of time.

Allegations of sexual assault, harassment, and other misconduct are in no way confined to those in positions of privilege. As this book makes clear, it is an endemic result of a culture that devalues women, leaders who do not place a priority on respect and inclusion, and entrenched biases that bloom within structures and processes that fail to support systems to challenge those biases.

The Deflective Shield of Alcohol

In so many stories that victims share about their workplace experiences, alcohol plays a starring role. It remains, therefore, surprising the extent to which the serving of unlimited alcohol at business events remains embedded in workplace culture.

A young lawyer described an incident that arose as a result of alcohol-fueled behavior. She felt that reporting was not a safe option at this early stage of her career, but she at least made the effort to document the behavior for her own records:

> Male partner got drunk at a holiday party for clients and put his hands on my back and legs in an inappropriate and unwanted way. . . . I did make a contemporaneous written record of it.

This was but one of many comments in the Women's Bar Association of Massachusetts survey describing misconduct at a work-related social event where people were drinking. Similar examples were also provided by many of the women interviewed for this book and appear in other survey data.

Yet executives can be resistant to any change that would upend the expectations people have for the easy flow of alcohol during work social events. In a conversation with a senior-level executive about limiting the amount of alcohol that could be freely available at work events, the answer was a swift dismissal:

> There would be no possibility that you could tell our [senior leaders] that alcohol was being limited at our events.

It's Not About the Sex and It's Not Always Illegal

There are a wide range of behaviors that can be destructive to workplace engagement and morale without crossing the line into illegal sexual harassment. As subsequent chapters will describe, most workplace harassment has little to do with sex. Often, harassment emerges in such nonsexual forms as demeaning behaviors, hostility, exclusion or other forms of social ostracism at work, physical assault, bullying, and conduct that humiliates or degrades others. For example, in the course of many conversations that took place while researching this book, women shared examples of being objectified at work, or demeaned for their status as a mother, or dismissed because they were not part of the dominant culture.

A group of noted scholars wrote that: "harassment is more about upholding gendered status and identity than it is about expressing sexual desire or sexuality. . . . Even where unwanted sexual misconduct occurs, it is typically a telltale sign of broader patterns of discrimination and inequality at work such as sex segregation and gender stereotyping . . ."[15] And as they further stated, "Without the power and safety that comes with equal representation and numbers, women cannot effectively counter stereotypes or deter or resist harassment."[16]

The EEOC Task Force Report urged workplaces to implement policies that go beyond a strict definition of sexual harassment that focuses only on legally actionable behaviors. Indeed, as the EEOC emphasized, a comprehensive range of conduct must be identified and addressed. Hostile behaviors extend beyond the realm of unwanted sexual attention, and the negative consequences can be equally severe, both in terms of physical and psychological health.

Accordingly, this book addresses a range of bullying, demeaning, and other negative workplace behaviors that operate behind the shield of silence that protects perpetrators. As one example, experts recognize bullying as a form of control that subjects targeted individuals "to overt and covert behaviors that prevent them from performing their jobs and cause significant physical and psychological harm."[17]

To truly achieve a respectful and inclusive work environment, it will be necessary to look closely at organizational culture and the messages that are sent even in everyday conversation. One young woman described a culture consumed by the constant malicious comments of the organization's leader:

> She was completely focused on the appearance of other women. She'd comment on their looks and was very status-oriented, gossiping about their nannies, their shoes, their clothes . . .

If people feel pitted against one another, or as though they can never measure up to an arbitrary standard of physical expectations based on status considerations, it can be as debilitating as other behaviors, all of which undercut the substantive work of the organization.

Interviewees for this book and respondents to surveys, including the one conducted by the Women's Bar Association of Massachusetts in partnership with the Rikleen Institute for Strategic Leadership, described offhand but frequent remarks by key managers that, while not illegal, left women feeling as though they would never be viewed as equal professionals in that work environment. Such comments reinforced women's exclusion from those business and social activities that help build careers and cemented a view of women as occupying a subordinate role in the workplace.

It Should Always Be About Accountability and Transparency

Just as forms of harassment can be different, the ways in which people are held accountable can vary, depending on the nature of the conduct. There can and should be a range of responses appropriate to the findings of an investigation. The responses, however, must be sufficiently transparent to convey that the workplace sets high expectations for how people behave at work and demands that those expectations be taken seriously at every level of employment.

But these goals are thwarted when employers worry more about the economic impacts of reputational damage and the risk of potential litigation that may result from internal complaints. When this occurs, the end result is a failure to provide a consistent and aggressive response to allegations of misconduct, as policies and procedures are ignored.

As will be described, however, the fear of potential risks has its own costs. The antidote is to provide a transparent process for reporting and investigating complaints of improper conduct—one that supports victims through every step of the process, including full protection from any retaliatory behaviors in the future.

To achieve these goals, it is necessary to break from long-held beliefs about what is and is not possible. For example, protecting the privacy of accused individuals does not mean that victims and others in the workplace must be kept in complete darkness about the process. When no one can see that steps are being taken, rumors continue to run rampant, promoting the belief that no one cares and nothing is ever done.

Trust is a critical element of an effective process to address workplace complaints of negative conduct. Without trust, people assume the worst and stay silent. They view the ongoing rumors and the lack of information as evidence that inappropriate behaviors are tolerated.

The Price of Despair

For so many observers of Dr. Ford's testimony before the House Judiciary Committee, it was especially painful to see the president of the United States subsequently mock her at a public rally. Reflecting on the women sitting behind the president who cheered and laughed as he demeaned Dr. Ford and discounted the truth of her experience, playwright Eve Ensler wrote about the denial of women who turn away from the pain of another female who endured such an experience. In recounting the impacts of sexual assault, Ensler wrote:

> *Violence against women destroys our souls. It annihilates our sense of self. It numbs us. It separates us from our bodies. It is the tool used to keep us second-class citizens. And if we don't address it, it can lead to depression, alcoholism, drug addition, overeating and suicide. It makes us believe we are not worthy of happiness.*[18]

Even if an employer is completely unmoved by the personal pain inflicted by harassment, the actual costs to the organization should be incentive enough to take preventative measures. For example, the EEOC Task Force reported that, for fiscal year 2015, the agency secured $125.5 million through its administrative process for employees and $39 million in lawsuits involving harassment.[19] This does not include legal fees and other costs of litigation, such as expert witness fees, nor does it include lawsuits that resulted in monetary settlements. Here is how the EEOC's report described the business impacts:

> *The business case for preventing harassment is sweeping. At the tip of the iceberg are direct and financial costs associated with harassment complaints. Time, energy, and resources are diverted*

from operation of the business to legal representation, settlements, litigation, court awards, and damages. These are only the most visible and headline-grabbing expenses. They also only address employees who report harassment, which . . . may account for only a fraction of the harassment that occurs.

The business case extends far deeper. It encompasses employees who endure but never report harassment, as well as coworkers and anyone else with an interest in the business who witness or perceive harassment in the workplace. When accounting for all those affected by it, harassment becomes more insidious and damaging. In addition to the costs of harassment complaints, the true cost of harassment includes detrimental organizational effects such as decreased workplace performance and productivity, increased employee turnover, and reputational harm.[20]

The costs of workplace bullying reveal a striking parallel:

Common psychological effects include stress, depression, mood swings, loss of sleep (and resulting fatigue), and feelings of shame, embarrassment, guilt, and low self-esteem. Some targets have developed symptoms consistent with Post-Traumatic Stress Disorder. Common physical effects include stress headaches, high blood pressure, digestive problems, and impaired immune systems.[21]

Employers do not escape the costs of bullying. Studies demonstrate that there are direct costs such as medical expenses, increased worker compensation claims, and litigation costs; indirect costs that include negative impacts to employee morale and engagement from working in an abusive environment, and costs relating to higher turnover and absenteeism; and opportunity costs such as workers who are performing far below their potential because of the impacts of their work environment.[22]

Ashley Judd was the first actress to openly speak about Harvey Weinstein's advances, recounting both his harassment and its detrimental impact on her career as a result of her refusal to acquiesce.

In an interview with *New York Times* journalist Jodi Kantor, Judd identified the damaging financial and career impacts:

> *The power dynamics at play are revealed in a worker's trajectory and in her paycheck. Being able to have the legal basis for remedy is crucial. The promotion that doesn't materialize, the shift that's reassigned, the opportunities for advantageous overtime . . . those are all ways that women are punished. Bringing that to light and having economic and legal remedy is an integral part of the strategy of moving the American work force forward.*[23]

For organizations that are ultimately held accountable for their failure to protect victims, the costs can be staggering. For example, Penn State has reported that, to date, it has paid over $100 million in civil settlements to child sexual abuse victims of assistant coach Jerry Sandusky.[24] It is hard to conceive of any negative circumstances that could come close to the monetary and other costs the university absorbed in negative publicity, including loss of reputation and community standing, impaired ability to recruit and retain talent, and expenses associated with litigation, had it instead chosen to exercise appropriate stewardship from the outset.

The Pervasiveness of Misconduct

No Escape

Harassment and negative behaviors in the workplace are not new problems, nor are they restricted to women. The EEOC Task Force Report identified numerous studies that revealed harassment based on sexual orientation, race, ethnicity, disability, age, religion, and harassment against men. The Task Force also highlighted research looking at intersectional harassment, where the target of the negative conduct holds multiple identities. This research underscores the substantial damage caused by any form of harassment.

The stories of misconduct are ubiquitous, but the circumstances differ in degree, timing, and intrusiveness. They are blatant and subtle, public and private. But their impact is the same regardless of the circumstances; victims are left feeling diminished, demeaned, and powerless.

Consider the experience of Miranda, a young professional who attended a social event with a male colleague. At the event, they had the opportunity to meet Steve, a successful leader in their field who introduced himself to Miranda and her coworker. The next day, Miranda sent Steve a note thanking him for taking the time to speak with her. Miranda had long ago been told the importance of sending personal notes as a way of expressing appreciation, especially to those who take time to offer advice to young professionals. What follows is the rest of Miranda's story, as she told it, but it is also a story that countless young women have similarly experienced:

> Steve responded to my note by saying that I should feel free to call or text if there was anything he could ever "help me with," attaching his cell phone number. I thought that it was a bit odd . . . He then invited me to come to his workplace [as an opportunity to observe], and told me I could invite my colleague. I invited my colleague and we went—Steve talked to us for about an hour, which was very nice. My colleague said that he got the feeling that Steve was really "interested" in me, but I just thought that he was being nice and at most a bit overenthusiastic. The next day, I received a friend request from Steve. I called my colleague, who confirmed that he had not received a Facebook request and also had not received Steve's cell phone number, despite also emailing to thank him after our first meeting. Even if he was just being nice (and nothing more than that), it did put me in a really uncomfortable place, as I was afraid that he would be offended if I did not accept his Facebook request. I ended up deleting my profile for awhile.

This is an example at its most subtle. A young professional meets someone well established in her chosen field. He offers to be helpful. But then it gets uncomfortable. The attention veers from the professional setting to a Facebook friend request and the giving out of a cell phone number—behaviors not shown to her male colleague, similarly situated. As a result of her discomfort, Miranda removed herself from social media—and the attendant benefits that go along with it. She also questioned herself and her own judgment, worried that she was being too harsh in her assessment of Steve and his intentions, and wondered if she came across as vulnerable to more senior colleagues.

These are the doubts that plague so many women who find workplace interactions veering from the pleasant to the awkward. This is the point at which the more senior person's intentions may not become known because the other person took steps to remove herself from contact. But the lack of an actual incident does not mean a lack of impact. Women who share Miranda's experience understandably may seek to avoid contact with someone who makes them feel uncomfortable, but they are also removing themselves from potential interactions with that person's professional network.

Miranda's example reveals the complexities that can exist for women in the workplace. Her example matters because it demonstrates the subtle ways in which unwanted conduct can begin, starting with different cues sent to her than her similarly situated male colleague. Generally, however, negative workplace behaviors will be more obvious, even as they pose similar dilemmas about how they should be handled in the absence of clear guidelines in the workplace.

The stakes for victims are daunting as they try to figure out how—or if—to respond to inappropriate behavior or misconduct by people of seniority, or stature, or notoriety. But the longer such behavior is ignored or hidden, the more entrenched the power of the perpetrator can become.

The torrent of publicity that followed the Harvey Weinstein accusations crossed all sectors and focused on egregious behaviors. But even as it is important to aggressively address these significant transgressions, it is also necessary to identify and respond to the full range of behaviors that can thwart and undermine careers.

To do this successfully, every workplace must first learn from its history and take responsibility for—and be prepared to change—its own culture. This requires understanding the nuanced relationship between culture and negative behaviors. For too many sectors, bias and workplace misconduct are inextricably entwined and long-standing. The following are some examples of the way in which silence becomes a learned behavior—indeed, a part of the culture—in various fields.

I'm Not Here for Your Entertainment

In the glamorous world of Hollywood and high-profile television, 2017 and 2018 were not very good years. Scores of well-known men suffered irreparable career damage following accusations of sexual harassment and sexual assault. But the circumstances that led to these moments of reckoning often revealed an organization that was complicit, either through its knowledge or its unwillingness to see what was in plain sight.

For example, a *Washington Post* investigation reported that, as far back as 1986, concerns had been raised about the behavior of Charlie Rose, the cohost of *CBS This Morning* and a *60 Minutes* correspondent. Rose was fired in November 2017 after the *Post* reported on numerous allegations of sexual misconduct against him. The *Post* had interviewed 107 current and former CBS News employees, as well as people who worked with Rose at other stations. According to the report, CBS had stated that no complaints against Rose had been made to human resources.[25]

It should be no surprise, however, that employees would be reluctant to report the negative behavior of a key network star. This is one of many examples that demonstrate why employers can never rely on a lack of reporting as proof that there is nothing to report.

Other scandals involving sexual harassment at CBS have implicated key leaders of its legendary *60 Minutes* franchise. Overshadowing these, however, has been the investigative reporting by Ronan Farrow in the *New Yorker* that led to the removal of Les Moonves, the former chairman and CEO of CBS Corporation and one of the most powerful men in the media. The articles revealed a dozen instances of sexual assault and misconduct that included career-altering retaliation measures taken against those who rebuffed him. Moonves released a statement denying the allegations and admitting to what he characterized as three consensual relationships more than twenty-five years ago. CBS Corporation's statement spoke of its commitment to a thorough investigation.[26]

Moonves had a great deal at stake in the investigation. According to media reports, his eligibility for a $120 million severance payout depended on whether he was terminated for cause. Subsequent to his departure, the *New York Times* raised substantial questions about whether the former CBS chief was honest in his statements to the company's hired investigators.[27] A week later, the *New York Times* confirmed that, based on a draft report of the investigation prepared for the board of CBS, Moonves destroyed evidence and misled investigators to save his severance:

> The report . . . says Mr. Moonves "engaged in multiple acts of serious nonconsensual sexual misconduct in and outside of the workplace, both before and after he came to CBS in 1995." The report includes previously undisclosed allegations of sexual misconduct against him.
>
> The lawyers who conducted the inquiry wrote that they had spoken with Mr. Moonves four times and found him to be "evasive and untruthful at times and to have deliberately lied about and minimized the extent of his sexual misconduct."[28]

After the investigation results were presented, the CBS board voted that sufficient grounds existed to terminate Moonves for cause and deny him the $120 million severance package. The CBS board's decision could also spur a change in the historical trend in which senior executives accused of harassment are paid millions in severance, while the victims are left with far less or nothing at all. As one commentator noted:

> By fumbling his exit payout, Leslie Moonves may have inadvertently created a turning point in the baffling pattern of harassment settlements. And it could signal a shift in the #MeToo quest to hold abusers accountable. . . .
>
> The revised package of zero dollars is a significant reversal of fortune, and maybe not just for Moonves. Until now, harassment math has been upside-down: The accused often receive bigger payouts than those subjected to their behavior. Information is scarce and mushy, but it seems more profitable to abuse than to be abused.[29]

After more than two decades as the host of the *Today* show, Matt Lauer had what appeared to the world outside of NBC to be a shockingly swift fall. But the perception of the speed of his departure may have depended on one's vantage point.

Following his November 2017 firing, the CEO of NBCUniversal directed the company's general counsel to supervise an investigation into whether corporate leaders had information about inappropriate conduct by Lauer and, if so, whether they were reported and addressed appropriately. Not surprisingly, the final report exonerated NBC leadership, stating that the company was unable to establish that anyone in a position of authority knew of Lauer's behavior. The report's carefully chosen words presented the picture of a well-liked *Today* show host who flirtatiously engaged in sexually oriented banter and held back when his suggestive comments were ignored.[30]

Yet soon after Lauer's firing, news outlets reported that his behavior around women was well known within the organization, but his stature and power served as a protective shield.[31] The report noted that interviewees were provided an opportunity to raise other examples of inappropriate workplace conduct, and only "a small number" expressed concerns. But as the blatant examples of Roger Ailes and Bill O'Reilly at Fox News demonstrated, a culture that enables one perpetrator to act with impunity is likely to be a safe harbor for others.[32]

NBC reported that it consulted with outside law firms who concluded that the investigative steps taken were appropriate. But the media reports of Lauer's past conduct should have been sufficient for NBC to conclude that employees who were unwilling to come forward over a period of decades would not suddenly feel safe speaking openly to a leadership team of investigators and internal lawyers.

There is a wide gulf between "appropriate steps" and an investigation that is designed to provide unfiltered and honest responses. Such a self-investigation is premised on the misguided notion that, in a workplace where bad behavior has been perceived to be tolerated or ignored, the veil of fear and secrecy will be lifted simply because management is finally asking the right questions.

Money Makes the World Go 'Round (for Men)

Sex discrimination in the financial services industry is deeply entrenched. In a business where the financial rewards can be enormous,

#MeToo moments are buried under a shroud of secrecy in the ultimate protection of money and power.

A stunning glimpse into a world straight out of *Mad Men*, however, can be seen in the lawsuits that had been filed against financial services companies in the past. In the 1990s, litigation against Smith Barney and Merrill Lynch contained chilling details about a hostile work environment in which women were sexually harassed and discriminated against in terms of pay and promotion. Complaints were also filed against such other major companies as Citigroup, Deutsche Bank, and Goldman Sachs. Media accounts described multimillion-dollar settlements and expressed hope that the culture would finally change.[33]

Rather than changing, however, Wall Street figured out how to ensure that the rules worked to their advantage. They silenced victims, rather than fix their culture.

Employees were required to sign agreements that forced employment disputes into a private system, making it increasingly difficult to seek justice in the courtroom, where most cases are publicly accessible. Experts writing about the negative impacts of required arbitration in the legal profession identified issues of concern that apply when professionals in any field have little choice but to acquiesce:

> *Binding arbitration clauses in legal employment and partnership agreements are on the rise, making a public lawsuit even less of a threat. Without public accountability for the firm and named partners, law firms have little incentive to have reasonable policies . . . or to enforce them to protect victims and punish perpetrators.*[34]

Moreover, once these cases settle, the widespread use of nondisparagement and nondisclosure agreements (NDAs) and settlement confidentiality provisions ensure that perpetrators are forever protected behind a wall of silence.

In the few more recent cases that have managed to find their way into the court system, the allegations were distressingly similar to the challenges that were described decades ago. A 2016 lawsuit filed against Bank of America described a "'bros club' that favored male employees."[35] That suit settled for an undisclosed amount four months after it was filed. In 2014, on the eve of trial, Morgan Stanley settled a sex discrimination lawsuit for $54 million and agreed to establish an internal program focusing on promotional opportunities for women.[36]

In an example of extraordinary perseverance in the face of a daunting process, Cristina Chen-Oster filed a discrimination claim against Goldman Sachs before the EEOC in 2005. After an investigation that took five years to conclude, the EEOC dismissed Chen-Oster's complaint, but authorized her initiating a lawsuit in federal court. Joined by several other plaintiffs, Chen-Oster subsequently sought class-action status, alleging that "Goldman allowed managers, almost all men, to make biased pay and promotion decisions, with the result that women were systematically denied the opportunities they deserved."[37]

Thirteen years after she first began her pursuit of justice, Chen-Oster's patience was rewarded when a judge granted class-action status for female associates and vice presidents within three divisions at Goldman, bringing approximately 2,300 women into the lawsuit. As of the completion of this manuscript, the suit was continuing to move forward. Chen-Oster's saga represents, as a *Bloomberg Businessweek* article noted, "the sobering reality of what it takes to challenge Wall Street's problem with women. In an industry adept at keeping embarrassing details quiet, with a culture that fetishizes secrecy and loyalty, the question isn't why so few women speak up. It's why any speak up at all."[38]

Stemming the Misogyny in STEM

Women have long been significantly underrepresented in the science, technology, engineering, and math (STEM) fields. Research has long demonstrated biases that provide continued advantages to men. Science faculty are more likely to hire and mentor male lab managers, as well as pay them and rate them higher than female candidates with identical resumes; respond to more emails of prospective male PhD students than female students; and overall offer greater access to men over women.[39]

Ironically, however, when STEM faculty were asked to assess the quality of research showing some bias against women in STEM, as compared to fake research showing no such bias, the faculty were more likely to favor the false data. The research team offered an insightful analysis as to how scientists can prefer false data to the truth:

> *Why do men in science devalue such research and the data it produces? If anyone should be willing to accept what the peer-reviewed research consistently shows and use it to correct the underlying assumptions, it should be scientists.*
>
> *But it is in large part because they are scientists that they do not want to believe these studies. Scientists are supposed to be objective, able to evaluate data and results without being swayed by emotions or biases. . . .*
>
> *Even more pernicious, however, is the understanding that results from reading these studies, the realization that those who have succeeded in science (and in many fields—the implications reach far beyond science) have not done so entirely due to their own innate brilliance. Statistically speaking, just being male will automatically give you a leg up. And no one wants to believe that they achieved their success, even in some small part, based on their gender or ethnicity. We all want to feel that we deserve the success and accolades that we have received based on our own merit.[40]*

Another study also provided a window into the way that social media can foster explicit expressions of bias against women. The research revealed the gender stereotyping that can occur when the anonymity of online conversations provides the conditions for people to speak in a more unfiltered way than in conversations where social pressure may serve as a moderating influence.[41]

The study examined content in an online forum, Economics Job Market Rumors, that facilitates the opportunity for graduate students in PhD economics programs to share information about job applications and hiring. The research combined an analysis of text mining, machine learning, and econometrics in a review of over 1 million posts on the forum over a two-year period.

The analysis found significant differences in the types of conversations that occurred when female terms were used, as compared to male terms. For example, in discussions relating to women, the conversations contained, on average, "43% significantly less academic or professional terms, and 192% more terms about personal information or physical attributes."[42] In addition, the study found that "a post tends to deviate more drastically from being academically or professionally oriented if its prior post is related to women."[43]

Even more disturbing, the research revealed the pervasiveness of gender stereotyping through a word selection model that analyzed the use and frequency of certain terms (e.g., *tits, horny, hot, bang*, among others). The study reported: "Words with the strongest association with *female* are mostly inappropriate, and the occurrence of these words in a forum that was meant to be academic and professional exposes the issues of explicit biases in social media."[44]

This research not only demonstrated the pervasive biases that women in the STEM fields face, it also brings to light the way in which anonymous online forums exacerbate conscious stereotyping through unfiltered words used to denigrate and humiliate women. As the study's author noted:

> *In conclusion, my results suggest the need for changes to maintain an inclusive online environment for everyone in the academic community. The casual setting of this online forum cannot be an excuse for gender stereotyping conversations, and the freedom to express one's opinions anonymously should not be abused to create a sense of isolation, which can be discouraging and harmful to the academic and professional development of all genders.*[45]

As in other professions, the data for women of color in STEM reveals significant disparities. For example, in a national survey of more than 400 astronomers and planetary scientists, 40 percent of the women of color respondents and 27 percent of the white women respondents:

> *. . . reported that they had felt unsafe in their current career position due to gender; further, 28% of women of color reported feeling unsafe in their current position due to race. Significant proportions*

*of women compared to men, as well as men and women of color
compared to white men and white women, reported that they had
even skipped a class, meeting, fieldwork, or other professional
event because they did not feel safe. . . .*

*Thus, the disproportionate gender- and race-based harassment
experienced by women of color in astronomy and planetary science represents a clear condition under which women of color are
less likely to have social support, less likely to feel engaged in the
workplace, and less likely to wish to stay. Rather than seeing the
dearth of women of color in the astronomical community as a
passive circumstance, these data indicate that their numbers are
at least in part a result of being pushed out by hostile workplace
experiences.*[46]

The National Academies of Science, Engineering, and Medicine
undertook a study of the impacts of sexual harassment and found that
the fields of academic science, engineering, and medicine share characteristics that make harassment more likely to occur. For example,
career advancement is heavily dependent on advisors and mentors,
there is a system of meritocracy that won't recognize the impacts on
morale or productivity arising from harassment, and a "macho culture" that exists in some fields. The study also found that women more
generally cope by "ignoring or appeasing the harasser and seeking
social support." Far less often they formally report the behavior for
fear of retaliation and other negative outcomes.[47]

The Glamour of Google

For years, Google has been the prototype great place to work, offering perks that include abundant food, games and other ways to unwind
at work, and great parties. Its image has been that of a still young, hip
company that has avoided the workplace errors of older, more staid
corporations. But with respect to negative workplace behaviors and
sexual harassment, apparently not so much.

A *New York Times* investigation of the company described a world
in which high-ranking executives were paid tens of millions of dollars

following explosive allegations of improper relationships.[48] When sexual misconduct allegations were made against Andy Rubin, the creator of the highly successful Android mobile software, Google reportedly investigated and found the claims credible. Mr. Rubin's sanction? A $90 million exit package and Google's investment in his next venture.

According to the *New York Times* investigation, when it was revealed that Google's general counsel had a relationship with a subordinate, the woman was transferred to a different department and left the company a year later. The general counsel continued to rise within the organization, reportedly receiving an estimated $190 million and remaining eligible for more than $200 million in other options and equity awards.

The *New York Times* article reported other examples of accused senior executives being protected by the company, even as it included a statement from the "vice president for people operations" that the "company takes harassment seriously and reviews every complaint."[49] It is hard to imagine that, in light of the incidents reported in the article, the culture of Google fostered the reporting of misconduct. Other Google employees likely learned that silence was the safest course of action.

In response to the revelations in the *New York Times* article, and as an example of the way technology has changed the nature of worker resistance, more than 20,000 Google employees around the world simultaneously staged a walkout. Their action has ramifications for all sectors, as employees grow increasingly frustrated with negative workplace cultures amid stories of large payouts to those accused of harassment, as this CNBC report noted:

> *Many demonstrators at Google's Mountain View headquarters leaned into the idea that the only way to achieve their demands— which include the end of private arbitration, a transparency report about sexual harassment, more disclosures about compensation and an employee representative on the company's board—were only possible if all employees at every level of the company were active and included.*[50]

Heal Thyself

Women comprise approximately half of the students in medical school but only just over a third of practicing doctors. And as in so many other fields, there is significant research demonstrating the disparate treatment women face in their medical school training and in practice settings.[51]

One study found that female medical students were more than twice as likely as men to base some part of their specialty choice on concerns about gender discrimination and sexual harassment. The study's authors also noted the importance of influencing the pipeline:

> *Most notably for women physicians, gender discrimination and sexual harassment behaviors have been shown to persist into medical practice, suggesting that any truly comprehensive response to the problem not be restricted to any one segment of medical training. Still, to the extent that such behaviors are learned during undergraduate education—especially core clerkships—students should be educated to recognize and encouraged to report incidents of gender discrimination and sexual harassment, and a satisfactory organizational response should be assured.[52]*

A *Boston Globe* article reported that at an AAGL (American Association of Gynecologic Laparoscopists) medical conference—an organization consisting of 7,000 gynecological surgeons who practice minimally invasive surgery—a surgeon included a crude image in his PowerPoint. Following the presentation, more than 100 surgeons sent a petition to the AAGL board stating that female members of the professional association have experienced sexual harassment, sexual assault, and workplace intimidation and have felt unsafe at AAGL functions. They further described feeling undermined in their career advancement and requested that the organization institute a variety of changes, including standards for member behavior at events, a process for investigating complaints, and third-party reporting options to protect members who fear retaliation.[53]

In an article addressing #MeToo in the medical field, the author identified the profession's hierarchical culture as responsible for the perpetual silence by noting that "unwanted advances happen so frequently, it becomes normalized to the point where no one wants to report it. . . . Part of the problem is what sexual harassment is rooted in. It's often a form of intimidation—a way to show someone where they stand in the pecking order, and make them feel that their status has been lowered."[54]

Among her interviewees, the author spoke with a doctor who was sexually harassed while a resident at a medical center, and then reported the institution's unsurprising response: the surgeon in question had not worked at the medical center for years and there was no record of a report. Once again, a high-level person against whom one or more allegations have come to light is no longer employed in that setting and, by the way, the organization has no records of any report of bad behavior.

The article demonstrated how secrecy reigns at every level. Generally, people in the workplace don't know why the alleged offender is no longer in that workplace. Did the offender leave because of rumored allegations yet departed with his reputation intact, free to continue similar behaviors at other institutions? Did any independent investigation follow?

In an analysis of data that demonstrated a higher level of care provided by women doctors, the authors noted that the barriers women in medicine face should be viewed as a quality of care issue: "The field is routinely under-promoting, under-supporting, under-rewarding, and under-training female physicians. And yet, despite these implicit and systemic barriers, female physicians continue to persist and achieve better outcomes than their male colleagues. . . . Allowing things to continue as they have for women in medicine is accepting a system where potentially higher-quality care is denied to patients due to sexism and bad practices."[55]

An Education Students Do Not Need

In 2014, Chessy Prout, then a freshman at the elite St. Paul's School in New Hampshire, became the victim of a long-standing school tradition known widely as the "Senior Salute." The Senior Salute marked the experience of males nearing graduation who competitively sought to have sexual encounters with younger female students. Chessy was one senior's prey.

Notwithstanding the long history of silence from others who had endured similar experiences that year and in years past, Chessy reported her assault to the school and to law enforcement. As a result of her reporting, Chessy was revictimized. She was shunned by her friends and made to feel increasingly uncomfortable for the negative publicity that the school faced—as though Chessy was responsible for these impacts from the reported assault. She subsequently left St. Paul's, further traumatized by the school's lack of support and what she viewed as a rape culture that even included fund-raising efforts among alumni and students for her attacker's defense.

Prosecutors in New Hampshire, however, indicted St. Paul senior Owen Labrie for rape and for other charges. After a trial at which Chessy testified about her experience, Labrie was found guilty of using the internet to solicit sex, committing misdemeanor statutory rape, and endangering the welfare of a child. He was acquitted of the felony rape charge.

Over time, it became clear that the Senior Salute was part of a more pervasive problem at St. Paul's. An independent investigation identified faculty and staff alleged to have sexually abused students over a period of decades. How could students possibly have felt it was safe to report assaults by their peers when the institution had a history of ignoring the behavior of the staff entrusted to protect them?

In reflecting back on her time at the prestigious prep school, Chessy wrote about St. Paul's as a place:

> . . . *where everything was about status, tradition, and hierarchy—and guys ruled all three. They ran most of the clubs, dominated class discussions, and determined girls' worth by whether or not they wanted to score them. . . . It wasn't just the students who reinforced this male hierarchy. When we gathered at the oval wooden table for my humanities class, the teacher listened intently to the boys and fluffed their egos while dismissing girls' opinions as "wrong."*[56]

St. Paul's is but one example of elite schools that have a history of protecting their status over their students. An investigation of the prestigious Phillips Exeter Academy revealed multiple instances of sexual abuse by staff as well as peers, spanning multiple decades. The report even identified separate record-keeping systems that kept confidential information out of HR files, a dual system that continued past 2010.[57]

When an institution's priorities are to maintain the façade of status and prestige, the result is to see no evil. And when seeing is unavoidable, a light penalty may help ensure that minimal attention is drawn to the problem. An investigation at the prestigious Hotchkiss School in Connecticut found decades of ignored sexual misconduct. One teacher was found with a student in a motel room, only to receive a one-year suspension. He was finally terminated more than a dozen years later and after more allegations surfaced.[58] And in an example reminiscent of USA Gymnastics doctor Larry Nassar's abuse of female gymnasts, the Hotchkiss School's gynecologist was found to have performed unnecessary gynecological exams and have children disrobe without reason. Astonishingly, this doctor's time working at the school spanned from 1972 to 2005.[59]

A former student at the elite Horace Mann School in New York interviewed more than a hundred other former students who described the culture of sexual abuse of students at that school.[60] And a student at the Groton School, frustrated by the institution's failure to respond to his report of being sexually molested by students, spoke at an assembly about the experiences he had endured. The faculty and students responded with anger, not at how he was treated, but for bringing shame on their prestigious school by speaking out. Like Chessy Prout, he left the school and completed his high school education elsewhere.[61]

In 2015, Stanford student Brock Turner was spotted by two graduate students behind a dumpster, sexually assaulting a woman he met at a frat party. When he tried to run, the students tackled him; he was subsequently arrested, charged, and convicted of three felonies. In a powerful impact statement, the survivor of the attack described the humiliating questions she endured from investigators and the defense attorneys, the depression and anxiety that consumed her since the attack, and the bewilderment of seeing constant media coverage that referred to Turner as a star swimmer at Stanford, rather than as an alleged rapist.[62]

Turner could have been sentenced to fourteen years in a state penitentiary; the prosecutor recommended a six-year sentence. Instead, the judge ordered a far lighter sentence of six months in a county jail and probation, based on, among other things, Brock Turner's many strong character references.[63] Turner's dad, in a statement released after sentencing, defended his son by pointing to his athletic and academic accomplishments, and then stated: "His life will never be the one that he dreamed about and worked so hard to achieve. That is a steep price to pay for 20 minutes of action out of his 20 plus years of life. . . ."[64]

To be sure, Turner's father experienced a deep anguish seeing his son's life in shambles, far from the dream of unlimited opportunities that would emerge from the glory of a Stanford education and stellar athletic achievements. The judge, too, presented a detailed explanation of why he was sentencing Turner to six months in a county jail—an explanation that also recognized the shattered life of a promising student.

But the words of both conveyed an undercurrent of privilege and an objectification, even a nullification, of the victim. Just as at St. Paul's and the other elite schools that embed privilege and power in those who pass through their halls, women's voices have been devalued, breeding the silence that becomes a lifelong pattern.

The Glory and Hypocrisy of Sports

Americans glorify sports and athletic achievements. We hero-worship athletes and watch them perform with avid fervor. Our devotion, however, has an unintended consequence. Organizations continually protect their sports-generated revenue over the athletes whose skills support that income.

Larry Nassar had the distinction of being an esteemed doctor for the USA Gymnastics team and Michigan State University for decades. During that time, as he sexually abused hundreds of young women and girls dating back to the 1990s, he was treated with the reverence that those who serve and surround elite athletes frequently encounter. That meant rumors and complaints were ignored and his access to young girls continued unabated.

When Nassar was finally sentenced for his crimes in early 2018, more than 150 victim-impact statements revealed to the world the way in which institutions protect their image and status above all else, turning away from the voices of victims. At least in Nassar's case, the victims were transformed into an "army of survivors" who had their opportunity to confront their abuser in court.[65]

As additional information about USA Gymnastics is revealed, it has been shocking to learn the extent to which silencing was institutionalized. In October 2018, criminal charges were filed against Steve Penny, the former chief executive of USA Gymnastics, for tampering with evidence. The indictment alleged that Penny ordered the removal of documents relating to Nassar's work as a doctor at the Karolyi Ranch, which, for decades, was the place where elite gymnasts trained under the watchful eye of famed coaches Bela and Márta Karolyi. Penny purportedly removed the documents with the intention of impairing the investigation. Those documents have never been found.[66]

Notwithstanding Penny's indictment, the USA Gymnastics leadership remained tone deaf to the harm caused, as his two successors served only a short time before being forced out. One successor, interim chief executive Mary Bono, was forced out within days of assuming the role. Ironically, a primary concern raised against Bono was an earlier tweet in which she defaced a Nike logo after Nike featured civil rights activist and former NFL quarterback Colin Kaepernick in its ads. Her downfall was her seeming desire to silence Kaepernick for his own outspoken advocacy against police misconduct.

More than a hundred lawsuits representing over 350 survivors of Larry Nassar's sexual abuse have been filed against USA Gymnastics. Moreover, the U.S. Olympic Committee (USOC) has taken steps to revoke USA Gymnastics' certification. USA Gymnastics responded by filing for bankruptcy in December 2018.[67]

For Michigan State University, the sentencing of Larry Nassar marked the beginning of investigations and lawsuits that will continue to shine a harsh light on the way in which leadership and governance failed the very people they are there to serve.

For example, in the wake of Nassar's lengthy sentencing hearing and the resignation of Michigan State University's president and athletic director, additional facts emerged that again reinforced how ethically deficient decisions are made. An ESPN investigation described a culture of institutional indifference as numerous allegations of sexual assault against student athletes were withheld from the Michigan State University's reporting channels and were instead handled internally by athletic department officials.[68]

Reporting further revealed that at least fourteen Michigan State University representatives learned of abuse allegations against Nassar, starting as far back as 1997, when two high school gymnasts participating in a youth program at MSU told the university's head gymnastics coach about Nassar's behavior during his so-called treatment sessions. The coach responded with an admonishment that pursuing such a claim would result in serious consequences for Nassar and the girls.[69]

Three other coaches over the next few years were similarly informed of Nassar's abusive treatments and took no action, further revealing a climate in which Nassar could prey on young women in the guise of practicing medicine.[70] One dismissed a young victim by stating that Nassar's credentials as an Olympic doctor were proof that his treatment methods were sound.

It seems incomprehensible that Nassar was able to molest young athletes for so long without any of the institutions he served intervening on behalf of the victims. But the reality is that all the signs were there—and then ignored. The USOC board of directors hired a law firm to conduct an independent investigation of Nassar's long history of abuse. The firm was retained to determine when individuals first became aware of Nassar's abuse, what was—or was not—done with that information, and what were the systemic deficiencies and cultural conditions that supported the abuse. The findings provide a deeply disturbing roadmap for the ways in which organizations can institutionalize cultures that support harassment and abuse, and reflexively protect the perpetrators. Specifically, the report stated:

> *While Nassar bears ultimate responsibility for his decades-long abuse of girls and young women, he did not operate in a vacuum. Instead, he acted within an ecosystem that facilitated his criminal acts. Numerous institutions and individuals enabled his abuse and failed to stop him, including coaches at the club and elite level*

trainers and medical professionals, administrators and coaches at Michigan State University . . . and officials at both United States of America Gymnastics . . . and the United States Olympics Committee. . . . These institutions and individuals ignored red flags, failed to recognize textbook grooming behaviors, or in some egregious instances, dismissed clear calls for help from girls and young women who were being abused by Nassar. Multiple law enforcement agencies, in turn, failed effectively to intervene when presented with opportunities to do so. And when survivors first began to come forward publicly, some were shunned, shamed or disbelieved by others in their own communities. The fact that so many different institutions and individuals failed the survivors does not excuse any of them, but instead reflects the collective failure to protect young athletes.[71]

No organization is immune from the possibility of a predator in its midst, nor should any individual be beyond the reach of accountability. Penn State's Jerry Sandusky abused young boys for decades, including while serving as a defensive coordinator for legendary football coach Joe Paterno. As with Larry Nassar at MSU, Penn State officials were told in the late 1990s that Sandusky was acting inappropriately with young boys that he brought to the college's athletic facility. Sandusky's abuse continued unfettered until he was arrested in 2011, found guilty in 2012, and sentenced to thirty to sixty years in prison. Several other university officials, including Penn State's president, also served time for their failure to report allegations.

Without vigilance, predators can operate with impunity. Better reporting procedures alone, however, are not the answer, although certainly the failure to report and follow up at Penn State and MSU were shocking in scope. It is equally important for institutions to understand the underlying human motivations that create a climate in which predators can thrive and maintain the respect of their peers.

For major sports organizations—including professional and college-level sports, as well as the USOC—the common denominator that allows negative conduct to thrive is money. And in the highly lucrative world of the National Football League (NFL), players embroiled in allegations of abuse of women are more likely to be protected than held to account for their behavior.

NFL commissioner Roger Goodell has administered punishment like a father who tries to compel obedience by grounding his kids. In 2014, the commissioner purportedly toughened the NFL's response to allegations of domestic violence.[72] Yet Goodell continued to impose minimal suspensions on behaviors in which women were allegedly assaulted—for example, issuing suspensions lasting four games or less for such behaviors as assaulting a woman in a hotel; throwing a mug at a bartender; exhibiting road rage; assaulting a spouse and breaking her nose, and, in the same incident, throwing a shoe at her toddler; creating revenge porn; and endangering a child by putting a plastic bag over a toddler's face. And consistent with the silence so endemic in the workplace, the female victims refused to press charges.

By not being held accountable within the criminal justice system, the alleged abusers avoided the harsher penalties that the NFL imposes on players found guilty of a crime. Absent that intervening factor, the commissioner can impose lighter penalties that allows players who have committed a range of abusive behaviors to hasten back to the field. Moreover, notwithstanding the intense scrutiny following some of the high-profile domestic abuse incidents involving football players, the NFL has continued to hire new players and retain existing players accused of, among other things, domestic violence or assaults involving women.[73]

As the commissioner was putting in place its allegedly stronger policy in 2014, the NFL Players Association (NFLPA) created a Commission on Violence Prevention. Its appointees included Deborah Epstein, a professor of law and co-director of the Georgetown University Law Center's Domestic Violence Clinic, and Susan Else, the former president of the National Network to End Domestic Violence. By May 2018, both resigned from the Commission.

Professor Epstein explained the reasons for their resignation in a *Washington Post* op-ed that demonstrated the pernicious way that silence can operate on several levels. She described how she dove into the work of the Commission, collaborating with Lisa Goodman, a

Boston College research psychologist, to survey players' wives about their perspectives on family violence in a community that is always in the spotlight.

In undertaking this survey, Professor Epstein was required by the NFLPA to sign a confidentiality agreement that prohibited her from speaking publicly about the research findings. In effect, the NFLPA silenced the researchers and, by extension, the players' wives, who may have had stories to share about their experiences. Their survey was completed in 2016, and according to Professor Epstein, the Commission met a mere three times in the following two years.

In her op-ed, Professor Epstein wrote about the NFLPA's response to her research and the duplicity of the silence the organization demanded:

> When I was asked to join the commission, I told NFLPA Executive Director DeMaurice Smith that I was leery of associating with an organization that might just be paying lip service to the defining issue of my career—so that, in essence, the NFLPA could say it was confronting domestic violence abuses long enough for the Rice story to fall out of the news cycle. Smith assured me, repeatedly, that this commission would be a serious working group and that our efforts would help produce necessary reforms. But clearly that has not been the case. Authorizing a single study, and then burying it through a confidentiality agreement and shelving its recommendations does not constitute meaningful reform. Because I care deeply about violence against women in the NFL and beyond, I can no longer continue to be part of a commission that is essentially a fig leaf.[74]

After years of prodding by advocates who had been trying to move the USOC to take action to combat sexual abuse in the Olympic movement, the USOC finally opened the U.S. Center for SafeSport in March of 2017. By August 2018, the Center had received 1,200 complaints of sexual abuse, most of which stemmed from recent incidents.[75]

The NFL, the USOC, Penn State, and Michigan State demonstrate how the machinery of high-profile sports allows the victimization of the vulnerable to continue, while vast resources are used to protect their brand at the expense of the victims.

But it is not only in the world of high-profile athletics where coaches and others prey on vulnerable athletes who are taught never to question those who are ostensibly building or otherwise supporting their athletic prowess. For example, a Massachusetts Appellate Court decision revealed how a small community college betrayed students to protect a coach and the school's reputation.

The facts described in the court's decision showed that as early as the 1979–1980 academic year, administrators at Northern Essex Community College, including the college president, had knowledge that its athletic director and coach, Marshall Hess, was providing alcohol to underage students and asking female students to engage in sex. As a result of the complaints, the college created sexual harassment policies and procedures but took no action against Hess, notwithstanding complaints that continued for the next seven years.

Finally, in 1987, the college undertook an investigation that identified a series of allegations:

> *Female athletes had been made to feel beholden to Hess for getting them scholarships or playing time; Hess had, during walks or lunches with female students, encouraged them to confide in him about intimate details of their lives, their relationships with boyfriends, and whether or not they had had abortions; he made liquor available to female students, some under the legal age for drinking alcohol; he pulled their shorts, patted bottoms, and undid bra straps; he walked in on female students in the bathroom in his house; he had them drink liquor out of his mouth; he kissed them; he engaged in sexual intercourse with female students during the frequent trips he organized; and he discussed his vasectomy and made "dirty vasectomy jokes."*[76]

The court also described how Hess threatened to reveal compromising pictures he had from when they were drunk. Hess effectively silenced his victims and profoundly affected their lives, resulting in a decision to leave the team they loved, ceasing to attend classes, and even withdrawing from college.

The college's response proved more shocking than the allegations. The school entered into an agreement with Hess in which he continued to be employed but would no longer coach female teams. Two and a half years later, however, the agreement was modified to allow Hess to attend field trips with female students and to permit him to serve as head coach of the women's basketball team.

In February 1994, two student athletes complained to the college that they were being sexually harassed by Hess and were the victims of retaliatory behavior for refusing his demands, including being benched from their sport. Ultimately, both students left the school. Hess was suspended in August 1994.

The appellate court opinion was procedurally significant in that it overturned a lower court's dismissal of the plaintiffs' claims against the college on statute of limitations grounds. Ultimately the case against the community college was settled.

Injustice in the Justice System

Whether in the courthouse, a law firm, or other settings, those within the justice system have a special obligation to provide a respectful workplace. Lawyers have particular power and influence, with a seat at the table in important board rooms of major businesses and institutions. Corporations today rarely make important decisions without attorneys at their side. Law firms serve as training grounds for those who become societal figures of influence.

As gatekeepers of the justice system, lawyers should serve as role models, setting a standard for others to follow in complying with, and going beyond, legal obligations in the workplace. The reality is, however, that workplace harassment in the legal profession exists as it does in other fields. For example, in the United Kingdom, complaints against lawyers have increased significantly. According to the Solicitors Regulatory Authority (SRA), misconduct complaints have increased 58 percent in just the first seven months of its fiscal year, between November 2017 and June 2018.

A partner in the London office of one of the world's largest law firms, Baker McKenzie, was alleged to have sexually assaulted an associate following a firm social event. The matter was reportedly resolved quietly by the firm through a payment to the associate, the obligatory signing of a confidentiality agreement, and the subsequent departure by the associate while the partner remained. Media reports eventually emerged of the incident and settlement, prompting an internal investigation by the firm. The SRA undertook an investigation to determine whether the firm's use of a confidentiality agreement could effectively preclude the SRA from investigating a complaint of professional misconduct. The firm responded by acknowledging shortcomings in its handling of the incident and implementing a firmwide code of conduct.[77] Ironically, a multimillion-dollar judgment had been assessed against the firm in 1994 arising out of a lawsuit alleging that a partner sexually harassed his former secretary. In 1991, the firm had been sued for age and gender discrimination by its first woman partner.[78]

A partner at another global law firm, Dentons, was suspended and subsequently left the firm following allegations of inappropriate behavior. The behaviors were alleged to have occurred when the partner was at a predecessor firm, which subsequently merged into Dentons. Although Dentons was reported to have taken prompt steps to resolve the matter when they were disclosed, media reports indicate that, at the predecessor firm, multiple women had come forward with allegations about inappropriate sexual behavior, and at least one had been warned against making a formal complaint.[79] The women's voices that were previously silenced were, in this instance, vindicated by the effectiveness of sunshine.

Several months after the partner issue at Dentons was publicized, a lawsuit was filed against the firm by a business development specialist alleging ongoing sexual harassment from her supervisor. Of particular note, the complaint states that, after enduring many months of this behavior, the plaintiff reported the allegations and met with representatives of the firm's human resources department, who directed her not to "discuss the allegations with anyone else inside or outside the firm." The plaintiff also stated in the complaint that the firm interviewed other witnesses who also were directed to remain silent about the allegations.[80] The firm's response stated that the complaint was meritless and a misappropriation of the #MeToo movement.[81]

Such lawsuits are a rarity in the legal profession. When they occur, the troubling allegations raised are firmly denied, but little else is learned about the firm's culture because the underlying litigation is usually resolved through a settlement or arbitration procedure. For example, in a discrimination suit filed against another global law firm, the plaintiff alleged that the firm "has one exception to its general practice of denying women professional development opportunities and compensating women less than men. [It] . . . prioritizes, pays and promotes women who have intimate relationships with Firm leaders or who acquiesce to sexualized stereotypes. . . . [The firm] sends female shareholders the unwelcome message that the only way women can shatter the glass ceiling . . . and otherwise circumvent the discrimination that otherwise runs rampant is by sexualizing their professional relationships at the Firm."[82] The firm vigorously denied the allegations and sought to move the case to arbitration. Ultimately, the matter was settled in mediation; the terms of the settlement are confidential.

In June 2018, a complaint was filed against another global law firm alleging, among other things, pay discrimination. In the complaint, the plaintiff described:

> . . . a fraternity culture that centers on male attorneys, their clients, their relationships, and their female conquests. Male partners often initiate happy hours and pub nights, where conversations center around sporting events, sports stories, and tales of bad-boy behavior. . . . As part of the Firm's fraternity culture, the Firm's male leaders often make sexist comments and rate the attractiveness of female lawyers, paralegals, staff, and officers of the Firm's clients. Business development events, too, often center on degrading stereotypes of femininity and cater to a preference for sports and alcohol. Within this environment, female attorneys are undervalued and marginalized.[83]

The complaint referenced trips to strip clubs and further described an annual business development event in which male partners invited their female clients to a spa, and female partners "were expected to disrobe in front of the clients and to serve as 'hostesses.'"[84]

In any organization, such lawsuits can serve as silent cancers. They are usually strongly opposed by an indignant management that may seize on perceived differences in the underlying facts as proof that the allegations are all false. It may be a natural protective reaction, but it can result in a missed opportunity to look inward to find the truth within the differing perceptions. Once an individual goes to the extreme step of filing a suit, employees are likely quite aware of what is alleged to have led to this point. Blanket denials absent an internal investigation or other measures demonstrating concern and a commitment to unearth the facts have a negative impact on employee morale, engagement, and trust in the organization.

Surveys provide another opportunity for a more in-depth analysis of a particular sector. Such research offers a more nuanced understanding of the way in which pervasive workplace misconduct and the failure to report can impact people's lives and livelihoods. Fortunately, some bar associations have elicited this type of information in surveys of the legal profession. For example, in a poll of California lawyers, 50 percent of the women respondents reported they had been sexually harassed, and 70 percent reported receiving inappropriate comments regarding their physical appearance.[85]

A study conducted by the Florida Bar Association asked respondents about conduct they had experienced within the past three years:

> *Approximately one out of every 25 male lawyer respondents and one out of every seven female lawyer respondents indicated that they have experienced harassment or bullying within the last three years due to gender. This amounts to an average of eleven lawyers harassed or bullied due to gender per work day. Only 23% of female respondents and 19% of male respondents who reported the incident to a supervisor indicated that the issue was resolved to their satisfaction.*[86]

The Florida Bar Association's glimpse into the daily lives of people in the legal profession is of particular interest because its focus was on experiences within the three years prior to the survey date, confirming that harassment and bullying are not behaviors confined to the past.

Challenging behaviors extend beyond bullying and harassment, yet are infrequently captured in survey data. A survey of law firm conduct by the Women's Bar Association of Massachusetts, in partnership with the Rikleen Institute for Strategic Leadership, undertook such a comprehensive analysis by addressing a wide range of negative behaviors that impact people in the workplace on a daily basis. The survey also included anecdotes and data that demonstrate why reporting rates are so low. This study can be found in the Appendix to this book.

There are few roles in our justice system as exalted as that of members of the judiciary, leaving those who may be victimized by a judge feeling not only overpowered, but also not likely to be believed. In an essay in the *ABA Journal*, a lawyer who had been sexually assaulted by two judges early in her career wrote of her fear of career repercussions if she identified the perpetrators. She noted that, notwithstanding their unique position of power, judges are not above committing the same transgressions as others in the workplace:

> *There are very few men who have more power than a judge. . . . But a judge should never use his power to sexually pressure court staff, lawyers, litigants or others. A judge should never use his power to grope, kiss, massage or rape someone who trusts him because of his position, and who feels powerless against him. A judge should never use his power to silence or retaliate against someone he sexually assaults.*[87]

Her own story can find validation in the results of a public records request to the California judiciary. The response to this request included sixty-four pages of settlement agreements showing that the court had paid nearly $645,000 in the settlement of sexual harassment and gender discrimination claims since 2012. The heavily redacted documents revealed a range of amounts paid, and although most details were missing, it appears they frequently contained confidentiality clauses.[88]

Too often, victims must sign away their voice for a modicum of justice. Demands for confidentiality agreements may benefit the employer by keeping the resolution out of the public eye, but it leaves other employees frustrated by further silence. The matter is settled, but the underlying problem likely remains.

Looking Back after the Mighty Fall

What does it mean when organizations tolerate sexual harassment at the most senior levels? What is the impact when hurtful comments in the guise of "joking remarks" are abided? Are there greater societal impacts when the daily work experiences of employees are impacted by, in some cases, outright bias and, in other instances, a disregard for the effect of one's words or deeds and the tolerance of a culture of disrespect?

Boston Globe columnist Margery Eagan suggested a critical connection between workplace misconduct and the long history of gender inequality. For example, noting the "gross sexual demands" of Fox News founder Roger Ailes, Eagan wrote of the work culture he created and perpetuated throughout the Fox network of stations that spread his misogyny far beyond the targets of his direct sexual harassment:

> *Plus he presented to the world just one kind of woman: the Barbie doll anchor. The gorgeous young blondes he hired wore sleeveless dresses, skirts the size of Band-Aids, cleavage-revealing necklines, and enough makeup to fill an aisle at Sephora.*

Eagan also noted the litany of men accused of rampant sexual misconduct whose names have been influential for decades, including Weinstein, Moonves, Lauer, Rose, and Trump. She also referenced the inexplicably lenient plea agreement engineered by top Miami prosecutor Alex Acosta that allowed well-connected Florida financier Jeffrey Epstein to essentially escape meaningful punishment for the alleged sexual abuse and trafficking of scores of teenaged girls that could have resulted in a sentence of life imprisonment. Alex Acosta subsequently became the labor secretary in the Trump administration, a position that includes oversight of human trafficking.[89] As Eagan wrote:

> What's the cost to American women when so many of the men who've run our most powerful culture-shaping institutions—CBS, Fox News, the White House, the Hollywood film industry—are sexual predators?
>
> Could the need of these men to degrade be linked to how few women make it to the top at the nation's biggest companies? Could it be related also to why American women, unlike those in advanced nations everywhere else, get so few basics like, say, subsidized child care? . . .
>
> And all, to a greater or lesser degree, shaped America's political perspectives, cultural norms and views on women for a generation. So you have to wonder, again, how much did men like these hurt not just corporate women but the efforts of everyday working women seeking simple fairness? The answer is obvious: plenty.[90]

Linda Bloodworth-Thomason, the famed creator of a CBS comedy that featured strong female protagonists, had been given the largest writing and producing contract in CBS history, only to have her career derailed when Les Moonves became president of the network. Her punishment was not for spurned advances, but for advancing a view of women outside the narrow vision of a corporate executive who seemed opposed to shows on his network that featured fiercely strong and independent females. Thomason's description of the devastation to her career is yet another example of the incalculable career damage that can be caused by leaders whose cultural views result in systemic exclusion of those who do not fit their misogynistic or biased vision.[91]

Most individuals who have felt the pain and humiliation of harassment and retaliation, whether in its overt or more subtle forms, have carried their silence like a weighted burden. It is that silence, however, that facilitates the conditions in which misconduct grows.

3

Building Structures That Victims Can't Access

The Evolving Terrain of #MeToo

Comedy writer Nell Scovell, describing her experiences working at *Late Night with David Letterman*, expressed her concern about whether too high a bar was being created as a result of the #MeToo revelations: "One of the unfortunate parts of #MeToo is that you look at Harvey Weinstein and Bill Cosby, and their transgressions were so grotesque that I actually worry that they've raised the bar—now, if a guy hasn't raped a dozen women, we think he's a gentleman."[92]

The fact is, sexual harassment and negative workplace conduct have long been endemic, with behaviors that include sexual assault as well as transgressions ranging from bullying to inappropriate humor to demeaning or harassing comments. The common element that supports these behaviors is the pervasive silence steeped in fear.

How Did We Get Here?

Much of the way in which workplaces address—or fail to address—gender discrimination and sexual harassment derives from decades of court decisions that have ruled in favor of employers. The root of many of these cases can be found in Title VII of the Civil Rights Act of 1964, which banned employment discrimination on the basis of sex, race, color, national origin, and religion. Twenty-two years later, sexual harassment was recognized by the U.S. Supreme Court as a violation of Title VII.[93]

In 1998, the Supreme Court held that employers are strictly liable for harassment by a supervisor that results in a tangible employment action—for example, a subordinate fired for failing to comply with demands of a sexual nature. Of critical importance to the way that training programs have evolved, however, is the aspect of the ruling that said that employers may be vicariously liable for a hostile environment created by a supervisor's behavior.[94]

Where such behavior did not result in a tangible adverse job consequence, the employer could have the opportunity to assert an affirmative defense that included two required elements. First, the employer would have to demonstrate that it exercised reasonable care to prevent and promptly correct sexually harassing behaviors. Second, the employer would need to show that the employee unreasonably failed to take advantage of any preventative or corrective opportunities provided by the employer or to otherwise avoid harm.

As a result of this ruling, employers sought to implement mechanisms that would allow them to take advantage of this defense by demonstrating that they undertook measures that would meet the Supreme Court's standard of reasonable care. In doing so, sexual harassment training emerged as a nearly impenetrable shield, protecting employers against a claim of a hostile work environment. Prudent employers required sexual harassment training of employees that was coupled with a system for reporting harassment to, for example, HR.

In those cases that actually have made it past this hurdle and into court, plaintiffs still encountered formidable obstacles to success. Over time, the courts erected steep barriers in front of plaintiffs, resulting in a justice system that has evolved to support employers far more frequently than it does employees.

In an article describing some of these key barriers, former federal district court judge Nancy Gertner noted that, under the Federal Rules of Civil Procedure, judges are only required to write decisions when they are granting summary judgment—dispensing of a case without a trial—for the defendants. Judge Gertner identified "Losers' Rules," written decisions against plaintiffs that resulted in "wholly one-sided legal doctrines that characterize discrimination law. In effect, today's plaintiff stands to lose unless he or she can prove that the defendant had explicitly discriminatory policies in place or that the relevant actors were overtly biased."[95]

As Judge Gertner described, judicial decision-making has resulted in a system that disadvantages those bringing employment discrimination and harassment claims:

> *Asymmetric decisionmaking—where judges are encouraged to write detailed decisions when* granting *summary judgment and not to write when* denying *it—fundamentally changes the lens through which employment cases are viewed, in two respects. First, it encourages judges to see employment discrimination cases as trivial or frivolous, as decision after decision details why the plaintiff loses. And second, it leads to the development of decision heuristics—the Losers' Rules—that justify prodefendant outcomes and thereby exacerbate the one-sided development of the law.*[96]

As a result of these "Losers' Rules," a body of one-sided precedent developed on behalf of employer-defendants who succeeded in having the plaintiff's case disposed of before ever getting to the trial stage. Noting that more than 70 percent of summary judgment motions granted involved employment discrimination claims, Judge Gertner emphasized:

> *[T]he problem is more than just the creation of one-sided precedent that other judges follow. The way judges view these cases fundamentally changes. If case after case recites the facts that do not amount to discrimination, it is no surprise that the decision-makers have a hard time envisioning the facts that may well comprise discrimination. Worse, they may come to believe that most claims are trivial.*[97]

Checking the Box, Neglecting the Substance

As employers implemented training programs to qualify for the affirmative defense in the event of a lawsuit, employees have been subjected to training programs that vary widely in quality and are often criticized as rote and stilted, without accomplishing a major change in workplace culture.[98] Yet the affirmative defense fails to require an answer to key questions. Has the training worked to change behaviors? What conduct should or should not be reported? Is there a triggering threshold? Should there be a statement of zero tolerance? Is the reporting process transparent enough to build trust? Do those reporting— whether victims or caring bystanders—feel supported? Does the workplace vigilantly guard against retaliation?

Moreover, as a means of changing behavior, most training programs are insufficient. Too many training modules address only behaviors that meet the legal standard of harassment that is severe or pervasive. As a result, conduct that may not rise to the level of actionable sexual harassment is given little or no attention, even as such behaviors can nonetheless demean workers, destroy confidence, and turn jobs into an obstacle course focused on avoiding aggressors.

Employers may also face an unintended consequence from focusing only on the prevention of legally actionable behaviors. When negative conduct is ignored, it sends a signal to others in the workplace that such conduct is acceptable. It also enables perpetrators to escalate their behaviors, possibly crossing into the realm of legally actionable misconduct in the future.

In addition, most training tends to focus on actions of "harassers" and rights of "victims," leaving trainees feeling uncomfortable with labels with which they do not identify. Workplace behaviors are not as simple as these labels suggest, so it is easy for attendees to reassure themselves that they are not the ones being described. As a result, the training misses the most important goal: influencing behavioral change.

And notwithstanding efforts to implement some type of workplace sexual harassment training over the years, there is little data that evaluates its efficacy. The lack of data is not surprising. Employers may not be motivated to incorporate assessment analytics into their training if they perceive that negative feedback will undermine the affirmative defense they are trying to create. It is important to note, however, the data on training that does exist casts doubt on its efficacy.[99]

Another flaw in programs developed with a primary eye toward defending against a potential lawsuit is that policies for reporting sexual harassment are generally underutilized. Based on its analysis of existing data, the EEOC Task Force reported that "approximately 70% of individuals who experienced harassment never even talked with a supervisor, manager, or union representative about the harassing conduct." Rather, those who experience sex-based harassment are more likely to avoid the harasser, deny or downplay their experience, or try to ignore or endure the behavior.[100]

The Complicity of Loyalty

What happens in a workplace where senior management is protective of those with whom they share a trusted relationship and HR is protective of senior management? That is a scenario that plays out in countless workplaces as a result of the convergence of unconscious biases, long-standing loyalties, and an instinctive desire to protect the organization's brand and its bottom line.

These factors may have influenced what is alleged to have transpired at the Huffington Post, following claims that a managing editor sexually harassed multiple young women he had hired for the publication's Editorial Fellows program in New York.[101]

According to reporting, Arianna Huffington knew that a trusted member of her editorial team and her former chief of staff, Jimmy Soni, was accused of sexually harassing young women, but she did not take any action.[102] An HR investigation began only after one of the young fellows told a more senior employee about her discomfort with Soni's after-hours Facebook messages, particularly as Soni's pressure on her to socially engage with him coincided with an imminent decision about whether any fellows would be hired as full-time employees.

After the HR investigation commenced, Soni was transferred to India, to launch Huff/Post India. As one commentator stated: "It is important to note that oftentimes, harassers in positions of power can continue to engage in sexual misconduct without consequence due to the complicity of those in their professional sphere. And that includes women."[103]

In the face of multiple allegations of sexual harassment, Soni's transfer to a foreign country—one where he had strong family ties—was positioned as a new internal opportunity, certainly not a disciplinary action.[104] Soni departed the Huffington Post altogether a short time later, during the time parent company AOL was conducting an investigation.[105] His stated reason was that he was leaving to write a book.[106]

This dynamic is one that plays out with frequency. People at the top of an organization develop close relationships with individuals who have demonstrated loyalty. When the rumor mill begins to sound the alarm about inappropriate conduct among a close lieutenant, the natural tendency for the leader is to choose to believe in the person they see each day—someone who comports himself or herself as a trustworthy and loyal employee.

Until an official complaint is launched, it is much easier for the senior leader to convince oneself that the rumors are the result of office politics or jealousy. To believe otherwise calls into question the leader's own judgment and ability to select key staff of strong character.

Yet even as the rumors appear to be ignored by leadership, they continue as the topic of internal conversations in the workplace. The inevitable conclusion that others reach is that the chief of the organization does not care about the allegations and only wants to protect his or her trusted lieutenant, leaving employees feeling demoralized.

The Huffington Post's response also demonstrated the discounting of women's stories. No information emerged regarding the results of the HR investigation, and Soni's transfer to India was presented as an opportunity. Left behind were the concerns expressed about Soni's behavior.

Takin' Care of Business

In many of the companies where the misconduct of high-profile individuals has been reported in the media, the response from senior executives has been to express surprise, justified by a claim of reliance on a purported lack of prior reporting to HR. This is then followed by a commitment to conduct an internal investigation. The initiation of an investigation, however, only after allegations become public suggests a flawed internal process and underscores how sexual assault and sexual harassment can continue unaddressed through a culture of plausible deniability.

It should be unacceptable to any workplace leader that journalists can discover multiple allegations of lewd and indecent behavior, yet the organization's internal structures lack sufficient due diligence to similarly bring such misconduct to light. As the humiliating revelations have shown, proclaiming a lack of knowledge tends to sound more like plausible deniability than meaningful reflection.

In an article in *Fortune*, the authors described the conflicting perspectives of the role of HR departments:

> *As nice and well-meaning as they may be, your colleagues in HR don't work for you. Management signs their paychecks, and their No. 1 priority is to serve and protect the company. . . .*
>
> *For every Harvey Weinstein, there are roughly 86,000 discrimination and retaliation cases filed with the U.S. Equal Employment Opportunity Commission each year. And behind every fallen offender and hostile workplace, it seems, there is a complicit HR department—the executor of a liability-avoidance strategy that ticks all the boxes (cookie-cutter antidiscrimination training, a perfunctory investigations process, silencing arbitration, and nondisclosure agreements).*[107]

If employees do not trust the respective roles and loyalties of workplace leaders, including those in HR, silence will always feel like the safest choice.

A Matter of Trust

The failure to report is not unreasonable. If the process cannot be trusted, then it is rendered ineffective.

Those who are considering whether to report misconduct often fear they will become subject to retaliation. In its overt form, retaliation can result in being denied a promotion or being transferred. Other forms of retaliation can include being ostracized in some way, such as physical or social isolation from one's peers, gossip about the victim that undermines her allegations, labeling the victim as a troublemaker, or other negative treatment that weakens any process for addressing negative conduct.

These concerns are fundamental to every person aggrieved by another individual in the workplace. The effectiveness of any system rests on the belief that the system will protect the victim from these impacts.

The question for every workplace, therefore, is whether the foundational elements of its policies and reporting process operate to support victims. Yet organization leaders—including human resources personnel—may see their primary role in these types of matters as protecting and defending the company. For example, in a lawsuit filed against Microsoft for gender discrimination, the complainant alleged that when people reported their concerns about disparity in pay and promotions to HR, their complaints were often ignored and, in some instances, their workplace circumstances worsened.[108]

Exposing the facts underlying a report of misconduct could be seen as a source of embarrassment or a potential financial drain in the event of litigation. When an executive's bonuses or salary increase depends on the organization's financial performance, which can also be tied to its reputation, protecting the entity can become an instinctive behavior.

A Gender-Neutral Challenge

It is not solely men who may engage in instinctive behavior to protect the organization. In interviews for this book, numerous women described their surprise when they reported negative behaviors to senior women, only to be met with an unsympathetic response.

For example, several described instances where senior women gathered information about misconduct and then, instead of facilitating a supportive response and offering strategic assistance, reported back to leadership and participated in damage control. In some instances, reporting resulted in greater scrutiny of the victims or bystanders who provided the information. Some noted that, for the first time in their careers, they received complaints about purported errors in their work product. One woman noted:

> *The errors that were pointed out were so minor. But when you are in the thick of it, you just start to doubt yourself and your work quality.*

Another described a social event at which a senior leader made nuanced sexual remarks and inappropriately touched a female subordinate. Shortly after she reported the behavior, she was told that her performance was no longer acceptable and that she was at risk of being terminated if she did not improve. In describing the events, she stated:

> *What struck me at the meeting where I was informed of this apparently sudden change in my performance was how angry the female senior manager was. I also learned that another woman suffered the same reaction after reporting. The manager became angry with her about a variety of things and accused her of not being a team player.*

Several interviewees described an additional level of bullying that resulted from senior women who supported the institution over the female victims. One interviewee shared her experiences of workplace misconduct, and then described being bullied via email by a senior female leader who levied a barrage of complaints about her work and her commitment.

Each of these interviewees expressed their bewilderment at the response of senior women who may have themselves experienced harassment in the early stages of their careers. They were dismayed that the women did not instinctively want to help and questioned the motivations behind their response. Was it to demonstrate that they remain good corporate players striving to protect the organization? One interviewee stated:

> *The senior woman had the attitude that "I've been here for 30+ years and as I near retirement, I'm not going to see this place tank now."*

For senior women in the organization, there may be an additional reason for their apparent lack of assistance. Women remain underrepresented in key leadership roles in most organizations. When there are relatively few, if any, women in top management, it is difficult to place the expectations for addressing these behaviors on those few senior-level women who themselves may feel they lack the authority to help without facing repercussions to their own position.

The Complicity of Silence

At the highest levels, the tendency to discount the credibility and experiences of women sends a message that reinforces silence as a safer alternative to reporting. As Professors Epstein and Goodman stated:

> *All too frequently, system gatekeepers also discount the importance of women's actual experiences and of the ways in which the system itself exposes women to additional harms. Such experiential discounting occurs when, regardless of the plausibility of a survivor's story and regardless of her personal trustworthiness—in other words, even when system actors believe her—they nonetheless adopt and enforce laws and policies that, in practice, re-victimize her.*
>
> *These issues—credibility discounting and experiential discounting—cannot be considered in isolation. Such an approach would fail to capture the way that each relies on and reinforces the other, both in practical reality and through the personal lens of survivor experience.[109]*

Workplace harassment and negative conduct survives in the protective embrace of entrenched responses. These behaviors cannot be erased with a video program and a flawed system of reporting.

To effectively address these challenges, employers must first understand the workplace conditions that allow negative conduct to exist. It is impossible to build an infrastructure that changes culture without understanding what drives that culture.

Do You See What I See?

The Contagious Misuse of Power

Young women in the workplace can offer a litany of examples detailing when they had to get past observations about their physical appearance before it was possible to move on to the business at hand. It may seem easy to dismiss such comments focusing on one's physical appearance as inconsequential, but in many settings, these remarks go far deeper than a simple compliment—or insult—and have a far more malicious impact. These are comments that have the effect of wielding power and diminishing competency.

An associate who worked as a litigator at a well-regarded law firm described the discomfort she felt with remarks that undermined her standing as a professional:

> *I frequently get comments about my appearance. One time, at a court hearing, a lawyer on the other side of the case asked me why I looked different and kept asking questions like, "Is it your hair?" or "Are you wearing glasses?" Then he said, "You look beautiful." Another time I was meeting with a witness prior to a deposition who I had not met before—just spoke to on the phone. His first words on meeting me were, "Wow! You look so much different than what I expected you to look like." A male walking into a room doesn't have to deal with these comments.*

Her observation points directly to challenges that feel formidable but become blurred by a hyper-focus on the legal definition of sexual harassment. The fact is, few comments rise to the level of legally actionable sexual harassment. But there are a world of behaviors that can leave employees feeling drained and diminished. That is why it is so important for employers to develop a contextual understanding of the broad range of behaviors that may not be legally proscribed but nonetheless undermine careers.

To lay a foundation for the sensitive conversations that will inevitably be necessary to create a more respectful work environment, it is instructive to begin with an analysis of academic research. For decades, researchers have been studying gender interactions and behaviors, as well as workplace power dynamics, but these studies are generally underutilized and difficult to access. This is unfortunate, as the studies offer an opportunity to serve as resources upon which sound policies can be built.

Consider, for example, the study of power, which has resulted in varied definitions and longstanding efforts to determine how it is wielded and how it persists within organizations. Professor Vincent Roscigno, who analyzed nearly 70,000 discrimination cases, detailed "the sheer prevalence of inequality within seemingly neutral institutional and certainly bureaucratic organization contexts, but also the ways in which power is specifically enacted and hierarchy/inequality reinforced."[110] He importantly noted that institutional rules do not necessarily constrain behavior and may even be the basis for justifying mistreatment:

> *Deeper immersion into case materials, however, which include narratives of victims, perpetrators and witnesses, reveals that conceptions of organizations and bureaucratic structures as constraining relative to malicious treatment and irrational conduct are both inadequate and overly determined. More often than not, in fact, and rather than constraining,* bureaucratic structures and procedures were invoked in a relatively discretionary way by powerful actors in a manner that reifies hierarchies and inequalities by age, sex and race. *Indeed . . . managers and supervisors often*

*draw from relatively neutral organizational rules and mandates
to isolate, harass, demote, retaliate, and in many cases, terminate
workers who were already being treated unjustly.*[111]

Professor Roscigno identified ways that individuals in positions of power actually relied on institutional policies to engage in
"discretionary policing" to reach an outcome that ostracized, penal-
ized, or resulted in the termination of minorities, women, and senior
employees:

> *The decoupling of formal procedure from everyday practice
> provides flexibility for more powerful organizational actors to
> exclude, to hoard, or to be particularistic, as long as behaviors
> can be justified relative to some formal policy. This allows power
> abuses, malicious behaviors and inequality to commence, often
> unabated.*[112]

In other words, organizational structures that appear to offer a
veneer of fairness can actually be at the root of behaviors that result
in inequality. Those who are less powerful may be viewed as either
problematic or not as worthy as others, allowing those in power to
hide behind institutional dictates in meting out what they deem as
appropriate, punitive measures. The organizational structure and its
"seemingly neutral policies" do not constrain, but rather enable the
"power imbalances and related inequalities" to flourish.[113]

In *The Tipping Point*, Malcolm Gladwell analyzed how behaviors
take hold within a population. Gladwell looked, for example, at the
rise of teen smoking in the United States to understand how someone's
negative behaviors could cause others to feel encouraged to similarly
engage. He noted that antismoking efforts have long focused on changing attitudes toward smoking through such measures as public health
messages, the curtailment of advertisements, and limiting access to
minors. These efforts, however, have not had the desired impact on the
behaviors of young adults.

Instead, as Gladwell noted, the initial step—the first time a teenager
lights a cigarette—depends on that teen's exposure to someone who

appears cool, "who gives teenagers 'permission' to engage in deviant acts."[114] This is what Gladwell describes as the "contagion" side of the Tipping Point, as distinct from the "stickiness" component that turns a casual smoker into someone addicted to cigarettes. While Gladwell focuses on the "stickiness" issue as possibly holding the key to combating teen smoking, it is the "contagion" element that may have more relevance to the way in which negative cultures in workplaces are perpetuated through permission-giving—that is, individuals observe people in powerful or interesting roles (perhaps people they may want to emulate in some way) engaging in deviant behaviors that seem to provide permission to others to behave accordingly.

Stanford professor Robert Sutton described the contagion of bad workplace behavior, citing research in which exposure to a rude person in a negotiation will increase the likelihood that the exposed individual will carry that rudeness into a subsequent negotiation with someone else. He also pointed out that the ability to wield power and influence over others increases the likelihood of engaging in negative behavior:

> *Regardless of how kindly, cooperatively, and empathetically you've acted in the past, power can cause you to have less empathy, to exploit others more, to focus on your own needs, to be rude and disrespectful, and to act like the rules don't apply to you.*[115]

These perspectives help demonstrate that organizations cannot rely on their existing policies as proof that negative behaviors, if they occurred, would be anomalous. Scholarly research provides an abundance of evidence showing that human beings are far more complex and hierarchies are too well entrenched to assume that a simple policy will deliver the desired behavior. Research offers helpful guidance for the development of more coherent workplace policies as well as a far more meaningful approach to a supportive and respectful workplace culture.

The Man in the Mirror

In late 2017, the *New York Times*, in collaboration with the polling and media company Morning Consult, conducted an online survey of

615 men who worked full-time, asking them about their own conduct in the workplace. Although a limitation of such a study is the extent to which people will honestly self-report bad behaviors, even with this cautionary factor the results were illuminating.

Approximately 25 percent of the men reported that they engaged in such activities as telling crude jokes or stories or sharing inappropriate videos—behaviors the researchers called *gender harassment*. Ten percent reported that they engaged in unwelcome sexual attention such as touching or commenting on someone's body or continuing to ask them on a date even after the person said no. And 2 percent said they engaged in sexually coercive behaviors such as pressuring a person into having sex by threatening retaliation or offering a benefit.[116]

The survey also revealed a worrisome link between less benign and more aggressive behaviors: "Men who admitted to telling sexual stories or jokes were about five times as likely to report other harassing behaviors."[117] This reinforced a key point: workplaces that dismiss some hurtful behaviors as "just a joke" minimize its implications, including as a harbinger of other negative behaviors.

It is important to note that the *New York Times*/Morning Consult survey respondents encompassed a broad range of demographics, including younger and older age cohorts, those from blue- and white-collar backgrounds, married and single, as well as Democrats and Republicans. The key behavior differential was in the culture of the workplace:

> *A major difference between those who harass and those who don't is the culture at their workplace. Behaviors associated with harassment are especially prevalent among men who say their company does not have guidelines against harassment, hotlines to report it or punishment for perpetrators, or who say their managers don't care.*[118]

The study also drew a link between feelings of resentment at work and harassing behaviors. Specifically, the research showed that those who were more likely to acknowledge their own harassing behaviors included respondents "who described a feeling of resentment, saying they were unappreciated by coworkers or superiors or that colleagues received undeserved promotions."[119]

This study showed how workplace culture infuses behavior. Accordingly, if the goal is to foster a culture of civility and respect, it is necessary to create a climate where negative behaviors are not tolerated and clear standards are set regarding the way people interact with each other as colleagues. Employers who articulate expectations about conduct and provide a transparent process for addressing complaints may be far more likely to achieve a culture of civility and mutual respect.

Another aspect of achieving a respectful workplace, however, requires that people honestly appraise themselves. Too often, we tend to minimize our own shortcomings. Professor Sutton described how the human tendency to be overconfident can lead to misconduct in the workplace:

> We are prone to developing distorted and overly positive self-images—and to deny, disregard, or never notice negative information about ourselves. For most of us, coming to grips with when we act like jerks, or encourage others to do so, requires overcoming some mighty potent predilections. . . .
>
> Consider that more than 50 percent of Americans say they have experienced or witnessed persistent bullying, but less than 1 percent admit to doing it.

He encouraged leaders in organizations to be open to the truth about themselves and encourage feedback that may be painful to hear.

Perceiving What Isn't There

The dismissive reference to an uncorroborated allegation as "he said/she said" demeans victims while empowering perpetrators. The phrase is used to justify a lack of follow-up, even as it lets the workplace look like it takes matters seriously—but apparently only when there are witnesses. The lack of a witness to harassing conduct, however, is hardly proof that it did not occur.

Employers would benefit from a deeper understanding of research that helps to explain potential reasons for harassment and other negative behaviors in the workplace. These studies offer a wealth of knowledge that can help inform training programs as well as policy development.

Researchers have long studied how men and women perceive sexual intent differently. The results generally show that men more frequently misperceive women's level of sexual intent and infer greater sexual interest from women than women themselves report. A comprehensive review of numerous studies analyzing gender differences in sexual intent perceptions noted:

> We conclude that gender-based differences in sexual intent perceptions are reliable.... Furthermore, they are most pronounced when the target is female; the target's behaviors are mundane; the situation has the possibility of friendly or sexual outcomes; and the rater has pejorative attitudes about women, sex, and heterosexual relationships.[120]

Another study sought to understand the role of personality in these misperceptions, and whether such misperceptions can lead to sexual aggression when not resolved.[121] The researchers first analyzed past studies that demonstrated a positive correlation between hostility toward women and narcissism, as defined by a grandiose sense of self-admiration and importance, among other characteristics. They noted that those high in narcissism are more apt to seek casual sexual relationships, finding partners who can reinforce their positive self-image. They also reviewed research into the quality of sensation-seeking, which is:

> ... defined as the enjoyment of exciting and potentially dangerous activities. Men who frequently misperceive women's sexual intentions appear to be acting impulsively. They "jump to conclusions," eagerly interpreting friendly responses from women as a sign of sexual interest. They then act immediately rather than gathering further evidence of women's level of interest.[122]

The researchers sought to determine the impact of these two personality constructs—narcissism and sensation-seeking—on men's misperception of women's sexual intent. The study results suggested "that it is narcissists' distrust and suspicion toward women, rather than a proclivity toward short-term and casual relationships, which increases their risk for misperception." Moreover, because it is difficult for narcissists to accept rejection, when they do misperceive intent, such "experiences might already exacerbate their already hostile views of women."[123]

This research may help inform workplace policies. For example, a simple admonishment or a policy that offers a prescriptive series of "do's and don'ts" may not work for those executives or other employers who demonstrate these personality characteristics. The study's authors stated:

> Selective prevention programs are needed for men at risk of committing sexual assault because of their distorted cognitions, narcissism, and hostility toward women. Different prevention messages may be needed for men who are impulsive, enjoy casual sex, and are often drinking in casual sex situations. In their rush to fulfill their own sexual desires, these men may cross the line into sexual assault because they did not pay sufficient attention to their partners' cues.[124]

Other research has sought to assess how individual differences in attitudes about engaging in short-term sexual relationships that lack emotional bonds ("sociosexuality") relate to studies showing that men misperceive sexual intent more frequently than women. Researchers looked at whether attitudes about casual sex, more than simply gender, contributed toward the variances previously identified in how men misperceive sexual intent more than women.

The study found that men show a greater interest in sociosexual behaviors than women and that men are more likely to rate female faces as more flirtatious than women do when asked to rate both male and female faces. The study sought to determine if the results were driven more by the underlying views of the survey participants or by their gender, and found that attitudes toward short-term sexual behaviors were a better indicator of perceptions than gender alone: "Our findings demonstrate that it may well be one's propensity to engage in, or attitude towards, casual short-term sexual relationships that is the most important mediating factor in perceiving the sexual intent of others."[125]

Another study looking at perceived sexual intent analyzed whether the order in which questions were framed could bias responses of self-reported interest among men and women. That is, would responses about one's own intentions differ if research asked about how they perceived the intentions of others before they were asked about themselves? Among other findings, the results "corroborated the conclusion that men *over*estimate women's sexual intention and women *under*estimate men's sexual intention."[126]

Another study looked at the effect of power on sexual perceptions, finding that "power leads to the perception of intentions and desires in others that are consistent with the power holder's own motives."[127] In analyzing how this study builds upon prior research demonstrating the potential of power to bring out antisocial tendencies, the authors stated:

> . . . *power sexualizes social interactions in part because it biases the perceived intentions and desires of others. Hence, power can set the stage for harassment, because it leads to a fundamental misperception of the social environment.*

The myriad studies identifying ways that intent can be viewed differently by men and women may be helpful in developing more comprehensive training programs, particularly as traditional approaches have not resulted in significant behavioral changes.

Still another area where academic research may inform workplace training and policy development is that of consent. For example, notwithstanding decades of educational and preventative programs on college campuses, there has not been a corresponding decline in the rates of sexual assault.[128] In response to this data, a group of researchers sought to analyze the link between sexual assault and sexual consent.

They explored, in particular, gender differences in how college students defined sexual consent as well as how they communicated their consent and lack of consent.

The study found that there was little gender difference in how males and females responded to questions asking how they defined consent. They both saw the giving of consent as an explicit communication in which they were agreeing to engage in sexual activity.

There were, however, gender differences in the way in which men and women perceived consent from their partner. Men, for example, were more likely to rely on nonverbal cues in assuming consent to sexual activity, where women were more likely to assess verbal cues in interpreting their partner's consent. Men were similarly more likely to rely on nonverbal cues in interpreting nonconsent. The authors noted: "It may be the case that a man might think that a woman is giving him signals of consent, when in fact she does not intend to consent to engage in sexual activity; this type of miscommunication could lead to sex that the woman perceives as unwanted or coercive."[129]

The study pointed to the importance of understanding "how individuals communicate and interpret nonconsent, as nonconsent that is not recognized and honored by a partner could lead to sexual assault."[130]

The interpretation of this data has particular applicability to a workplace setting where sexual overtures are made in the context of power imbalances, a reporting process that is not trusted, and a looming fear of retribution for resistance or for speaking up. Silence interpreted as consent may rather represent a hope that the behavior will stop.

Of relevance, the researchers interpreted their findings of verbal versus nonverbal cues in this way:

> [W]omen may tolerate a certain level of sexual activity, even surpassing a level of intimacy with which they are comfortable, hoping that men will stop at that behavior rather than progressing to more intimate behaviors such as sexual intercourse. However . . . men may interpret that silence as permission or consent to continue to engage in increasingly more intimate behaviors. . . . Furthermore, some men may also interpret a woman's refusals,

either verbal or nonverbal, as token resistance, even if the refusals are genuine, and continue to progress in sexual behavior. . . . Both situations could result in a man unintentionally having sex with an unwilling woman without him realizing that she was not consenting to the sexual activity."[131]

These findings do not ameliorate how individual conduct is addressed under existing laws. Rather, they are offered to add context to a complex topic in which, all too often, actions occur without consequence. The researchers saw these differences as relevant to sexual assault prevention programming, to ensure that "perceptions of sexual consent and gender power norms" are appropriately addressed.[132]

In the Workplace, It's More About Status, Not Sex

Studies analyzing the different ways that men and women perceive intent provide a helpful understanding of how behaviors can be interpreted—and misinterpreted. This can assist in understanding a subset of workplace behaviors and in considering policies and accountability measures that would fit these circumstances. Of great significance when analyzing the full range of negative conduct in the workplace, however, is the emerging data on sex-based harassment as a form of gender discrimination.

University of British Columbia professor Jennifer Berdahl's work provides insight in explaining the root cause of workplace harassment. She argues that, underlying all workplace harassment is a desire to protect one's own social status and that the focus on sexual harassment as based on sexual desire impedes the ability to recognize that the basis of harassment is actually sex discrimination:

Instead of viewing sexual harassment as inherently driven by sexual desire, a desire in men to dominate women, or both, I suggest it is fundamentally motivated by the basic desire, present in everyone, to protect or enhance one's social status against threat. Sexual harassment occurs because the motive for social status takes shape in a context of gender hierarchy.[133]

Professor Berdahl stressed the need to step back from the view of harassers as being flawed human beings. Instead, she described sex-based harassment as rooted in gender hierarchy and supported by the incentives that exist in a culture that allows social status to be based on sex. In analyzing decades of research on harassing behaviors, Professor Berdahl notes that harassment occurs through the use of "organizational, economic, physical, or social power . . . which explains why organizational subordinates can, and do, harass their superiors."[134] Moreover, sex-based harassment can be inter- and intra-group in its form, arising out of the desire that all individuals have to protect their social status.

In her own research, Professor Berdahl analyzed whether women were more likely to be sexually harassed if they met traditional feminine ideals, or whether they were more likely to be harassed if they deviated from those ideals. Her hypothesis was based on other studies showing a link between gender harassment and sexist hostility, as opposed to sexual desire: "Women threaten male identity when they blur distinctions between men and women and thereby challenge the legitimacy of these distinctions and the status they confer upon men."[135]

Her findings revealed that women whose personalities were more masculine as well as women who worked in male-dominated organizations experienced more sexual harassment than both men and women in female-dominated occupations. Women who demonstrated more masculine qualities were, on average, more than twice as likely to be harassed as other women and more than eight times more likely than men.

Berdahl concluded that workplaces must shift the focus away from viewing sex-based harassment as rooted in desire and recognize it as rooted in issues of power and control:

> *The current research suggests that sexual harassment as traditionally defined for women—as consisting of sexual and sexist comments, unwanted sexual attention, and sexual coercion—is primarily targeted at women who step out of place by having masculine characteristics, or "uppity" women. By implication, this*

suggests that sexual harassment is driven not out of desire for women who meet feminine ideals but out of a desire to punish those who violate them.[136]

A *Yale Law Journal* article noted several of the power disparities that arise in the workplace sexual harassment context:

> *Employers who respond to the #MeToo movement by looking solely at unwanted sexualized behavior are likely to miss the forest while uprooting particular trees. By contrast, examining the allocation of power in contemporary workplaces helps identify where and in what form sexual harassment is likely to occur. Not only are top-level employees uniquely situated to sexually harass their subordinates, their disproportionate influence and control makes any form of harassment, or any implicit threat of adverse consequences, more menacing.*[137]

A study analyzing the intersection of sexual harassment and masculinity examined the social practice of "girl watching." The research focused on the way in which such behavior is often treated as both normal and trivial—a form of play among males where they share a masculine identity and that is often dismissed as "boys will be boys." The study's author noted the themes that emerged:

> *First, girl watching appears to function as a form of gendered play among men. This play is productive of masculine identities and premised on a studied lack of empathy with the feminine other. Second, men understand the targeted woman to be an object rather than a player in the game, and she is most often not the intended audience. This obfuscation of a woman's subjectivity, and men's refusal to consider the effects of their behavior, means men are likely to be confused when a woman complains. Thus, the production of masculinity through girl watching, and its compulsory disempathy, may be one factor in gender differences in the labeling of harassment.*

> *... In its most serious form, girl watching operates as a targeted tactic of power. The men seem to want everyone—the targeted woman as well as coworkers, clients, and superiors—to know they are looking. The gaze demonstrates their right, as men, to sexually evaluate women. Through the gaze, the targeted woman is reduced to a sexual object, contradicting her other identities, such as that of competent worker or leader.*[138]

In order to perpetuate their own sense of masculine identity, the men ignore any pain their behavior causes the women. The men have, in essence, traded empathy for their shared behavior, failing—or refusing—to recognize the harm caused by their actions, and how those actions may contribute to a hostile work environment.

The study further pointed out the implications for sexual harassment training that arises from the men's lack of empathy and their objectification of women. In the study, men viewed a sexual harassment training video and judged the women in it who complained as inferior women, sending the message "that women who complain are those who fail at femininity."[139]

The author reported that some harassing behaviors "are mechanisms through which gendered boundaries are patrolled and evoked and by which deeply held identities are established."[140] The study concluded by stating that, for sexual harassment training to be effective, it will need to help people understand the way in which empathy is relinquished to masculinity.

This study helps explain why workplace programs designed to meet the letter of the law are generally ineffective. Too often, such programs are premised on the notion that negative behaviors are caused by a lack of knowledge about what conduct is and is not acceptable. As this research shows, however, men may not identify their behavior as meeting the definition of sexual harassment:

> *... the source of this contradiction lies not so much in ignorance but in acts of ignoring. Traditional sexual harassment training programs address the former rather than the later.*[141]

Ultimately, the success of training to stem harassment will depend on programs that convey an understanding of the underlying motivations and gendered identities that result in these behaviors.

Changing the Framework from Sex to Equality

Yale Law School professor Vicki Schultz identified the pernicious way in which developing legal doctrine that has addressed workplace sexual harassment has harmed women, as well as men, who do not conform to male norms of behavior. She meticulously analyzed case law that emerged under Title VII to demonstrate the harm that has emerged from the courts' hyper-focus on the sexual nature of the perpetrator's conduct, rather than the far more debilitating impacts of other negative and harassing behaviors.

Schultz described how courts have relied on a narrow sexual desire–dominance paradigm to analyze whether the alleged offending conduct rose to the level of a claim for sexual harassment under Title Vll. In most cases, the judges disaggregated sexual and nonsexual conduct into separate claims, rather than view them together as part of the harassment claim.

By failing to move beyond a restrictive focus on sex, however, and by excluding from consideration the humiliating and debilitating impact of non-sexual harassing behaviors, the courts missed an important opportunity "to expand the concept of hostile work environment harassment to include all conduct that is rooted in gender-based expectations about work roles and to recognize that harassment functions as a way of undermining women's perceived competence as workers."[142]

By this disaggregation, Schultz argued, courts ignore workplace cultures and conditions that can create hostile work environments, resulting in the trivialization of both the hostile work environment claim as well as the disparate treatment claim:

> *When removed from the larger discriminatory context, the sexual conduct can appear insignificant. For this reason, courts often conclude that the harassment was not sufficiently severe or pervasive*

to alter the conditions of employment and create a hostile or abusive work environment.

By the same token, when women are denied the training, information, and support they need to succeed on the job, or when they are subjected to threatening or alienating acts that undermine their confidence and sense of belonging, they can easily be made to appear (or even become) less than fully proficient at their jobs. This lack of proficiency then becomes the nondiscriminatory reason that justifies the hostile treatment that has undermined their competence. Furthermore, when separated from sexual advances and other sexual conduct, the nonsexual actions may appear to be gender-neutral forms of hazing with which the law should not interfere. For these reasons, courts frequently rule against plaintiffs on the ground that acts were not directed at them because of their sex.[143]

Schultz also expressed concern about "sexual paternalism"—the focus on sexual advances that results in courts protecting women for the wrong reasons, such as concern for their virtue. When courts are focusing on a women's sensibilities, rather than the gender bias they encounter, the result is generally not only sexist, but also classist:

To conform to the image of the proper victim, women must comport themselves as sexually pure, even passive, beings who have been violated by their coworkers' sexual predation. This requirement is not only sexist, but also class-biased in nature, for working-class women are less likely than more privileged women to be perceived as pure . . . Regardless of their backgrounds or their underlying motivations, women who participate in sexual joking and ribaldry become fallen women, no longer capable of finding harassment unwelcome—even when that harassment consists of nonsexual actions with the purpose of driving them away from the job or undermining their competence or authority on the job. Within the sexual desire-dominance paradigm, the focus on protecting women from sexual violation deflects attention away from such nonsexual assaults on their capabilities as workers.[144]

Where Gender Bias and Racism Intersect

The research tells us that workplace policies are far less likely to be effective unless built upon an understanding of why people engage in harassing conduct. This also means recognizing that neither the experience nor the root cause of harassment or negative behaviors are identical for all victims. The intersection of race and gender has significant implications for women and men of color: "In general, people who experience sex-based harassment are more likely to experience racial-ethnic harassment, further suggesting the importance of intersectional analysis . . ."[145]

Studies support what we anecdotally already know: women of color experience higher rates of harassment than white women. For example, an analysis of demographic trends in reported cases to the EEOC over two decades revealed that, although there has been a decline in complaints filed by white women, there has been no change in the number of claims brought by women of color as well as older women:

> Women of color and older women are reporting just as much harassment as they were 20 years ago. This certainly looks like a cultural issue within companies, as evidenced by the fact that the biggest employers made the least progress in reducing sexual harassment claims. . . .
>
> Managers and human resources departments should understand that while existing techniques may have reduced sexual harassment among some groups, they're not working for everyone. New training and reporting mechanisms, ones that recognize the seeming disparity in the progress that we've made, are necessary.[146]

In a study investigating the sexual and racial harassment experiences of African American women, the researchers found that the negative conduct described by the study participants did not fall within neat categories of either racial harassment or sexual harassment. Rather, they intersected in a pattern of racialized sexual harassment.

The study identified three specific patterns of bias. Most frequently, the study participants described covert harassment reflecting an overall bias. A particular example reported by several participants in supervisory roles was the refusal of white female subordinates to undertake tasks they regularly performed previously for white supervisors. A second form of harassment was described as subtly overt bias that occurred when sexually harassing behaviors were infused by stereotypes about sexuality and African American women. The third category consisted of overt behaviors that combined racist and sexist conduct—for example, where white males made sexual overtures while referring to the victim's race.

The study examined the way in which these patterns of bias emerge to serve as "a subtle reminder that Black women should not be in positions of authority."[147] The authors noted:

> *In extreme cases, this behavior can take the form of contrapower sexual harassment (e.g., a female professor being harassed by a male student). Black women may be more vulnerable to harassment from male or White subordinates because their achieved status or formal organizational power does not mitigate their lower ascribed status as members of a marginalized group . . .*[148]

The study also found that many of the sexualized racist acts were perpetrated by white women. This has particularly important ramifications for workplace strategies to address racialized sexual harassment and warrants a rethinking of old assumptions. For example, the authors highlighted that "some of the safeguards against harassment, such as working in an all-women environment, may not offer protection for African American women."[149]

When a woman of color seeks to report a perpetrator's behavior, she is at high risk of experiencing the credibility discounting described previously:

> *Indeed, a wide array of women may be viewed as untrustworthy because of who they are—women, Black women, poor women, women who exhibit trauma symptoms that are easily conflated with a lack of credibility, and women who are many or all of the above. This distrust, in turn, creates a broader hermeneutics of*

suspicion, through which the listener interprets the substance of her story. In other words, once a listener has discounted a woman's trustworthiness, he will be hyperalert for signs of deception, irrationality, or narrative incompetence in her story. He will tend to magnify inconsistencies and overlook the ways in which any inconsistencies might be explained away.[150]

It is important to emphasize that the full scope and impact of the intersectionality challenge remains to be more fully defined in the research. As the EEOC reported, much of the sexual harassment research is based on the experiences of white women, and much of the research on ethnic harassment is based on men's experiences:

As a result, current research may underestimate the extent and nature of intersectionality harassment. . . . The bottom line is that there is a great deal we do not know about the prevalence of harassment that occurs because of an employee's race, ethnicity, religion, age, disability, gender identity, or sexual orientation. This is so despite the fact that there is no shortage of private sector charges and federal sector complaints that are filed claiming harassment on such grounds.[151]

The Reach of Harassment Extends Beyond Gender

Once the definition of harassment is understood as conduct that can extend far beyond a narrow view of sexualized behaviors, the full scope of its impact on those outside conforming norms in the workplace can be recognized. Same-sex and LGBTQ harassment are areas where negative behavior has little to do with sex and much more to do with the punishment of people who do not conform to gender norms, as studies focusing on LGBTQ individuals in the workplace demonstrate.[152]

The limited data that exists makes clear that LGBTQ individuals experience extraordinarily high rates of harassment and derogatory comments.[153] Professor Schultz described a prevalent form of harassment by men against men who do not conform to masculine norms. She analyzed numerous court cases in which men suspected of being gay were cruelly harassed, but because the harassment did not involve a more powerful person seeking sexual demands or favors, the employers escaped liability.

Courts, Schultz argued, should include in their analysis the ways in which work cultures detrimentally impact those who do not conform. Schultz's competence-centered analysis framework would result in a redirection of the court's focus "toward the processes through which men create work cultures that sustain their own idealized definitions of masculine mastery to the detriment of men who cannot or will not conform."[154]

A respondent to the Women's Bar Association of Massachusetts survey described being subject to inappropriate touching and comments by a senior male attorney and succinctly explained his unwillingness to report the conduct:

> *He was a highly respected partner who would have denied the claim and made it clear I would be fired if I told anyone.*

If the focus on #MeToo is to bring about workplace change, all communities must be included in its scope. It is also important to understand that the ability of employees to share their story will vary significantly depending on their circumstances. An article in the *Nation* highlighted this challenge:

> *Women in marginalized communities are more likely to be victims of sexual assault and often face more hurdles to being believed when they come forward. . . .*
>
> *Industries in which women of color workers are strongly represented are also particular hotbeds of sexual harassment and assault.*[155]

The article noted studies reporting the high rates of workplace harassment that black women and Latinas who work in the fast-food industry experience as well as the vulnerabilities of home health care workers. The author concluded with a cautionary note for those committed to creating respectful and inclusive workplace environments:

> Women and men living at the margins of American society are far from immune to sexual assault, and it is the duty of those of us who feel safe enough to tell stories without fear of retribution, jail time, or deportation to make a little more space, to consider that not everyone feels like they can say #metoo.

Undermining Female Authority

Even as many studies have analyzed the power imbalance seen in harassing behaviors experienced by women in subordinate roles, there is also research into the negative behaviors experienced by women in positions of authority. The results should be a warning to any organization that thinks that women in leadership roles, absent critical mass, can alone effect organizational change.

For example, one study analyzed the power-threat theory in the context of behaviors against women who have obtained supervisory roles, particularly in male-dominated organizations. The study found that a woman's supervisory status can actually increase the likelihood she will experience sexual harassment. In explaining why women in authority were targeted, the study authors noted:

> Women supervisors repeatedly spoke about feeling isolated and of harassment by co-workers and subordinates directed towards putting them "in their place." Still, they tolerated such harassment to keep their jobs. . . .
>
> In particular, we find that female supervisors are more, rather than less, likely to be harassed, supporting the notion that interactions between workers are not driven strictly by organizational rank. Instead, co-workers' relative power is also shaped by gender. Although women supervisors' authority is legitimated by their employer, sexual harassment functions, in part, as a tool to enforce gender-appropriate behavior.[156]

Another study analyzing contrapower harassment reported an interesting correlation with age. Female supervisors between the ages of thirty and forty-four were more likely to be harassed than women without supervisory authority. Male supervisors, however, were significantly less likely to be sexually harassed, as compared to their counterparts without supervisory roles. The study offered important advice to employers:

> *More women are climbing the career ladder and breaking the glass ceiling, yet the organizational and legal responses to sexual harassment have not kept pace with this evolution. Sexual harassment is often still merely regarded as the male boss abusing his position in the workplace to harass his female secretary. The reality proves to be far more complex and it is necessary for organizational policies and training to reflect the diversity of harassment experiences. In cases of contrapower harassment, organizational policies, and more broadly, organizational culture should allow victims to come forward without undermining their own authority.*[157]

A critical takeaway from this research is that sexual harassment, bullying, and discrimination do not necessarily diminish when a woman achieves more power in the workplace. In fact, the opposite can occur from both other supervisors and subordinates.

The research demonstrates that workplace leaders cannot make assumptions about who may be safe from negative behaviors. A more comprehensive approach is warranted. Workplaces must ensure that their training extends far beyond the more culturally ingrained image of a sexual harasser who is in a position of power and a victim who is subordinate with no base of power.

If organizations can understand the dynamics underlying negative conduct and harassment—whether or not such conduct meets a strict legal definition—they will be better equipped to design more effective training programs and policies. Employers should learn from the decades of research on harassing behaviors and the related power dynamics that have fostered their continued existence in the workplace. To be effective, training and policy development should incorporate the valuable lessons learned from this research.

The Power of Assumptions

The Pernicious Effects of Unconscious Bias in Perpetuating Gender Inequality

The study of unconscious bias—the way in which our minds operate outside our conscious awareness—can provide important insight into underlying causes of negative behaviors, including harassment and sexual assault.

Unconscious biases impact how we make decisions and choices at work. From a positive perspective, the outward expression of explicit biases and overt sexism in the workplace has diminished over the past decades, both because of increased laws and greater social awareness. Today, the challenges to diversity and inclusion can be largely found in the realm of implicit biases, which can thwart equality just as much as explicitly expressed biases do. The result, however, can be more pernicious because unconscious biases hide in the shadows.

There are many patterns of unconscious bias that research has identified as having a direct impact on our actions. For example, confirmation bias is at the root of our tendency to accept facts and information that conforms to our beliefs and reject information that is contrary to those beliefs. Confirmation bias helps explain the motives that drive people to turn a blind eye to conduct that deviates from established views or that threaten a way of life.

Confirmation bias is sometimes more accurately referred to as *myside bias*, since we only seek to confirm our own preexisting beliefs, not those of others with whom we disagree. In the workplace, as well as in any institution with which we have an affiliation, myside bias fuels the way in which institutional loyalty and pride impacts our behaviors, effectively resulting in the ability to ignore information that would diminish that pride.

In a compelling analysis defending the science of implicit bias research, the authors pointed to ten studies that demonstrate the way in which unconscious biases affect the judgment and behaviors of people in all walks of life, noting "These studies should not be ignored by anyone who is responsible for hiring, firing, interviewing, managing, or evaluating others . . ."[158]

One of the studies, for example, demonstrated that job candidates with names pretested to be white-sounding were 50 percent more likely to be called for job interviews than candidates demonstrating equal qualifications but who had names pretested to be associated with someone who is African American. Another example from this research revealed gender discrimination even among women and men of equivalent skill:

> . . . although research participants regarded female manage-rial applicants who presented themselves as confident, competitive, and ambitious (i.e., agentic) as highly qualified for a leadership role, the participants still discriminated against them (relative to men who were identically described) with respect to hiring deci-sions because the agentic women were perceived as dislikable and therefore thought to be deficient with respect to social skills. . . . These findings suggest that the prescription for female "niceness" which is often internalized at an implicit, unexamined level of awareness, penalizes agentic women in the workplace . . .[159]

Unconscious biases impact the way in which women and minori-ties are evaluated, the opportunities they are given, and their access to important work and networks vital to career success. For example, there is no shortage of articles telling women how to fix themselves and become more "leadership ready." These messages persist, notwithstanding clear evidence that it is the organization itself that needs to be fixed: "In reality, the dilemma women have faced for the last several decades is that their advancement has been limited by their exclusion from the internal sources of power."[160]

It is also not about a simple pipeline that, once filled, will spill out a cadre of women and minorities who will take their place at the helm. Comedy writer Nell Scovell dispels the notion that the exclusion women and other minority groups have faced will be resolved by a simple filling of the pipeline: "I have long believed that there is not a pipeline problem when it comes to women and people of color. I call it a broken doorbell problem: There are competent, capable women and people of color standing on the doorstep ringing the doorbell, and the door is not being opened."[161]

That door will only be opened when leaders in the workplace understand that developing diverse and inclusive leadership requires measures to identify and minimize both structural and personal unconscious biases. Moreover, leaders must also recognize that there is a direct relationship between negative workplace conduct and unconscious—and, sometimes, conscious—bias, as the studies discussed in this book make clear.

Feeling Confident—but Looking for Warmth

Women are frequently subjected to the canard that a key to their success is to develop more self-confidence and to demonstrate that self-confidence to others. One important study has demonstrated, however, that the appearance of self-confidence does not translate into equal influence:

> For women, but not for men, influence was closely tied to perceptions of warmth—how caring and prosocial they seemed. Moreover, women's self-reported confidence did not correlate with how confident these women appeared to others. While self-confidence is gender-neutral, the consequences of appearing self-confident are not. The "performance plus confidence equals power and

influence" formula is gendered. Successful women cannot "lean in" on a structure that cannot support their weight without their opportunities (and the myth) collapsing around them.[162]

One of the study's authors emphasized that, not only is it a myth to tie women's success to their appearing more self-confident, but it also imposes an unfair burden by placing expectations on women to care for others in a way that does not factor in to how men are evaluated and promoted: "This prosocial (double) standard does not appear in any job description but it is, indeed, the key performance indicator against which access, power, and influence will be granted to successful women. Men are held to a lower standard."[163]

Indeed, the longstanding problem of inequality in the workplace, whether in the form of unequal pay, lack of advancement, or sexual harassment, will not be eliminated by advice to women about how to act differently or suggesting they lean in more. In general, women have been spending so much time leaning in they are at risk of toppling over.

Professor Berdahl's research demonstrates that women who act outside gender norms face greater risk of harassment and fare even worse when their perceived masculine personalities are combined with less warmth and femininity:

> *These results highlight the double bind faced by women who are dismissed and disrespected if feminine but scorned and disliked if masculine, limiting their ascent up the organizational ladder . . . There appears to be little that women can do to avoid being victims of sex discrimination. The onus should not be on victims to avoid a wrong but on those in charge to create structures and incentives to prevent it.*[164]

Confidence May Be Dangerous for Your Workplace Health

Although confidence is touted as a critical workplace trait, a working paper from the Harvard Business School suggested that an abundance of confidence may actually be toxic to workplace health. Using a data set of 50,000 workers across eleven different organizations, the study looked at characteristics that lead to toxic behaviors—that is, behaviors harmful to organizational performance.

In particular, the study analyzed those toxic behaviors that can result in termination such as sexual harassment, violence, falsifying documents, and other forms of egregious workplace misconduct. Among its findings, the study linked overconfidence to a greater propensity for misconduct, stating: "someone that is overconfident believes the expected payoff from engaging in misconduct is higher than someone who is not overconfident, as they believe the likelihood of the better outcome is higher than it really is. Hence, all things equal, those that are overconfident should be more likely to engage in misconduct."[165]

This research has a lesson for employers whose hiring decisions are influenced by the degree of confidence exhibited by a candidate in an interview. The analysis showed a potentially costly trade-off. Confident workers were identified as more productive, at least in terms of output quantity. The correlation, however, between more confident workers and the potential for engaging in toxic behaviors suggests, as the authors indicate, the dangers of hiring based on a unidimensional reason.

The study further noted that the higher productivity likely helps keep toxic workers in an organization longer than their behavior warrants, but they further report that the actual gain is illusory. If managers were to consider the outcomes of productivity and toxicity together, "the net consequence in terms of profit is still net negative. . . ."[166] These costs can include: loss of customers/clients; the impact on employee morale, which affects engagement and productivity; increased attrition; and even a potential loss of credibility among external stakeholders.

In other words, "avoiding toxic workers is still better for the firm in terms of net profitability, despite losing out on a highly productive worker."[167]

The study concluded that it is less costly to the organization to avoid a toxic hire than it is to hire a "superstar" (i.e., someone considered to be within the top 1 percent of productivity). Workplace performance is enhanced more by the avoidance of toxic workers than by the addition of highly productive ones.

This study suggests that employers exercise caution before making a hiring decision that is blinded by the appeal of an overconfident candidate while ignoring the potential of the candidate whose greater modesty can lead to a more cohesive work environment.

The EEOC Task Force Report similarly noted the financial impact of ignoring the costs of an apparent superstar performer who engages in negative conduct:

> *No matter who the harasser is, the negative effects of harassment can cause serious damage to a business. Indeed, the reputational costs alone can have serious consequences, particularly where it is revealed that managers for years "looked the other way" at a so-called superstar harasser.*[168]

As noted in a *Washington Post* analysis of the dangers of superstar workers, employers who focus on a star system that greatly rewards some employees over others are facilitating a power imbalance that is likely to be more costly over time. Such organizations are, in effect, "setting up a power differential that can overlook or excuse bad behavior. There's a chance that companies that have extreme differentials between employees in incentive pay, that are highly focused on individuals rather than team-based work or that don't consider workers' behavior enough in performance evaluations could be more at risk."[169]

The Myth of Meritocracy

Much is revealed about the culture of an organization in the way it describes itself. For example, many organizations consider themselves to be meritocracies—that is, places where people succeed solely on merit and skill. In these alleged meritocracies, no barriers exist to hold back women or other minority groups; it is all about working hard. But when an organization describes itself this way, its real message generally is that individuals succeed by working long hours to demonstrate dedication and commitment. Those who cannot meet that idealized vision simply lack the merit that others demonstrate.

The reality is far different. There is no such thing as a pure system of merit, as issues of privilege, individual networks, family commitments, and many other challenges have an impact—for better or worse—on everyone's performance at work. How those challenges are viewed and evaluated can make all the difference to one's success.

A study analyzing purported merit-based compensation systems revealed gender and racial disparities in wage growth and promotions, even following positive performance evaluations. This research looked at the aftermath of the performance evaluation process to determine whether people rated of equal merit were treated similarly in their pay and bonuses.

The findings revealed that equivalently rated employees received different salary increases—the salary growth for women was lower than for men, and African American and Hispanic American employees were given lower salary increases than similarly performing white employees. In effect, "women's and minorities' performance appraisals are significantly discounted, meaning that they need to work harder and obtain higher performance scores in order to receive similar salary increases to white men."[170]

The study importantly noted the way in which the concept of a meritocracy can be illusory. The author stressed that equating meritocracy with fairness, while popular to do so, is less accurate than equating the term with consistency: if rewards are consistent, they are less likely to be arbitrary or discriminatory. Employers may see a system that links performance appraisals with merit-based salary increases, but the research demonstrated that bias still manifests itself in the reward-distribution process.

To address this, the study's author stressed the importance of transparency and accountability in the way people are evaluated and compensated:

> . . . because the results of this study imply that merit-based policies with high transparency and accountability may reduce bias and increase equity, this is an important contribution to our thinking about how employer practices can counteract discrimination and remediate bias. . . . I suggest that the lack of both

accountability *and* transparency . . . *explains why, in an organi-*
zation such as this, neither employees nor administration seem to
be aware of performance-reward bias. According to experimental
research on accountability, when decision makers know they will be
held accountable for their decisions, bias is less likely to occur . . .[171]

A study of nearly 500 managers at a large financial services corporation looked at performance evaluations and promotions to determine
whether female managers in line jobs are more strictly evaluated than
both male managers and men in staff roles. The study also analyzed
whether women who were promoted were held to higher performance
ratings than similarly promoted men. The study showed "that even
when women are well on the way toward breaking through the glass
ceiling, they face greater obstacles than their male counterparts."[172]
The research revealed a connection between the gender of the manager and the type of position held, demonstrating that women in line
positions were more negatively evaluated:

> *Not only were women in line jobs rated lower than men in either*
> *line jobs or staff jobs, but they were also rated less favorably than*
> *other women holding staff jobs. Because line management posi-*
> *tions are likely to be perceived as more strongly male gender-typed*
> *than staff management positions, these results support lack-of-fit*
> *ideas, which specify that more negatively biased evaluations of*
> *women mangers will occur when there is a greater perceived lack*
> *of fit between job requirements and attributes of women. . . .*
>
> *Moreover, we found that promoted women had received higher*
> *performance ratings than promoted men, suggesting that women*
> *had to be regarded as more stellar in their accomplishments than*
> *men if they were to be promoted. In addition, we found that per-*
> *formance ratings had more direct career consequences for female*
> *managers than male managers. Our data demonstrated that*
> *women's performance ratings were more strongly related to pro-*
> *motions than were men's, indicating that the standards for promo-*
> *tion of men were more flexible than the standards for promotion*
> *of women. . . . These findings . . . also are consistent with anecdotal*

claims that women have to work harder to get to the same place, doing more and doing it better than men in similar positions.[173]

The study's authors pointed out the implications for aspiring female managers. On the one hand, women are encouraged to seek line positions as an important building experience on the way to higher-level roles. On the other hand, these results revealed that women are held to more stringent standards for promotion, and women in line positions were evaluated more negatively than all other managers, including men in staff roles. As the authors stated: "Line positions may be critical for advancement, but they also are rife with potential hazards for women."[174]

You Can't Always Get What You Want

The impacts of unconscious bias extend beyond the structural barriers that prevent equal opportunities for mentoring and sponsorship, access to influential networks, high-profile assignments, and gender-neutral evaluations. Unconscious biases also influence how we view our life experiences and the choices we make. In that regard, they even can protect us from some of the harsher realities of the workplace. As a result, however, in reframing our own perceptions of our circumstances, we risk leaving behind the impacts of bias in the workplace as a problem for others to solve.

The fact is that everyone wants to feel they have some control over important life decisions, so it is natural to view such decisions as a choice, rather than the result of circumstances. For example, the popular narrative is that when women leave high-pressured jobs, it is often attributed to their desire to spend more time with their children.

For leaders in the workplace, this narrative allows the status quo to remain firmly in place. If women continually leave because of their biological imperative as mothers, there is no need to make significant structural changes, as the exodus will nonetheless continue.

This thinking allows workplace leaders to hide behind their own existing—and generally flawed—reduced-hours policy as an example of why other changes won't matter. After all, employers lament, they "accommodate" new moms by "letting them" work reduced hours, yet women still leave in disproportionately higher numbers.

This flawed analysis ignores the diminished opportunities, changed perceptions, unilateral shifts in the status of assigned work, and the myriad other ways in which the day-to-day life of someone at work can be altered following a change in schedule. Women who move from a full-time to a reduced-hours status continually fight against a stigma—one that reinforces a perception that women are less committed to their careers. From that misperception and implicit bias, diminished opportunities further stall careers.

As a result, women reach the point where leaving feels like a better alternative than staying. But because they see a need to preserve their professional relationships for the future, they refrain from an honest conversation about the barriers that drove them out.[175]

Instead, women may be more likely to say they chose to leave, allowing them to maintain a sense of control and personal responsibility for their own decisions. But by framing their departure as a choice, the structural barriers that likely contributed to their decision to leave remain unaddressed. Even worse, they remain unacknowledged.

That is exactly what researchers found when they looked into the choice framework that women express after leaving their jobs. One study questioned whether stay-at-home mothers perceived their decision to be a choice and, if so, analyzed the consequences arising from that framing.

The study found that the mothers "strongly endorsed the choice framework to explain their own workplace departure."[176] Relying on this framework resulted in greater individual well-being for the women, "but less recognition of the structural barriers and discrimination that still hinder American women's workplace advancement, compared with women who did not rely on the choice framework."[177]

The implications for the workplace are significant:

> Given the ubiquity of the choice framework in American society, such effects could intensify over time through repeated encounters. Regular exposure could create a vicious cycle that helps to

maintain women's underrepresentation at the top of high-status fields. For example, if choice decreases recognition of the structural barriers in institutions (i.e., inflexible policies that constrain mothers' options), it might also decrease people's motivation to make the workplace more accommodating to working mothers (e.g., by increasing flexibility). Ironically, then, this choice framework might foster and maintain the very barriers that often push mothers out of the workforce by limiting their ability to simultaneously manage a professional career and family responsibilities."[178]

The authors posit that another long-term implication arising from an acceptance of this choice framework is that women may be less likely to support each other in the workplace. After all, if everything is viewed through the lens of individual choice, there may be less interest in collective advocacy for change.

The decision to leave can also have an unintended impact on those who remain, particularly when the decision is driven by work-life considerations. For example, mothers in the workplace report feeling more vulnerable when supervisors question their commitment to their jobs if they seek flexibility in their hours or in working remotely. They also can be viewed with suspicion as others wonder whether they, too, will leave. This often results in lessened commitment and engagement by employers to the career growth and development of mothers in the workplace.

In the Women's Bar Association of Massachusetts survey, numerous respondents described being the recipient of inappropriate conduct during their pregnancy and following their return from maternity leave. They were asked questions about their bodies, their sex lives, and their breasts and breastfeeding, and often felt particularly vulnerable about reporting such behaviors.

Women who leave the workplace due to either changes in how they are treated or how they perceive themselves or their opportunities for professional development are indeed making a rational choice. But it is driven by the biases that exist at work—biases that make staying feel untenable.

Unconscious Bias Is Not an Excuse

The growing body of research regarding the impact of unconscious bias on our decision-making process, including how we evaluate and promote people, is critical to the ability to change workplace culture. It infuses everything we do. Yet few workplaces appreciate the strategic importance of understanding and incorporating this research into the development of sound policies and systems that minimize the potential intrusion of biases we neither acknowledge nor recognize. Doing so, however, is a critical component of creating a respectful and inclusive workplace.

The Sound—and the Cost—of Silence

How Power Silences

The reluctance to report negative conduct and harassing behaviors is pervasive—and sadly logical. All too often, victims feel they have nowhere to turn, so they develop coping strategies as an alternative. A woman who worked in a legislative setting described this dynamic:

> *On more than one occasion, a male lobbyist or another Sen-ate staffer . . . entered my office during a late night session. I was alone in my office. The individual blocked my exit and wouldn't let me past him until I agreed to kiss him. At least once, I smelled alcohol on the individual. I never complied with the request and became more savvy in avoiding the situation (e.g., locating an exit door through a conference room; humoring him until I could get past and into the hallway; hanging out with another female, being careful not to be alone).*
>
> *We were powerless. . . . I learned to handle matters on my own and in my own way. Prevention was the key. I became aware of my surroundings and tried to avoid getting into potentially compro-mising situations.*

A woman who had worked in law enforcement talked about a senior officer with a well-known reputation for requesting more junior personnel to engage in affairs. She did not report the behavior, noting:

> *Who would have cared? Seems to have been accepted practice that the solicited just needed to say, "no thanks" and the solicitor gets to move on to the next prey.*

And even if workplace leaders have put in place a policy and reporting process, it still cannot compensate for a flawed implementation. One study demonstrated how a strong policy is insufficient in the face of a culture that impedes efforts to assert one's rights under that policy. The study explored whether women who were the recipients of unwanted sexual attention in their large university workplace sought to access the complaint process.

In establishing its policy, the university did most things right. It promulgated a broad-based antiharassment policy that went beyond the limits of a strict legal definition of sexual harassment, including the recognition of worker dignity. Moreover, the policy provided a flexible process for resolving complaints, offering multiple avenues for reporting and a commitment that there would be no retaliation against complainants.

The study found that:

> . . . *the harassing conduct addressed through the grievance procedure was considerably more serious than the prohibited conduct as defined in the Written Policy. Women were most likely to complain—and management most likely to act—when the complainant had proof of the harassing behavior, when the harassers bothered more than one person, or when the conduct was truly outrageous. But incidents that did not meet these rather narrow standards were likely to go unaddressed. . . .*
>
> . . . *[M]anagers rarely exercised their broad mandate to protect employee rights, and instead often shielded the harassers— and the University—from women's complaints. I also show that women anticipated these management practices in fashioning*

their responses to unwanted sexual attention. These interactions
reshaped—and narrowed—the meaning of sexual harassment for
working women.[179]

The study identified a series of practices that discouraged reporting. For example, supervisors often had closer organizational ties to the harasser arising from their similar status. They were, therefore, more inclined to take the side of the person accused of wrongful conduct, rather than serve as a neutral problem-solver.

This resulted in a dynamic where the supervisor effectively became the harasser's representative throughout the process, thwarting a nonbiased, neutral investigation. For example, they would respond to a complaint against a powerful faculty member by stating that, because of the person's importance to the university, nothing could be done. Or they might create a step that was not in the policy by recommending that the accuser first confront the harasser about the behavior.

Moreover, supervisors would narrowly construe the policy by offering "restrictive, legalistic interpretations that narrowly construed the Written Policy's protection and, in effect, dismissed employee complaints because the conduct did not violate the policy."[180] For example, even though the policy addressed worker dignity and equality, supervisors would respond to a woman's complaint by stating that the incident was not serious or offensive enough to trigger the policy.

And notwithstanding the policy's commitment to protect complainants against retaliation, respondents reported a variety of ways in which they experienced retaliatory behaviors, including negative performance reviews, removal from job responsibilities, removal from projects, and demotions. The unfortunate result of these management practices was that a well-crafted policy became meaningless in application:

And as a result, women's understanding of sexual harassment
reflected the adversarial nature of the complaint process, shrinking
to include only those behaviors they could prove. For these women,
supervisors did not need to dismiss complaints for failing to violate

the policy. Women's narrow interpretation of sexual harassment accomplished this task by censoring complaints before they ever formed.[181]

As the study's author noted, the women came to view the policy as the way in which the workplace protected its more powerful employees, rather than protect the victims of harassment. The result is that the university met its legal obligations through the policy's existence, but the protection was largely illusory.

Not Telling What Is Already Known

Respondents to the Women's Bar Association of Massachusetts survey similarly stated they did not report misconduct because it was already widely known. One of the more common reasons given by respondents for their unwillingness to report was that the firm already knew of the perpetrator's behaviors, so there was every reason to believe they would ignore the transgressions. Noted one respondent:

> [E]veryone "knew" this partner was a creep. Yet nothing ever happened.

Another respondent described a partner's highly inappropriate and frequent sexual comments to women and stated:

> Female coworkers knew about it and talked frequently about it, tried to avoid the individual particularly [in] 1 on 1 situations. It was one of those situations that everyone knew about it (including supervisors) but no one did anything about it.

Other common reasons for not reporting included fear of retaliation. For example, a respondent who described ongoing and unwanted touching stated:

> I was new to my role and was afraid to lose my job.

Another respondent described an incident that she did not report because she did not think she would ever be believed when it was her word as a young lawyer against a key partner in the firm:

> *I was a [new lawyer and the most senior partner] called for a meeting at his office to review a case. . . . [H]e closed the door, grabbed me from behind and tried to kiss me.*

The studies and shared anecdotes demonstrate that, notwithstanding the wide range of harassment that occurs in the workplace, the notion of senior leaders preying on young women who stay silent for fear of retribution remains a troubling theme. A survey respondent described partners who pursued associates, notwithstanding efforts at avoidance:

> *Another partner showed up at associate's hotel room in the middle of the night while traveling together on business. The firm was aware of the behavior already and did nothing. Firms care about rainmaking more than associates.*

An employee of a corporation described her experience in a setting where there was no place to turn because the perpetrator was in charge of the company. Here, too, fear of losing her job predominated:

> *The CEO . . . massaged the back of my neck then . . . continued to make strongly suggestive remarks about getting sexually involved. I had not realized that he was sexually involved with many employees before his conduct with me. I pretended not to catch on to what he was saying, but it was very touch and go because I felt I could easily lose my job if I didn't finesse things and keep him from feeling upset and realize I was rejecting him. He seemed to just think I was dense, which was what I was going for. . . . I mentioned to a . . . friend but not anyone at the company. There was no one to report it to except the CEO . . .*

A Women's Bar Association of Massachusetts survey respondent described her efforts to fend off a senior leader:

> *The managing partner asked me to work over a weekend, and when I was leaving . . . he put his arms around me, pushed me up against the wall and groped and tried to kiss me. I . . . didn't know what to do but I pushed him off and avoided him after that. . . . After that incident, he left expensive gifts in my office and continued to ask me to meet him at [a hotel] bar after work for "drinks and some fun." I never took him up on his offers but I was always afraid that he would fire me if I refused to work overtime.*

Even beyond fear of retaliation, and as described by Professors Deborah Epstein and Lisa Goodman, a range of harms can arise when institutions ignore or discount a woman's experiences. For example, "survivors develop a sense of powerlessness and futility," believing that "nothing they say or do" will ever make a difference. They also can "develop a sense of personal worthlessness"; if nothing is done to address such a painful experience, then the victim is left feeling she simply does not matter. And lastly, the survivor develops her own "sense of self-doubt" resulting from the response to her experience— suggestions that she is not remembering it clearly or the myriad other ways her story may be discredited, leaving her questioning herself.[182]

The Illusion of Silence

Too frequently, workplace leaders take pride in the fact that no incidents of sexual harassment or other negative conduct have been reported. As stated in a *Boston Globe* op-ed: "As recent events have proved, lack of reported incidents does not mean there is no harassment; and intimidation can pervade a workplace below the surface despite a stated zero-tolerance policy."[183]

So as employers may draw false confidence from the lack of reported incidents, victims retreat into further silence. In its analysis of empirical data, the EEOC Task Force Report noted that the extent of nonreporting is striking. Rather than report, victims devise a range of self-help measures to respond to negative conduct: "Common workplace-based responses by those who experience sex-based harassment are to avoid the harasser (33% to 75%); deny or downplay the gravity of the situation (54% to 73%); or attempt to ignore, forget or endure the behavior (44% to 70%)."[184]

A culture of silence is debilitating. Silence serves only to exacerbate the negative behaviors and worsen the impacts on victims. The hushed whispers of rumored negative conduct, absent internal reporting within the workplace or external reporting to law enforcement, is like the tip of the iceberg to an oncoming ship. For those not privy to the rumors, significant damage ensues from being caught in the perpetrator's path. For those lucky enough to have been forewarned, a self-imposed avoidance of the harasser—particularly if that person has stature in the organization—can result in lost assignment opportunities and a loss of access to influential social networks.

Federal circuit court judge Alex Kozinski resigned in December 2017, following more than a dozen public accusations of sexual misconduct from former employees and a long history of rumors about inappropriate behavior toward women.[185] Author and lawyer Dahlia Lithwick, who had professionally crossed paths with Judge Kozinski for years, poignantly expressed her regret for staying silent. Her words illustrated how silence empowers the harasser to operate in an unchecked environment:

> *I am thinking of all the ways in which "open secrets" become their own spheres of truth, in which the idea that "everybody knew" something awful absolved all of us of the burden of doing anything. . . .*
> *Everybody knew. This is the problem with a system of "open secrets." All of the clerks and former clerks in Kozinski's ambit knew and understood that you assumed the risk and accepted the responsibilities of secrecy.*[186]

The Price of Silence

Another important study of workplace behaviors analyzed what happens to employees who speak up against mistreatment. The study built on research that previously identified two types of retaliatory victimization that can occur when someone vocally opposes an employment practice.

The first type of retaliatory behavior is work retaliation victimization, a tangible action that has a direct negative impact on the complainant's personnel file, such as demotion, poor reviews, or some other adverse documentation in the employee's record. A key aspect of work retaliation victimization is that the person imposing the adverse action intends, or the target perceives, that it is directly related to the employee's complaint.

The second type of retaliatory behavior is social retaliation victimization, which consists of those verbal and nonverbal actions that impact the employee's interpersonal relationships with others in the workplace. Social retaliation victimization is less tangible than work retaliation victimization. Rather than consisting of negative responses that are generally documented in the HR records of the victim, these interactions can result in a wide range of antisocial conduct, such as ignoring or ostracizing the employee who raised the complaint, or blaming, threatening, or harassing the person.

The researchers also highlighted past studies that analyzed the primary ways in which victims give voice to their workplace concerns. One is to report concerns to an appropriate authority within the organization, a behavior traditionally viewed as whistle-blowing. The second is to seek support from colleagues about behaviors of concern, called *social-support seeking*. The third way is to directly confront the perpetrator of the negative behavior. The study focused on the latter two in particular as the more common strategies when an employee uses his or her voice to address concerns.

The study sought to better understand retaliation behaviors, particularly where the social power of the victim is less than that of the perpetrator. The researchers noted that because vocal resistance violates workplace norms, an employee may be treated harshly when questioning the behavior or ethics of a person in a position of power, thereby challenging organizational hierarchy. The researchers noted:

> *More specifically, exposing the misbehavior of a highly placed member of the organizational hierarchy—thus characterizing that*

person as unlawful, unethical, or inappropriate—questions that
hierarchy. The organization's dominant coalition, including the
wrongdoer, may therefore retaliate against the victim to correct
this challenge to authority. . . . Further, organizational peers who
are typically supportive of the victim could respond to the victim's
voice expression with distance and rejection—particularly when a
powerful wrongdoer is involved—as the peers may fear reprisals
for aligning with the less powerful (and thus more deviant) vic-
tim. Peers may also retaliate as a means of signaling to the victim
that she or he has deviated from behavior prescribed by social-
structural norms. . . .[187]

It is important to add that, in addition to fear of reprisals, another
reason why peers may join the perpetrator in retaliating against a victim is to curry favor, particularly if that perpetrator is in a position of
authority. This would logically flow from an additional conclusion of
the study demonstrating that power in an organization was central to
whether and how retaliation processes occurred:

[L]ower status employees experienced more retaliation victim-
ization. . . . [W]rongdoers' power relative to victims' also related
to retaliation, with greater [social retaliation victimization] and
[work retaliation victimization] experienced by lower status vic-
tims voicing against higher power wrongdoers. . . . The greater the
power disparity between wrongdoer and victim, the more that
the victim's resistance deviates from behavior prescribed by his
or her social position; thus, organizational members sanction the
insurgent victim. . . . In addition, retaliation fear might motivate
colleagues to instigate [social retaliation victimization]. That is,
the more deviant the victim's behavior, the more that colleagues
may distance themselves from that victim—worried about being
punished themselves for supporting an employee who challenges
authority.[188]

An additional troubling finding was revealed in the study. Among
those employees who were highly mistreated and vocal about it, the

health impacts resulting from retaliation were significant, including psychological and physical distress.

A ray of hope for the ultimate importance of speaking up emerged in an interesting additional finding connected to the psychological and physical implications that may result from remaining silent. The researchers reported:

> *Of particular interest, restraining from speaking out against frequent mistreatment was associated with the most psychological and physical harm. Although unexpected, this finding is highly consistent with research documenting that self-silencing, emotional suppression, and repressive personality and coping styles involve labor that takes a toll on the body—disrupting emotional regulation and exacerbating psychosomatic processes. The result can be rumination, depression, memory impairment, reactivity to stress-related cues, poorer immune response, and disease progression. Conversely, disclosing the thoughts and emotions associated with a stressful event has various benefits for the individual: greater sense of control; less effortful processing; and the ability to see structure, logic, and meaning in a formerly chaotic and overwhelming event. This can enhance adaptive coping, reduce rumination, and yield closure—resulting in improved immune function, psychosomatic and subjective well-being, and fewer medical visits or absentee days . . .*[189]

The concluding point is one that should resonate with hope for those who weigh the risks of silence in the future: "In short, health risks may accompany silence in the face of injustice."[190]

One of These Wrongs Is Not Like the Others

Women sometimes describe feeling conflicted when deciding whether to report workplace misconduct. For example, they worry that their speaking up will negatively impact the perpetrator's family or career. In other instances, they describe having these conflicts imposed on them by investigators. This can be very different from the experiences of those who report other types of wrongful activity.

When she was a young graduate student, UC Davis professor Simine Vazire was groped in the buttocks by a professor at a conference. Years later, when that same professor was teaching at Dartmouth and under investigation for complaints of sexual misconduct, Vazire spoke with one of the investigators about her own encounter with him years back.

The investigator questioned Vazire about her experience, asking how it made her feel and what she thought the outcome should be as a result of the incident. These questions, Vazire noted, made no sense in any other context where a violation has occurred. So why is it acceptable in the context of sexual assault or harassment? Vazire observed that if someone's house is burglarized or a bike is stolen, the feelings of the victim are not part of law enforcement's decision as to whether or how to respond, but not so with incidents of harassment:

> We interrogate the harassed as much as the harasser, not just about the specifics of what happened during the incident but about their feelings and opinions about what happened, how it affected their life, and what they think should happen next. . . . My emotional reaction is not relevant to determining that the harassment was wrong. I know it was wrong not because of how much it upset me; I know it was wrong because human beings should not have their asses grabbed out of the blue at professional meetings.
>
> What do I think the consequences should be? I think it doesn't matter what I think. We have experts who are paid to evaluate this. I'm not the employer, or the investigator, or even a friend or acquaintance of the harasser, so to be honest, I haven't given much thought to what the consequences should be. If that sounds callous, that's my point—it wouldn't sound callous in the context of reporting a burglary. I don't know what the punishment should be for the person who stole my bike for the same reason I don't know what the punishment should be for the person who touched my butt: It's not my job. The fact that I'm expected to know exactly what should happen to my harasser is one thing that makes it more difficult for people to report sexual harassment. I did think long and hard about the accuracy of my report, and I was careful about the parts of the investigation that were my responsibility. But I hope you'll forgive me for leaving the rest to the experts.[191]

Such concerns about the potential impact on the victimizer's future is a continual theme seen in interviews with and surveys of victims of harassment. In the Women's Bar Association of Massachusetts survey, for example, a respondent described a partner's escalating inappropriate behavior. She ultimately moved to a different floor to avoid encountering the senior married partner, yet she was reluctant to take any further steps to report the behavior:

> *I was young and naïve, hoping that . . . this was not a pattern of activity. I didn't want to ruin his career and family . . .*

Similarly, a female who noted highly improper behavior from a married supervisor stated that she did not report the behavior because:

> *I knew he was married and I decided to ignore it because I didn't want to disrupt his life.*

A respondent who described being groped expressed concern not only about the impact to her career but also to the perpetrator's life if she reported. As she did, she also noted the personal toll:

> *Afraid not to get hired anywhere, to destroy a family, and very short statute of limitations was over before I realized how much it had impacted me.*

These concerns add a further burden to victims, unfairly placing upon them a role that more appropriately belongs to employers. A victim should not have to be worried about the impact of reporting; it is the responsibility of the workplace to have in place the mechanisms to manage a fair process.

Do You Want to Know a Secret?

Another way that victims are silenced is through the ubiquitous use of nondisclosure agreements (NDAs). Such agreements effectively silence those who seek to vindicate their rights, resulting in a loss of their right to speak.

Julie Ruvolo was a freelance writer and contractor who was unable to secure permission to be released from a nondisclosure and nondisparagement agreement she signed. She described how she felt having been silenced when other voices were emerging following the *New York Times* coverage in the fall of 2017:

> *I can't tell you about what happened, I can't tell you if it happened more than once, I can't tell you who else was there when it happened or if I was alone. I can't tell you how it made me feel, I can't tell you about the power dynamic between myself and the person or persons the incident happened with.*
>
> *I can't tell you who I reported it to at the company, nor what their response was. I can't even tell you if or how their response changed over time. I can't tell you who I asked for advice, or what they told me. I can't tell you what conditions I signed the agreement under, and I can't tell you what was said to me before or after I signed the agreement.*
>
> *I would love to share with other people out there, men, women, whoever, encourage everyone to view NDAs with care. Because when you sign one, you're signing away your constitutional right to free speech.*

Employers who reflexively think it is critical to maintain the confidentiality of a settlement may be wise to question the value of insisting on silence. In many instances, the workplace rumor mill knows that there has been a complaint and employees may be concerned about the perpetrator and perhaps others who engage in similar behaviors. When the resolution is cloaked in secrecy, the employees are left wondering whether the perpetrator was disciplined and whether the victim was fairly treated.

By not knowing how a complaint is resolved, employees may be fearful to report future misconduct. The lack of knowledge allows negative assumptions to continue, even when the settlement itself may be one that, if disclosed, would send all the right messages to the workplace.

While it is contrary to long-accepted practice, employers who are concerned about the signals that they are sending to their workforce should consider the value of greater transparency. Perhaps the choice need not be as stark as requiring an NDA or releasing the entire contents of a settlement. But an alternative that provides employees with enough information to develop trust and confidence in the organization's policy and process may prove to be worthwhile.

If You See Something—Then What?

Many harassing incidents purposefully take place where the behavior cannot be observed. But not all. Insulting humor, inappropriate emails shared with a group, remarks made within earshot of others, comments or behaviors during a business event where people are drinking—these are just some of the instances in which negative conduct is observed by others.

The impact of these behaviors on bystanders is too often overlooked. Bystanders may have a potential role in aiding the target of the remarks. They may also struggle with feeling complicit by not responding or helping the victim more directly. A group of scientists described the experience of being a bystander and its potential negative impact:

> *"Ambient" harassment—the second-hand smoke equivalent of sexual harassment, which consists of harassment witnessed by others in a work group who are not themselves the targets—can be as damaging as individually targeted harassment.*[192]

The EEOC Task Force Report stated that bystanders can suffer both mental and physical harm: "these effects can stem from empathy and worry for the victim, concern about the lack of fairness in their workplace, or fear of becoming the next target."[193] The negative impacts of the bystander's experiences can even extend further into the workplace. For example, the EEOC Task Force also pointed to research demonstrating that employees who experience "unfairness" at work are significantly less likely to recommend their workplace to others.

Bystanders who feel unable to intervene without risk of retribution reinforce the perspective among employees that the workplace culture is toxic. The impacts could be far-reaching. An organization that is perceived to be unfair or worse will also likely suffer negative impacts to its brand and image.

Many of the respondents to the survey by the Women's Bar Association of Massachusetts described behaviors they observed and offered reasons for their silence. For example, one respondent wrote about not reporting incidents in which male partners inappropriately touched and stared at younger female lawyers:

> *I was not the recipient of this behavior; I witnessed it. I spoke with the female associates involved, and it was clear to me that they did not want me to report this behavior. I felt that their privacy and wishes were decisive.*

Although honoring such a request is not unreasonable, it betrays a deeper institutional problem about the culture of the firm when both the victims and the bystander are choosing the likelihood of ongoing misconduct over reporting the misconduct.

Another respondent observed a partner regularly "hitting on" an associate but did not take any steps to intervene or report:

> *I worried that I would be retaliated against.*

Similarly, a respondent who witnessed a partner groping a junior associate did not report:

> *Because I was not the one groped.*

A respondent who described a partner inappropriately touching female lawyers stated:

> *I didn't want to embarrass either of the people involved.*

There is a need to pay greater attention to the role of bystanders and to provide them with tools to support victims. Fortunately, this issue is getting some high-profile attention. In 2017, Anita Hill was asked to lead the Hollywood Commission on Eliminating Sexual Harassment and Advancing Equality. In speaking about that position, Professor Hill noted that it provided an opportunity to work with people in a position to implement change. She also stressed the importance of taking new approaches:

> We need to be more effective in the kinds of rules we put in place. Like bystander training. Everyone maligns it, but I'd challenge the entertainment industry to make it effective, to create organizational cultures where everybody feels it's their responsibility to eliminate bias.[194]

Employers have an opportunity to empower bystanders to respond when they witness negative behaviors by implementing effective bystander intervention training. The normalization of safe intervention strategies will also send an important message to victims that they are not alone.

Fighting Back Against Backlash

Killing #MeToo Softly

The signs of backlash started early and have become increasingly disturbing. Consider the January 2018 Facebook post of Robert Brustein, founder of the American Repertory Theater and Yale Repertory Theater, who expressed concern that the achievements of the significant number of prominent men publicly accused of misbehavior were lost in the focus on #MeToo:

> *We had a Witch Hunt in the 17th Century, which singled out innocent women for imagined misbehavior. Today, the tables are turned and the Witches are doing the hunting. Should we stop reading the Republic and Doctor Faustus because Plato and Christopher Marlowe hankered after young boys? Or give up on Strindberg because he may have thrown a lighted lamp at his wife? Or close the book on Shakespeare because he had a Dark Lady in his life? . . . If the position of the culprit privileged some form of harassment, then that should be exposed and punished. But let's not ignore the important difference between private behavior and public achievement.*

As reported by the *Boston Globe*, responses to this post compared the seventeenth-century witch hunts with the decades of silent abuse suffered by victims of sexual assault and harassment. They also noted that the enabling behaviors of people who looked the other way facilitated conditions that allowed the accused to excel in their careers.[195]

Consider, too, the April 2018 speech delivered at Hillsdale College by Heather Mac Donald, a Manhattan Institute fellow, where she predicted destructive impacts from #MeToo:

> *#MeToo is going to unleash a new torrent of gender and race quotas throughout the economy and culture, on the theory that all disparities in employment and institutional representation are due to harassment and bias. . . .*
>
> *Pressures for so-called diversity, defined reductively by gonads and melanin, are of course nothing new. . . . But however pervasive the diversity imperative was before, the #MeToo movement is going to make the previous three decades look like a golden age of meritocracy. No mainstream institution will hire, promote, or compensate without an exquisite calculation of gender and race ratios.*[196]

In her remarks, Mac Donald criticized "professional feminist Susan Estrich" for commenting on the exclusion of female op-ed writers in the *Los Angeles Times*. Her dismissive title for Estrich left out a few key points for audience members not familiar with Estrich's work; for example, the first female president of the *Harvard Law Review*, clerk to Supreme Court Justice John Paul Stevens, author of several books, first woman to run a major presidential campaign, and law professor. In other words, Mac Donald did to Estrich what women have experienced throughout history—dismissed her accomplishments while ridiculing her beliefs.

The backlash to #MeToo has significant potential to further diminish opportunities for women at work, as some men claim to be fearful of engaging in mentoring and other relationships important to career advancement. In but one example, a survey reported that "65% of men say it's now 'less safe' to mentor and coach members of the opposite sex."[197] Some survey respondents expressed concern that the work environment has become too sterile and that women are not being held accountable for their work because managers fear being accused of gender bias.

The Fear of Illusion

Days after the Harvey Weinstein story broke, a *New York Times* article identified a "heightened caution" experienced by men who fear their own careers could be ended as a result of "one accusation or misunderstood comment." The article also noted the potential negative career impacts on women who lose valuable mentors and sponsors when men take steps to protect themselves from hypothetical accusations: "But their actions affect women's careers, too—potentially depriving them of the kind of relationships that lead to promotions or investments."[198] Further to those career impacts, the article identified one survey in which 64 percent of senior men and 50 percent of junior women indicated that they avoided interactions that could give rise to the risk of rumors.

This analysis by the *New York Times* of industry sectors where men reported their fears and avoided interaction with professional women provided a sweeping—and worrisome—indication that women are at risk of losing career-critical relationships. In identifying where the potential impact on women was greater, the article reported a wide range of workplace settings: "People were warier in jobs that emphasized appearance, as with certain restaurants or TV networks; in male-dominated industries like finance; and in jobs that involve stark power imbalances, like doctors or investors."[199]

Business sectors are expressing fears that, ironically, will result in further disadvantaging women in the workplace. An article about the potential backlash in the legal profession noted: "The fallout is that some male lawyers are so fearful of being tainted with sexual harassment charges that they're running for the hills, dodging close working relationships with women."[200] Similarly, in an article about backlash in the financial services field, the author wrote: "I've heard men say that they're less likely to hire or associate with women as a result of the intensity of MeToo. . . . I have heard directly from male executives at two prominent Wall Street firms that they are moving their female direct reports to female bosses."[201]

The sad fact is that these fears are countered by significant research demonstrating the infrequency with which actual victims report sexual harassment. The notion that the #MeToo movement has put men at greater risk is contrary to the actual consequences women have faced from reporting, the continued power dynamics in the workplace that disfavor women, the greater likelihood that silence governs behaviors, and even the complicity of the courts in protecting the accused.

As discussed previously, research demonstrates that the court system has failed to adequately protect workers, erecting procedural, evidentiary, and other barriers for employees bringing discrimination, harassment, and retaliation claims. As documented in the book *Unequal: How America's Courts Undermine Discrimination Law*, there are a variety of reasons that the law has evolved to favor employer over employee rights.[202]

One such reason is the argument, adopted in a Supreme Court decision, that narrow rulings are warranted to protect employers from false claims. Yet research has shown this argument is not grounded in actual facts. For example, in 2013, there were 39 percent fewer cases involving civil rights employment claims than were brought ten years earlier in 2003. As the authors documented:

> *The number of federal civil rights claims is also not significant when compared to the total number of people in the workforce. In the twelve-month period ending in March 2013, only 12,665 cases were filed in comparison to 143,929,000 people employed in the civilian workforce. In other words, only a tiny fraction of the workforce files a discrimination suit in any given year. . . .*
>
> *Available social science evidence does not support any significant faker problem. Instead, it actually shows that employees are reluctant to believe that their employers discriminated against them. In circumstances when they believe discrimination has occurred, they are reluctant to complain to their employer, the*

EEOC, or a state agency. People can be reticent to make discrimination claims because they may fear retaliation.[203]

#MeToo as a Proxy

This brings us back to Heather Mac Donald's Hillsdale College speech. Mac Donald feeds the narrative that the #MeToo movement is bad for the workplace—indeed, bad for the economy—yet she seems unencumbered by the extensive research that undermines her arguments. She expresses concern that the #MeToo movement will lead to greater calls for diversity and gender equity, which will negatively impact decisions made on merit. For example, she referred to a public radio show's series on gender and racial inequities in classical music as "irresponsible," noting that, throughout history, "the greatest composers have been male. . . . We should simply be grateful—profoundly grateful—for the music these men created."[204]

But what about the music we have never been able to hear because female composers lacked the opportunities and networks to help their music reach the public? To Mac Donald, it is simply because the male composers had greater merit. Then how does she explain the transformation in the gender composition of most major orchestras in the decades since auditions have been conducted behind a screen, the candidate's gender unknown to those responsible for hiring? As one commentator noted:

Forced by the competition for skilled talent in a world of increasingly technical standards of playing (and also by widely available recordings that made it possible for people living anywhere to hear what a good orchestra sounds like) most orchestras realized that blind auditions were a better way of filling vacancies than the traditional alchemy of contacts, cronyism and personal recommendations. The music-lover has benefited: The growing use of blind auditions has been accompanied by a rise in technical standards as modern symphony orchestras demand more of their musicians.[205]

Mac Donald also pushed back on concerns about the lack of women in STEM fields:

> *Despite the billions of dollars that governments, companies, and foundations have poured into increasing the number of females in STEM, the gender proportions of the hard sciences have not changed much over the years. This is not surprising, given mounting evidence of the differences in interests and aptitudes between the sexes. . . . Females on average tend to choose fields that are perceived to make the world a better place, according to the common understanding of that phrase.*

Her data point for this sweeping assertion? Mac Donald referenced a preschool teacher who was profiled in an article and who, notwithstanding a bachelor's degree in neuroscience, chose not to go to medical school so she could work with poor and minority children. Mac Donald concluded her speech by acknowledging the abuses of power revealed by #MeToo, even as she again attacked any underlying effort for greater equality:

> *The #MeToo movement has uncovered real abuses of power. But the solution to those abuses is not to replace valid measures of achievement with irrelevancies like gender and race.*[206]

Mac Donald's speech sets forth a comprehensive attack on #MeToo as a rationale for resisting gender equality, a pairing that seems to be a particularly pernicious form of backlash. The dismissal of gender and race as irrelevant to the way in which achievement has been measured ignores decades of research demonstrating otherwise. Those who sow the seeds of a #MeToo backlash only serve to exacerbate the silence.

Beyond the Hashtags:
A Blueprint for Change

The Times They Are-a-Changin'

Every organization benefits by providing a safe, respectful, and inclusive workplace culture. These should not just be words to appear on a website. Rather, they should be a leadership commitment to a workplace environment that recognizes the moral, legal, and business reasons for doing so.

If the #MeToo movement and the ongoing revelations of negative conduct have taught us anything, it is that standard sexual harassment policies and related training programs are woefully inadequate. A far more comprehensive commitment is essential if meaningful changes are ever to be achieved.

This is a goal that is in the best interests of any organization. A workplace engaged in a culture of respect, civility, and inclusion performs better, and studies have long demonstrated the positive link between financial performance and diverse organizations.[207]

Developing such a culture, however, requires committed leadership and an engaged workforce willing to invest in data gathering, analysis, training, and systems that, together, create an environment in which intolerance and harassment can neither thrive nor be protected. Such a workplace must also be willing to move beyond bare-bones prescriptive training and reporting policies that infrequently help victims of negative behaviors and misconduct.

One of the more difficult aspects of writing this book was reading court cases and research detailing the demoralizing, humiliating, physically dangerous, and emotionally devastating harassment that individuals have been subject to at work. The physical and psychological harms suffered by victims whose sole transgression seemed to be their gender, race, ethnicity, sexual preference, or other way in which they differed from the dominant sectors in the workplace was and continues to be shocking. These examples span decades and continue today. It is unconscionable and remains unfathomable that workplace cultures continue to be so entrenched.

The recommendations offered in this chapter are based on the substantial body of research, articles, and other resources that have identified and analyzed negative behaviors in the workplace. A primary lesson learned is that, for change to happen, those in the workplace must have confidence that incidents will be addressed swiftly and fairly, without retaliation to the victim or others who report improper behavior.

There is nothing more important to the successful implementation of these recommendations than a workplace culture committed to an environment of respect and inclusion. As the EEOC Task Force Report noted: "workplace culture has the greatest impact on allowing harassment to flourish, or conversely, in preventing harassment."[208]

Accordingly, each of the recommendations that follow should be viewed as part of an overall strategy that will result in a respectful workplace environment that has the added benefit of providing greater opportunities to achieve true equality.

Change Depends on Understanding the Symbiotic Relationship between Leadership and Culture

Authors of a survey examining whether the #MeToo movement has resulted in workplace change reinforced that an organization's culture is directly tied to the ability to reduce sexual harassment at work: "Disturbing behaviors happen more frequently in cultures where misdeeds are given a pass. Leaders must create environments where people feel safe to report bad behavior and have confidence that concerns will be handled fairly and effectively."[209]

Cultural change requires leadership committed to fostering a positive environment where all are expected to treat each other with civility and respect, and where those at the top set an example and push for results. It also requires leaders to listen and to encourage communication among teams and across lines of authority.

Research from all sectors makes clear that the achievement of a workplace free of harassment and misconduct depends on committed leaders. As the authors of a broad-based study of harassment in academia highlighted:

> [W]e are encouraged by the research that suggests that the most potent predictor of sexual harassment is organizational climate— the degree to which those in the organization perceive that sexual harassment is or is not tolerated. This means that institutions can take concrete steps to reduce sexual harassment by making system-wide changes that demonstrate how seriously they take this issue and that reflect that they are listening to those who courageously speak up to report their sexual harassment experiences.[210]

It is not enough, however, for leaders to be committed to a workplace free of harassment if they are not equally committed to holding people accountable for achieving and maintaining a respectful work environment. As an American Bar Association (ABA) publication stated: "The willingness of employees to report incidents of sex-based harassment is tied directly to trust in the system. That is why leadership from the top is critical."[211]

The research makes clear that the most critical predicate to a cultural shift is leadership that models diverse, respectful, and inclusive values and then creates policies that support these values. The EEOC Task Force stressed that leaders must demonstrate urgency in these goals and noted that "an organization's commitment to a harassment-free workplace must not be based on a compliance mindset, and instead must be part of an overall diversity and inclusion strategy."[212]

The EEOC further observed the ways in which culture manifests itself in how expected behaviors are rewarded, both formally and informally:

> *If leadership values a workplace free of harassment, then it will ensure that harassing behavior against employees is prohibited as a matter of policy; that swift, effective, and proportionate responses are taken when harassment occurs; and that everyone in the workplace feels safe in reporting harassing behavior. Conversely, leaders who do not model respectful behavior, who are tolerant of demeaning conduct or remarks by others, or who fail to support anti-harassment policies with necessary resources, may foster a culture conducive to harassment.*[213]

If leaders are to be effective champions for change, their engagement should be visible and enthusiastic. As noted in a *Harvard Business Review* article: "Have these leaders—rather than HR—lead the initiative and any training you offer. Seeing leaders at all levels skillfully leading the charge shows the value they place on solving this problem, demonstrates commitment, and builds confidence that changes the organization is making aren't isolated to specific units or teams and aren't just lip service."[214]

To successfully accomplish this change, leaders should be specific about those behaviors that will not be tolerated and then demonstrate that consequences will flow from violating those expectations. Employees are astute observers of ways that people are rewarded in an organization and are well aware when bad behavior is seemingly unpunished. A panel of Harvard Business School faculty stressed that leaders must recognize the signals they send, which "starts with building a culture based on collaboration, teamwork, and respect—and not tolerating employees who dominate or treat other employees as if they are there to serve them. Leaders sometimes inadvertently send the wrong message by excusing—or even rewarding—employees for behaving aggressively toward colleagues, even if they're not being overtly sexual."[215]

Leaders cannot hide behind a lack of knowledge. Even when leaders are, or profess to be, unaware of negative behaviors, employees generally assume they have full knowledge. Respondents to the Women's Bar Association of Massachusetts survey and others interviewed for this book frequently described circumstances in which employees warned each other of those who should be avoided or grumbled quietly about the latest transgressions of a fellow coworker or senior leader. Their frustration was compounded by a belief that the behaviors were known to those in leadership, just as they were known to others in the organization. The reasonable assumption was that the perpetrators were acting with at least tacit acceptance from the organization.

Leaders should pay close attention to creating a workplace culture where there is no opportunity for someone to exercise unchecked power. As noted employment discrimination law scholars observed: "Heading private fiefdoms where they can hire, fire, and direct other people with impunity puts higher-ups in a position to indulge their biases; bosses can impose sexual demands or other sexist behavior on women, demean 'lesser' men, and punish those who resist such abuses."[216]

Even as power dynamics underlie so much of the interactions between people in the workplace, it is too often overlooked as an area of focus by top leadership. That leaves people to exercise their own power without close attention to the implications of such behavior. And one does not need to be a supervisor or manager to have power to exert.

To counter the impact of power and its potential to increase negative behavior, Professor Sutton recommended practicing humility:

> . . . giving credit to less powerful people, deferring to those who are less prestigious or wealthy than you, and doing them favors. . . . [F]inding ways to reduce the power distance between you and others decreases your employees' stress, increases their contributions, and changes how you see yourself in ways that can prevent you from acting like a selfish bully.[217]

Humility can be exercised in a variety of ways. In its simplest form, a supervisor or manager can exercise humility by purposefully getting to know people or by spending time outside his or her work environment to see how tasks are performed at all levels.

When leaders understand all aspects of their workplace culture, they are more likely to learn where there are negative behaviors to address. In addition, by staying alert to these challenges, leaders can avoid costs to the organization that result from low morale, accelerated turnover, reputational damage, and litigation risks.

One critical way that leaders demonstrate their commitment is through the allocation of resources. A leader cannot insist something is a sincere internal value if neither funds nor resources are dedicated to ensuring that the espoused value is inculcated throughout the workplace. To test leadership commitment to its values, it is important to ask: Are there budgeted resources? In an organization with multiple budgets across personnel, do the allocated dollars come out of already overstressed accounts for diversity or training? Is the entire process for reporting, investigating complaints, supporting victims, and reaching a resolution adequately funded? How extensive is the training budget? Are the funds sufficient to support meaningful, comprehensive programs, or mere online tools that simply cover the minimal amount of information needed to possibly qualify for an affirmative defense in the event of a lawsuit?

The availability of adequate resources to support an organization's values speaks volumes about its actual commitment to change. For example, several years ago, the National Association of Women Lawyers Foundation undertook a study of Women's Initiatives in law firms. The study sought to determine whether the initiatives' goals and objectives of advancing women had been allocated sufficient resources and whether the initiative had a strategy for how to accomplish its goals.

The study found that law firm Women's Initiatives were vastly underfunded, notwithstanding how frequently these initiatives were touted on websites or otherwise held up by firms as an important marker of their commitment to women's advancement. On average, the top 100 law firms spent less on their Women's Initiative than they did on the salary of a first-year associate. For those firms ranked 101 to 200, the amount spent was significantly less. Moreover, only 42 percent of the firms reported that their Women's Initiative was part of the firm's overall strategic plan.[218] Most Women's Initiatives lacked a clear strategic direction.

How, then, could firm leaders tout these initiatives on their website if their goals were not tied into the law firm's overall strategic mission nor given sufficient resources to meaningfully address internal barriers to women's advancement and equal compensation? Yet a Women's Initiative, as well as other workplace affinity groups, can provide an important structural opportunity to address issues of negative behavior and help exert needed pressure on organization leaders to act. As noted in an article by two law professors: "Safety in numbers is often what empowers women to come forward. And numbers are often what forces employers to settle and take preventive action. . . ."[219]

Implement Measures to Hold Leaders Accountable

An organization's reward system and its culture are inextricably entwined. The old axiom "What matters is measured" continues to hold true. Those who ignore or otherwise enable harassing or demeaning behaviors need to be held accountable.

All meaningful change requires accountability, and every organization uses metrics to track that which is important. For example, law firms painstakingly track billable hours, originations, collections, and yield, as key data points in determining a lawyer's annual compensation. Sales organizations track calls, individual production, profitability of each unit, growth trends, expenses, and other information showing how the organization is meeting its goals.

If the elimination of harassment is truly an organizational goal, then monitoring behaviors that help achieve—or detract from achieving—that goal should also be required. As the EEOC Task Force Report stated:

> *With regard to individuals who engage in harassment, accountability means being held responsible for those actions. . . . If weak sanctions are imposed for bad behavior, employees learn that harassment is tolerated, regardless of the messages, money, time, and resources spent to the contrary. Similarly, if high-ranking and/ or highly valued employees are not dealt with severely if they engage in harassment, that sends the wrong message loud and clear. . . .*

With regard to mid-level managers and front-line supervisors, accountability means that such individuals are held responsible for monitoring and stopping harassment by those they supervise and manage.[220]

Accountability starts with both tracking reports of and impacts from negative behaviors. This can include, for example, monitoring how many reports of policy violations have occurred, including by office location and department, and then seeing if there is a correlation with attrition rates in those departments and office locations.

Employers can identify a range of relevant metrics that can help them analyze how workplace culture is impacting morale, engagement, and productivity. As an additional accountability measure, the organization may consider a metric proposed by the Google workers—tracking how many victims and accused have left, and the value of any exit packages provided to either.

As noted in a Harvard Business School publication, "A common misstep companies make [is] allowing high-performing workers to get away with more than what is tolerated with others. The sales manager who brings in big bucks but acts in a hostile, domineering way with his team may be seen as the definition of success, yet letting 'a brilliant jerk be a jerk' could cost a company many other talented workers in the process. . . ."[221]

We have seen that negative conduct can be closely related to a culture that places barriers in the way of women's advancement. Part of the solution requires metrics to prevent both conscious and unconscious biases from thwarting the careers of women and minorities. A group of discrimination law scholars explained that workplaces can undertake a comprehensive approach to reducing harassment by eliminating sex segregation and inequality and building accountability into the process:

Organizations and industries must include women and men in equal numbers in every job at every level, especially in top positions. . . .

*Harassment policies should be linked to larger plans to elimi-
nate sex discrimination, facilitate full inclusion, and achieve equal
numbers of women, men, and gender nonbinary people of all races
in all jobs at every level throughout the organization. Both traditionally male-dominated and traditionally female-dominated jobs
should be integrated.*

*Organizations should hold owners, managers, and supervi-
sors accountable for implementing non-discrimination and equal
inclusion plans through measurable goals. Their own career
advancement should depend on success in meeting these goals,
along with success in preventing and remedying harassment.*[222]

People at every level of an organization should feel it is part of their
job responsibilities to contribute to a culture that promotes equal
opportunities and sets a tone that permeates throughout the workplace. This is where leaders make a difference by ensuring standards
to which people are held accountable.

One commentator described this comprehensive involvement as
the creation of counterincentives to sexual harassment: "Executives
and high-level managers are typically rewarded based upon stock
performance and other financial benchmarks. Employers might
consider rewarding these employees on such bases as the promotion
of women and minorities, efforts to equalize pay, and reductions in
Equal Employment Opportunity Commission filings."[223] Monetary
rewards as a counterincentive to harassment can be a strong moti-
vator, but employers may also choose to consider a monetary penalty where, for example, a particular unit or office is the recipient
of more complaints of negative behaviors than other parts of the
organization.

The EEOC Task Force Report noted that reward systems incentiv-
ize antiharassment efforts by managers. When people are rewarded
for behaviors that promote organizational values and an inclusive and
respectful culture, it sends a message that reverberates throughout
the workplace. This is at its most visible when accountability is built
into the evaluation process: "Maintain the policy by making offensive

conduct and sensitivity on diversity-related issues a factor in performance evaluation."[224]

A meaningful antidote to harassing behaviors is to ensure that there are more women in powerful positions. This must be part of a strategic focus that is clearly communicated throughout the organization. As the Harvard Business School faculty panel noted:

> *Sexual harassment is a power move: Powerful men forcing themselves on women behind locked doors, with the belief that they can get away with it. . . . Changing that dynamic requires making sure an organization hires a healthy balance of men and women. . . . Companies should make sure they are placed in high-ranking positions of power—on boards, in the C-suite, and in roles that others count on for innovation.*[225]

Of course, as some of the studies discussed in this book make clear, contrapower harassment can result in women and minorities bearing the brunt of negative behaviors even as they reach senior levels of an organization. It is, therefore, necessary to ensure that all of the measures implemented are fully accessible throughout the workplace.

A further cautionary note is needed. A leader's commitment to accountability for curtailing bias must be all-in:

> *One fairly subtle way in which the encouragement to perpetuate biases might occur tacitly is when employers fail to "walk the talk," that is, when they claim that they are in favor of equal opportunity but their behavior suggests otherwise.*[226]

In other words, accountability derives from leaders who demonstrate that everyone is responsible for a respectful work environment. Words in a policy are meaningless without full commitment and engagement at every level of an organization.

An additional way to measure accountability can be found in the disclosures that companies in merger negotiations demand. As the number of high-profile executives accused of sexual harassment grows, companies are scrutinizing potential behavioral liabilities that could arise following a corporate merger. To protect themselves, some companies are requiring that legal representations in merger documents assert that no senior-level executive or manager, nor any director in the acquired company, has been accused of sexual harassment.[227]

These representations are generally bounded by a time period; for example, no sexual harassment accusations have been made within the past five years. They can also cover a range of senior-level executives who manage a large number of people. The overall goal is to add a level of due diligence that considers social and cultural issues, beyond the typical focus on finances.

If an increasing number of transactions similarly require such representations, the result will lead to greater diligence and accountability. After all, as organizations plan for their own future growth and transactional opportunities, it becomes increasingly important that their workplace can stand up to scrutiny, knowing that a future partner may be looking at their culture as well as their balance sheet.

The Promise of the Policy

There is a high cost paid by those who are subjected—either as a victim or a bystander—to the behaviors of fellow workers who demean, disparage, or insult others, whether that treatment is against individuals or particular groups. Yet, too frequently, people who finally muster the courage to report negative behaviors are told that the words or actions did not violate policy nor meet a specific legal definition of, for example, sexual harassment. The resulting disengagement and lower employee morale also affects the organization's bottom line.

In addressing misconduct, workplaces should reach beyond a legal definition of sexual harassment and seek to address the full range of behaviors that could impact culture and employee engagement. Organizations should not require a strict legal definition to be met before they can respond to conduct that undermines a culture of civility and respect. Behaviors can be identified as unacceptable, regardless of whether they are legally actionable. If it is a goal of an organization to develop a respectful and inclusive workplace, then honest conversations about ways to promote those goals may actually become easier once removed from a legally constrained definition of harassment.

A comprehensive policy should leave no doubt about the conduct that it prohibits and should impose consequences for violations of the policy. A group of legal scholars recommended a broad-based approach:

> *Harassment policies, trainings, and reforms should cover all conduct that demeans, intimidates, excludes, undermines, or otherwise treats people differently because of sex, rather than focusing narrowly on unwanted sexual advances and other sexual behavior. . . .*
>
> *Harassment policies, training, and reforms should cover race-based and other types of harassment and discrimination (race, color, religion, national origin, age, and disability, for example, in addition to sex, sexual orientation, sex/gender stereotyping, and gender identity.) They should explicitly cover and explain harassment and discrimination that is intersectional (based on more than one factor).*[228]

Experts recommend that it can be helpful to include examples of prohibited conduct in sexual harassment policies to provide guidance. An ABA publication offered this example of inclusive policy language:

> *The type of conduct that is forbidden by this policy includes, but is not limited to, any one or a combination of the following:*
>
> *Demands for sexual favors in exchange for continued employment or for some benefit associated with a term, condition, or privilege of employment, including such things as favorable performance reviews, assignments, commendations, promotions, and bonuses;*
>
> *Sexual jokes, epithets, advances, or propositions;*
>
> *Verbal abuse of a sexual nature;*
>
> *Verbal commentary about sexual prowess, attractiveness, or deficiencies;*

> *Sexually degrading or vulgar descriptions of another individual;*
> *Leering, whistling, touching, pinching, or assaults;*
> *Touching of body parts;*
> *Suggestive, insulting, or obscene comments or gestures;*
> *Comments with respect to gender nonconformity and gender stereotypes;*
> *Bullying;*
> *Coercive sexual acts;*
> *Unwanted dating propositions or sexual advances;*
> *Display or transmission of sexually suggestive or explicit, demeaning, or hostile pictures, objects, posters, graffiti, or cartoons;*
> *Questions about sexual conduct, sexual orientation, or sexual preferences;*
> *Hostile, demeaning, or intimidating conduct that is consistently targeted at only one sex, even if the content is not sexual.*[229]

In their policy expectations, employers should also consider including the use of social media. As the reliance on and forms of social media continue to skyrocket, toxic ways of interacting has similarly increased. As the EEOC Task Force Report stated:

> *. . . harassment should be in employers' minds as they draft social media policies and, conversely, social media issues should be in employers' minds as they draft anti-harassment policies.*
>
> *For example, an anti-harassment policy should make clear that mistreatment on social media carries the weight of any other workplace interaction. Supervisors and others with anti-harassment responsibilities should be wary of their social media connections with employees. And, procedures for investigating harassment should carefully delineate how to access an employee's social media content when warranted.*[230]

Employers can also take measures to guard against concerns that the policy is too overzealous and inhibits welcome interactions. Generally speaking, that line is clearer in workplaces that have already taken steps to eliminate bias and promote equality at all levels. In a workplace where efforts at humor or relationship-building are not simply a guise for exercising power and control, banter is much more easily differentiated from comments that demean and humiliate. As one expert wrote: "Remember that the law is simply a floor for behavior, not a ceiling. If you strive for three things in your workplace: 1) awareness; 2) respect; 3) professionalism, you shouldn't need to worry about the law."[231]

Zero Tolerance Does Not Mean Equal Punishment

The term *zero tolerance* is used frequently, but its interpretation can vary greatly. A diverse, inclusive, and respectful culture should not tolerate harassment of any kind. But that does not necessitate a policy in which zero tolerance means equal punishment for all offenses. To do so is likely to further inhibit reporting because victims may not want to be the cause of someone receiving a significant punishment for what may be a far lesser offense than, for example, demanding sexual favors to be promoted.

An article in the *New York Times* raised a question that feeds directly into the proportionality argument. The writer, a journalist who had previously covered sexual violence, noted that perpetrators removed from one location tend to show up elsewhere, continuing to prey on new victims:

> Bad men are not just on our TV screens, but in our classrooms, our workplaces, our friend circles, even our families. Where should they go if they're fired from their jobs, expelled from their schools, kicked out of their homes or shunned by their communities?
>
> #MeToo is also supposed to reflect a spectrum of coercive behavior, not just crimes that should lead to prison sentences. Bill Cosby is one thing; but many women don't want the V.P. of sales who got too handsy at the Christmas party to be banished forever, let alone go to prison. If they're faced with what looks like no other option, will women be more likely to report him, or less? . . .

What do we want from abusers? Under what terms should they be allowed to return to normal life? Is there a way to explore possibilities of redemption that don't put more of a burden on the people harmed in the first place?[232]

It is clear that determining how to discipline someone who engaged in negative behaviors is complex and fraught with potential collateral consequences. Moreover, there are many factors to be considered, including, for example, the nature of the allegations, the power disparity between the perpetrator and the victim, whether there is a history of similar behaviors, and whether the alleged perpetrator has taken steps that could be seen as retaliatory to someone who has reported.

The EEOC Task Force Report recommended that a policy clearly articulate "that the employer will take immediate and proportionate corrective action when it determines that harassment has occurred, and respond appropriately to behavior which may not be legally-actionable 'harassment' but which, left unchecked, may lead to same."[233] The report noted that a statement of "zero tolerance" may be read as an approach to punishment in which all perpetrators are disciplined identically, regardless of the offending behavior. Rather, the EEOC recommends that once an investigation finds that harassment occurred, the follow-up discipline should be administered promptly, be proportionate to the conduct, and not create an appearance that employees may be treated differently.

Of course, the challenge is in developing a range of responses that are appropriate to the offense and respectful of and responsive to the victim's experience. Shortly after that *New York Times* article questioned how the workplace should appropriately respond to offenders, the paper published excerpts from readers who offered their own suggestions. For example, one reader recommended that offenders be required to volunteer their time helping abuse victims: "Maybe these men could take some time to reflect on the impact of their actions, demonstrate actual empathy for their victims, and devote their time, energy and money toward organizations that provide legal and emotional support to sexual abuse and assault survivors."[234]

Another wrote to suggest that offenders be required to attend a form of consciousness-raising classes: "What if predators go to classes, set up a bit like Alcoholics Anonymous, in which they learn that women are not subhuman life-forms and prey? It would be like court-ordered rehab combined with 'How to Be a Gentleman' classes."[235]

Still another spoke in support of restorative justice programs as raised in the original *New York Times* article as a way to bring victims, perpetrators, and other stakeholders together to discuss the wrongdoing and construct a response: "Victims are given the space to describe the harm they endured and to consider possible solutions. Perpetrators are given an opportunity to think through their actions. The premise of restorative justice is that people can learn through their mistakes."[236]

A therapist wrote to say that, although therapy has its limitations, "some form of self-reflection is essential for prolonged change. There needs to be a path for redemption that includes paying back a debt to the victims and society."[237]

Another reader responded by pointing to the Catholic Church's movement of pedophile priests from one church to another, noting that a key lesson learned is the importance of transparency. An additional key point, the reader argued, was money: "Like all things in life, if you want to effect change, then make those responsible pay. Money is something both the perpetrators and the institutions that protect them understand."[238]

An ABA publication suggested a wide range of potential disciplinary actions, for example:[239]

- Termination
- Counseling
- Coaching on proper behavior in the workplace
- Reductions in compensation and/or bonuses
- Removal from leadership positions
- Transfer of the perpetrator
- Mandatory training

The bottom line is to construct a policy that is sensitive to victims, that provides a disciplinary response commensurate with the nature of the offense, and that clearly communicates the workplace's insistence on a respectful environment.

Policy Implementation and Training Are an Ongoing Responsibility

In urging clear and comprehensive policies that are written in a user-friendly style, the EEOC Task Force Report stated that the policy "must be communicated on a regular basis to employees, particularly information about how to file a complaint or how to report harassment that one observes, and how an employee who files a complaint or an employee who reports harassment or participates in an investigation of alleged harassment will be protected from retaliation."[240]

In the study conducted by the Women's Bar Association of Massachusetts, nearly half of the respondents did not even know whether their firm had a policy for reporting. This is consistent with other research showing that people in the workplace often have insufficient knowledge of antiharassment policies and procedures. There is clearly ample room for improving communications on this issue.

Here is what the #MeToo movement tells us: when employers ignore the connection between their training and reporting policies and the existence of a respectful and inclusive environment, they may win the battle of legal protection, but they will fail to achieve a workplace that can compete for talent and engage workers in their common goals. Every organization should communicate its workplace conduct policies through frequent training programs for existing employees at all levels, including as part of the on-boarding process for all new employees.

Regularly implemented training programs offer an opportunity to provide comprehensive information about the organization's reporting options and subsequent investigatory process, accountability mechanisms, vigilance against retaliatory activities, and other information that will contribute to a positive workplace culture that promotes reporting. In addition, comprehensive training can help everyone in the workplace understand the way in which people develop assumptions and respond to the motivations of others. Training should also provide new insights into long-established beliefs, offering interventions to eliminate old behaviors. Training that keeps these considerations at the forefront has a much stronger likelihood of impacting behaviors and improving culture.

Finally, training need not—indeed, should not—wait until people enter the workforce. Business schools, for example, have a significant role to play as they are developing tomorrow's workplace leaders: "Now, with the steady stream of sexual misconduct claims set off by the Harvey Weinstein scandal, business schools are adding sexual harassment training to curriculums that are increasingly stressing ethics and values alongside finance, marketing, and economics."[241]

These programs can focus on a range of challenges that students will one day face—for example, creating an environment where people feel comfortable reporting harassment, teaching bystanders how to safely intervene, and learning to develop a respectful culture. Such programs should be implemented in all institutions of higher education. As graduates eventually ascend into intermediate leadership roles, younger employees have a special opportunity to influence changes in the workplace environment. The earlier they are provided the appropriate tools, the more influential they can be in establishing a respectful and inclusive workplace culture.

Train for Effectiveness, Not Liability Avoidance

A policy and reporting process that is designed as a mechanism to support an affirmative defense in the event of a sexual harassment lawsuit is likely to fail the employees it is supposed to protect. What may work in a courtroom will accomplish little in the office.

A workplace should not, therefore, consider its obligations complete when it posts a barebones policy, undertakes perfunctory training, and then is silent as to the results of any report of harassment, relying on privacy and confidentiality considerations as the reason for not providing feedback about the results of a subsequent investigation, if any.

Leaders must be fully engaged in promoting a culture of respect and treat that obligation as they treat other key strategic goals. The mere existence of training should not qualify as an affirmative defense to employer liability without standards for what is included in the training, how frequently it is provided and in what manner, and whether it strategically integrates with other efforts within the organization to create a respectful work environment. As one scholar on this topic noted:

> *Only those employers demonstrating efforts to reform educational programming and link it to comprehensive and holistic bias elimination efforts should be able to reference training as a shield from punitive damages. Creating doctrinal incentives for transformative prevention efforts can strengthen the impact of equal employment opportunity (EEO) law and make harassment a rare, rather than everyday, phenomenon.*[242]

Accordingly, training should be broad-based, extend beyond legal compliance, and set forth clear workplace boundaries around unacceptable conduct. In addition, training should emphasize that behaviors deriving from power imbalances and demonstrating disrespect should not be trivialized or treated as too unimportant to address. Each negative incident can be, at minimum, a distraction that impacts both the victim and the workplace or can be an experience that has more far-reaching ramifications for both.

Well-designed training is a critical tool for achieving a desired outcome in any workplace. Ineffective training is a waste of time and money. It is simply not useful to require employees to review an online course that consists of stock images showing women being menaced by a male figure, with simplistic language that superficially defines sexual harassment laws. When organizations resort to poorly designed training programs on sexual harassment, they are missing an educational opportunity to address the complexity of workplace experiences.

Training should be comprehensive enough to help all levels of employees develop a deeper understanding of a range of issues that can impact workplace culture. For example, incorporating social science research will provide a more nuanced, and concomitantly more useful, learning opportunity. As authors of the study that analyzed the link between power and misperceptions of sexual intent stated:

> *One solution to the potential problems caused by erroneous perceptions of sexual interest could be to build insight among those in power. . . . One simple addition to [sexual harassment] training would be lessons that teach individuals that positions of power can lead people to mistakenly infer sexual interest from members of the opposite sex. This training might also remind those in power that small differences in perception can translate into broad miscommunication or inappropriate behavior. Such lessons may offer an easily implemented and inexpensive addition to existing sexual harassment programs. In light of the massive financial, organizational, and physical and mental health costs of sexual harassment . . . insight training may be an effective preventative measure.*[243]

It should be a required element of training to address unconscious bias, particularly its impacts on how people are evaluated, paid, and promoted in an organization. Structural barriers with roots in implicit bias continue to inhibit opportunities for women and minorities to reach the highest levels of leadership and decision-making. In order to combat these biases, it is critical to understand how they are infused throughout an organization's structures and within every individual's own worldview.

For example, the study analyzing performance reviews and promotions in line positions noted that, if a workplace only looks for bias in evaluations by aggregating ratings, they may miss its occurrence in one level of employment (e.g., line managers) as compared to others. The study also cautioned that it may not be easy to discern whether bias is causing a group to be held to a higher performance standard:

> *Such subtle indications of gender bias could easily be overlooked by organizations unless they conduct detailed analyses of gender differences in performance ratings required for promotion and*

examine relative strengths of relationships between performance ratings and promotions for women and men.[244]

The lack of diversity in powerful roles in institutions reinforces a workplace in which the dominant culture makes and enforces the rules, leaving the organization vulnerable to abuses of power that can manifest in negative conduct and improper behaviors. To address this, unconscious bias training should be viewed as an integral component of training programs addressing sexual harassment and negative workplace conduct.

Training should also address the concept of credibility discounting and how it undermines women being seen as credible witnesses on their own behalf:

> *Credibility discounts and experiential trivialization harm women in an abundance of ways—up to and including the supremely destabilizing process of prompting women to question the truth of their own experience. Women are devalued and gaslighted from every direction, discouraging them from continuing to seek systemic support. Ripple effects discourage the broader community of women from seeking the help they need. And our entire society suffers from the failure to fully understand, credit, and value a substantial portion of the human experience. Together, these harms operate to form a formidable obstacle to women's healing, safety, and ability to obtain justice.*[245]

The EEOC Task Force Report recommended training for all levels of employees, including supervisory and managerial personnel. In addition, the EEOC stressed that training programs be supported by the highest levels of leadership: "The strongest expression of support is for a senior leader to open the training session and attend the entire training session."[246]

The EEOC also recommended that, to the extent possible, training should be undertaken live, rather than online, to provide an opportunity for creative, customized, and interactive programs. Each organization differs in culture and the challenges posed within, and training is most effective when developed for a particular workplace.

The authors of a survey addressing how workplaces are responding to the increased attention to sexual harassment offered suggestions for ways to create a more sophisticated training program:

> *People need to know how to coach, mentor, and meet one-on-one with members of the opposite sex without creating discomfort or running the risk of false accusations. Teach employees to address uncomfortable or awkward situations well before they rise to the level of harassment or misconduct. Rehearse the reporting process, including how to document, report, and escalate a problem. Create anonymized case studies that tell the story of how incidents of sexual harassment and misconduct are investigated, adjudicated, and punished.*[247]

The EEOC and other experts make clear that training can no longer be viewed as a perfunctory box to check in one's human resources manual. Training should be the vehicle through which all employees are offered a new way to understand the workplace and people's experiences. A workplace devoted to diversity, inclusion, and respect must invest the time and resources necessary to help people learn how to address difficult situations. Long-ingrained negative behaviors, supported by cultures that benignly—and sometimes overtly—allow their continued existence will not disappear without such sustained effort and hard work.

Undertake an Internal Assessment

A candid internal assessment provides an organization with the best opportunity to understand where it needs to focus its efforts and to identify the appropriate metrics by which to measure success. Every workplace has areas of vulnerability. Some have leaders who treat others dismissively, or who bully, or who engage in harassing behaviors. Other workplaces fail to address a culture where fear and stress take an emotional and financial toll. Many have poor systems for reporting and addressing negative conduct.

The specific issues of concern may differ across all organizations. But every organization should seek an opportunity to better understand its own challenges.

The EEOC Task Force Report described risk factors that may make organizations more susceptible to harassment. Noting studies that have demonstrated the predictive link between organizational characteristics and the likelihood of harassment, the EEOC identified a comprehensive list of risk factors:[248]

1. *Homogenous workforces: Workplaces that lack diversity increase the likelihood that someone outside the dominant gender, race, or ethnicity will feel—and be—isolated and vulnerable.*

2. *Workplaces where there are workers who do not conform to societal norms: When norms are based on stereotypes, a person who is seen as different may be more subject to ridicule such as an individual with a disability who is ridiculed for being different, or a male who is perceived to act more feminine in an environment that relishes crude banter.*

3. *Just as homogenous workforces have risk factors, so, too, can workplaces where a large number of workers are from a different nationality and speak a different language. Workers who do not speak English may be more subject to exploitation and less aware of their rights and laws that protect them.*

4. *Workplaces with high numbers of young adults and teenagers: Younger workers may be more likely to be taken advantage of by supervisors and those more established in their careers, as well as by other coworkers. Of particular concern, a young person new to the workforce may lack the confidence to resist unwelcome contact, so may be more vulnerable.*

5. *Workplaces that exalt certain employees who are perceived to bring high value and prestige may be less likely to intercede in a harassment complaint against that person or otherwise challenge their behavior.*

6. *In workplaces with significant power disparities, low-status workers are particularly susceptible to harassment. The EEOC*

Task Force noted the particular vulnerabilities of undocumented workers and women in gendered workplaces where most of the females are in support staff roles and most men are in executive positions.

7. Workers whose compensation is directly tied to customer or client satisfaction such as waitstaff or commissioned workers are also at risk of harassment. In addition, managers may tolerate harassing behaviors from clients or customers to retain their business.

8. Boredom may also exacerbate conditions for harassment. If people are not engaged in their work or otherwise have tasks that are monotonous or leave spare time, harassment may be a way to vent frustration.

9. Individuals who work in isolation, for example on a night shift or housekeepers alone in hotel rooms, may also be at risk as harassment tends to occur more in isolated areas.

10. Workplaces that provide alcohol are at higher risk for harassment, as drinking impairs judgment and reduces inhibitions.

11. Workplaces that are highly decentralized and offer limited communications across various organizational levels are also at higher risk, particularly those where the corporate offices are in a different location from where most workers do their jobs. Decentralization can pose a risk by emboldening those who feel their location provides some insulation and less accountability to other managers and leaders.

In identifying these risk factors, the EEOC Task Force Report stressed that situational awareness can help employers take more proactive measures to prevent harassment. By engaging in such self-analysis, workplace leaders can understand their own areas of vulnerability as creating the basis for individualized policies and programs.

This awareness can best be developed through an internal assessment designed to produce honest feedback and identify measures that can be implemented to improve culture and stop inappropriate behaviors. Toward that goal, firms should engage in a process to solicit confidential feedback from all levels of employees, including those in leadership. Such an assessment can be conducted in a variety of ways, including as a survey or a series of confidential conversations.

To ensure that interviewees and survey respondents provide information openly and confidentially, an organization should consider a neutral, independent party to conduct the assessment. The findings can serve as the basis for developing both short-term and long-term goals for improving culture and strengthening relationships among colleagues.

There are several examples of such assessments in the public domain. For example, an independent investigation revealed how Penn State's culture of reverence for its athletic programs permeated not only actual decision-making, but also the way in which staff perceived how decisions would be made, further discouraging efforts to report behaviors that were outside the expected norms. This culture impacted judgments at every level of employment, including janitors who first observed Jerry Sandusky behaving inappropriately with young boys in a shower but believed their jobs would be in jeopardy if they reported what they saw.[249]

Of course, the goal for any organization is to conduct an internal assessment long before such behaviors have had corrosive effects on the overall culture. This can best be accomplished if the organization is committed to addressing challenges identified in an assessment by, for example, creating a short- and longer-term plan for meaningful progress and change.

An interesting recommendation in the EEOC Task Force Report is to include in settlement agreements a condition allowing researchers to assess the workplace climate with respect to harassment both before and after training is implemented. This form of assessment will help determine the efficacy of the training programs.

Encourage Reporting—Then Encourage It Some More

A safe reporting process, free of retaliation or other negative consequences, is absolutely essential. Individuals should never feel they are risking their careers or their reputation within their organization if they report negative conduct. The simple fact is that people will not report unless they feel safe doing so.

Unfortunately, fear of retaliation frequently has a sound basis. Harvard Business School professor Rosabeth Moss Kanter described a simple dynamic that impacts reporting: people do not like complainers. This makes it critically important to put in place anonymous mechanisms that allow people to feel their identity can be protected if they come forward.[250]

The way in which a reporting process is handled speaks volumes to employees and directly impacts whether a policy is meaningfully implemented. Employees cannot have faith in a policy that, in actual implementation, results in retaliatory behaviors of any type. They also will not trust a process where reports do not appear to be taken seriously, or the confidentiality of the person reporting is not respected, or there does not appear to be any follow-up when reports are made.

Many organizations offer avenues of reporting to senior leaders, an HR department, or other designated individuals or groups. But as discussed previously, these mechanisms do not always work. For example, HR departments, no matter how well-meaning, may have conflicting loyalties when individuals come forward with information that may have negative consequences for the organization itself.

The reporting process is critical because it is the foundation for the follow-up investigations. An ABA publication recommended a variety of factors to consider when determining who should conduct an investigation, for example: "the nature and complexity of the conduct alleged; the position of the person or persons involved and/or accused; and whether there are employees within the organization who have the skill, resources, and training to investigate without any conflicts of interest."[251] In addition, the publication reinforced the need for the investigator to have the requisite skills and experience, to be impartial and neutral, and, related to the importance of trust in the process as previously discussed, to be removed from any influence or even the appearance that the employer could be influencing the process.

The EEOC Task Force Report suggested multifaceted reporting systems that provide alternative approaches to reporting:

> *Such a robust reporting system might include options to file complaints with managers and human resource departments, via multi-lingual complaint hotlines, and via web-based complaint processing. In addition, a multi-faceted system might offer an employee who complains about harassment various mechanisms for addressing the situation, depending on the type of conduct and workplace situation. For example, an employee may simply need someone in authority to talk to the harasser in order to stop the behavior. In other situations, the employer may need to do an immediate intervention and begin a thorough investigation.*[252]

Organizations may consider including within their policy an opportunity to report to someone who is independent from the firm's existing hierarchy. By providing access to a neutral third party, victims may be dissuaded from feeling they need to be silent to protect themselves from retribution.

Vigilantly Prevent Retaliatory Behaviors

Retaliation can be blatant or subtle. The blatant forms are easily observable—for example, whether a complainant is fired or demoted.

The more subtle ways in which a person's career can be damaged are equally pernicious. For example, a person can be socially ostracized, excluded from customer or client contact, become marginalized through fewer opportunities and less interesting and important assignments, or otherwise left out of opportunities that foster career growth and development.

In too many situations, the law provides little refuge for the aggrieved. The EEOC Task Force reported that there are well-founded reasons for victims to fear reporting:

> *One 2003 study found that 75% of employees who spoke out against workplace mistreatment faced some form of retaliation.*

> *Other studies have found that sexual harassment reporting is often followed by organizational indifference or trivialization of the harassment complaint as well as hostility and reprisals against the victim. Such responses understandably harm the victim in terms of adverse job repercussions and psychological distress.[253]*

The EEOC recommends that employers vigilantly guard against possible retaliatory behavior toward those who report harassment and implement measures to prevent its occurrence.

The U.S. Department of Labor's Whistleblower Protection Advisory Committee, a bipartisan labor-management group, developed best practices for establishing antiretaliation programs. The recommended practices include five key elements for inclusion in an antiretaliation program:[254]

1. *Management leadership, commitment, and accountability*
2. *System for listening to and resolving employees' safety and compliance concerns*
3. *System for receiving and responding to reports of retaliation*
4. *Antiretaliation training for employees and managers*
5. *Program oversight*

Also among its important recommendations is to develop independent channels for reporting retaliation that ensure an individual does not have to report to someone who may have been involved in the retaliatory behavior.[255]

The bottom line is that the workplace must step in to act where the courts have chosen not to do so. By broadly defining the scope of retaliatory behaviors that are unacceptable in the workplace, by protecting those who themselves side with victims of harassing behaviors, and by monitoring to ensure that these principles are upheld, employees are more likely to step forward without fear.

Seeing Through the Benefits of Transparency

There are few qualities that contribute more to a positive workplace culture than transparency. When workplace leaders are transparent about their mission, goals, metrics, personnel practices, and advancement opportunities, employees are more likely to feel that they matter within the organization. Another relevant reason for transparency is that research on millennials demonstrates that they will lead with transparency and seek that quality in their workplaces even at the start of their careers.[256] As millennials become half the workforce, offering a transparent work environment can be an effective recruitment and retention tool.

Accordingly, employers should consider every opportunity to add transparency to their policies addressing workplace conduct. This can be accomplished by providing clarity at each step of the process, including: identification of lines of authority; an explanation of the extent of responsibilities for each of the individuals who may be involved in the process; an approximation of the amount of time that the investigation will take; and information about the outcome.

Transparency also requires that everyone in the organization understands the potentially conflicting duties of loyalty that may exist in the reporting process. For example, and as described previously, an HR official may feel a conflicted duty of loyalty between their relationship with senior management and their designated role in this process.

We have seen examples where an individual who reports was told to ignore the person and the behaviors or was told that nothing can be done because of the stature of the perpetrator. But what may not be known is whether the person in HR or other senior official handling the matter is making that judgment to protect the company or their own standing. The policy should, therefore, address whether there are limitations on the HR department or other individuals involved in the reporting process, as well as set forth a process for reporting negative conduct by a senior leader.

Another area in which greater transparency is needed is with respect to the results of the process. Often, those who report are not informed of any follow-up, so it is not known whether any investigative or disciplinary measures were taken.

The lack of information leaves victims, and everyone who knows about the incident, feeling further demoralized. Reporting alone, without clear follow-up and transparency, is a disservice to the workplace.

As the EEOC Task Force Report noted: "Investigators should document all steps taken from the point of first contact, prepare a written report using guidelines to weigh credibility, and communicate the determination to all relevant parties."[257]

An additional practice that can help build trust and confidence among employees is to monitor the results of the reporting process. A third party can help engender trust in policies and follow up so employees know that the investigation, findings, and subsequent disciplinary steps, if any, are fairly and consistently implemented.

Provide Ongoing Support and Information to Those Who Report

Too often, victims of inappropriate behaviors inform a senior leader or their HR department but then ask that the conversation remain off the record and confidential. This reflects the victim's fear and discomfort with the process, yet it leaves the organization unable to respond appropriately. Without the complainant's willingness to participate in an investigatory process, the organization may find it impossible to move forward.

Encouraging a culture of reporting and then supporting those who do come forward is critical. It is insufficient to have a procedure for conducting an investigation or otherwise responding to reported misconduct without supporting those who report through every step of the process, and even beyond.

Both victims and bystanders who report often face difficult challenges, particularly if the results of an investigation lead to strong punitive measures or a judicial process. A story about the closing arguments in Bill Cosby's second sexual assault trial is instructive. One of the defense lawyers characterized the women who testified against the television icon as "promiscuous party girls out for cheap fame and a payday." The prosecutor responded to the defense lawyer who made that statement: "She's the exact reason why victims, women and men, of sexual assault don't report these crimes."[258] Indeed, the witnesses against Cosby had endured blistering criticism from Cosby and his defense team. For victims watching this case, the prosecutor's words rang true. Yet the prosecutor's steadfast support of the victims helped ensure that justice was achieved, notwithstanding the defense's attempted smears.

Workplace support should also include measures to keep victims from being revictimized. As a panel of Harvard Business School faculty observed: "A man accused of wrongdoing might point to a woman either remaining silent or laughing along with the crowd at sexist jokes or unwanted touching as a sign that she was OK with it or even enjoyed it."[259] Of course, such an accusation lacks any basis in reality and misses the difficult choices victims face in those circumstances. It is up to the organization to ensure the complainant that such a response will not be tolerated.

The level of support should be broad enough to help victims face each step of the difficult road ahead. Pitfalls include, for example, retribution, social isolation, hostile questioning, and skeptical coworkers. They may further face a negative reaction if the misconduct was not deemed egregious enough, either by colleagues or as a result of the subsequent investigation.

Organizations should provide in their policies that those who report may bring a coworker, a representative, or other support person to internal meetings. In addition, organizations can provide assistance through affinity groups that include within their mission a commitment to supporting those who report misconduct.

Victims of negative workplace behaviors face complex decisions. An effective reporting process will include support mechanisms throughout for those individuals who come forward.

Look for Patterns of Behavior

In too many workplaces, barriers to reporting are daunting. But the lack of reporting builds on itself, impacting a victim's willingness to be the first to raise concerns about a perpetrator's negative conduct.

The EEOC Task Force Report stated that victims are more likely to confide in close friends and family members than to report. As noted, nearly 70 percent of people experiencing harassment do not report the information to senior supervisors. Even fewer—6 to 13 percent—file a formal complaint.[260]

Informal sharing of information is an unsatisfactory alternative to the preferred result of an institutional response. Underreporting results in a culture that fosters continued negative conduct from perpetrators, emboldens others, and fuels the emergence of unconscious biases.

As a result of underreporting, workplace leaders may convince themselves that a reported or witnessed behavior is not part of a larger pattern. Without knowing more, however, such leaders may be lulled into a false sense of security. For example, individuals may be engaging in negative conduct, but because victims are reluctant to report, these behaviors may be occurring without the knowledge of those in leadership roles or in HR. If victims hesitate to report their experiences and if there is no repository of information indicating otherwise, it is too easy to assume that all is well.

Accordingly, this is an area where employers should develop creative solutions to help identify patterns of behaviors. To be effective, solutions should focus on the collection of information about individuals who engage in improper conduct.

As one person interviewed for this book stated:

> There is a need for the systemic compilation of data over time. People may want to share information for the greater good but not for themselves. Maybe even a confidential hotline can help.

Another described an incident in which she was at a business dinner with a senior work colleague and a client, both of whom were drunk. She was so uncomfortable with the experience, including her colleague's behavior after dinner, that she discussed it with her mentor, who helped her strategize about how to handle such a situation in the future. In retrospect, she realized that simply having a conversation with her mentor that was premised on confidentiality was an ineffective long-term solution. She noted:

There can be no accountability if everything is kept silent. Ideally, someone should have told him that he can't behave that way. . . . I could see a reporting mechanism working if, for example, my mentor was the one who reported to the system as a way of collecting patterns.

As part of an effort to identify patterns of negative behaviors, workplaces should also consider looking for patterns of bias. The research shows that negative behaviors are more likely to be found in an organization that allows other forms of bias to flourish. As noted previously, harassment seldom exists in a vacuum. Workplaces that harbor negative actors are also likely to see bias emerge in other personnel practices, such as assignments, promotions, and compensation. It is incumbent on the organization to look for patterns of both:

Organizations should monitor harassment and discrimination complaints for larger patterns of bias and broader hostile work environments. Responding to individual complaints and resolving them one by one is inadequate where they are part of a broader culture of stereotyping, discrimination, and inequality in the workplace.[261]

Vigilance in determining patterns of behavior starts with the identification and collection of relevant information. In the absence of reporting, the sharing of informal information can assist in identifying offenders and paving the way for future follow-up. For example, the EEOC Task Force Report offered an example of a company that created an internal group of key leaders who were informed immediately when a complaint of harassment was made (absent, of course, any conflicts of interest). This group was also kept apprised of outcomes and preventative follow-up measures. Such a group can also be an important vehicle for identifying and responding to patterns of behavior discussed in informal networks, but not formally reported.

Some victims who are fearful of choosing to report may be willing to share their story at a later time, when they can use their voice in support of someone else who came forward for similar reasons. We have seen from the decades of abusive behaviors that underlie so many #MeToo stories that the first report of bad behavior can be the hardest. Often, it is only after those first allegations are made that victims are more willing to speak up and corroborate the initial claim.

To encourage those first reports, an interesting idea that has emerged is the concept of information escrows. Information escrows serve to:

> . . . *allow victims to transmit claims information to a trusted intermediary, a centralized escrow agent, who forwards the information to proper authorities if (and only if) certain prespecified conditions are met. Specifically, the escrow agent would keep harassment allegations confidential, unutilized, and unforwarded until the agent has received a prespecified number of complementary harassment allegations concerning the same accused harasser.*[262]

The existence of an information escrow process can encourage a reluctant victim to share her story in confidence, not knowing if she is the first to report or the triggering mechanism in someone else's reporting. It provides a degree of control with respect to how the information is to be released and can allow the victim to revoke the escrow at any time and move forward with a complaint. The process is not a panacea, but it may present employers with an additional option for encouraging victims to step forward in the way that is most comfortable for them.

It is also instructive to collect information about patterns of behavior when reports are made but an investigation does not substantiate the reported allegation. A publication from the American Bar Association noted the following:

> *Records of all complaints of harassment, even those that cannot be substantiated, should be kept in a central and confidential place. This is the only effective way to monitor for patterns that may reveal undetected harassment. For example, even if a complaint is*

not substantiated, that complaint is relevant and should be taken into consideration when investigating a subsequent complaint about the same person. Incidents that do not appear serious in isolation assume broader significance when they reflect a continued course of conduct.[263]

It is critical to emphasize that efforts to observe patterns and act on such information should only be undertaken in the context of a comprehensive policy that supports victims and prohibits retaliation.

Even if formal reporting feels unsafe and no anonymous reporting mechanism seems available, there are still measures that can be taken. At the very least, an employee who experiences or witnesses harassment or other negative conduct should create a record by keeping copies of everything that could someday serve as evidence, including emails, texts, and voice mails. If the victim confides in friends and family, it can be helpful to keep a contemporaneous record of when that information was shared. The victim or bystander should also document whether any actions were taken to interrupt or stop the behavior.[264]

One professor suggested that workplaces consider the appointment of an ombudsperson—that is, someone who serves "outside of the traditional lines of organizational hierarchy who reports directly to the chief executive officer."[265] The duties of an ombudsperson could include educating and training employees, providing outreach, and even assisting in a dispute resolution role.

If an organization retains an ombudsperson, it is important to ensure that the individual be truly independent from management and is provided sufficient authority and resources to be able to meaningfully contribute. An ombudsperson does not advocate for nor represent the organization or its employees. His or her focus is to serve as an advocate for an accessible and fair process.

Do Not Treat Victims and Victimizers Like Couples Who Need Counseling

As part of the obligation to provide support throughout the process for those who come forward, organizations must avoid steps that emphasize the imbalance of power that generally exists between the victim and the perpetrator.

In the Women's Bar Association of Massachusetts survey, and in the course of many interviews for this book, women described being required to meet directly with the alleged perpetrator to discuss the accusations. None of these meetings had support mechanisms in place for the reporting individual, such as a neutral party who could facilitate a positive conversation. In fact, some described the meeting atmosphere as intimidating in tone and a reinforcement of the power imbalance.

One woman shared her experience fending off a senior colleague's advances at a conference. When she returned to the office, she reported the incident and was subsequently told that the head of the organization wanted to meet with her and the supervisor who propositioned her to discuss the incident. Concerned that such a meeting would be too uncomfortable, she requested that a lawyer be present on her behalf. The employer responded by taking measures against her perpetrator and against her.

Several women described forced meetings where the HR representative and company executives sat with the perpetrator, asking hostile questions throughout. Moreover, these meetings were held in rooms that lacked privacy, with glass walls open to the hall so anyone passing by could observe the attendees.

It is hard enough for someone to take the step of reporting. As discussed, the organization has an obligation to implement a process in which the individual feels safe and supported through each phase of the investigation. A forced meeting in which the only other attendees are part of the firm's power structure is a setting designed to intimidate someone already feeling victimized. Such a result further discourages others in the organization from reporting.

Avoidance Is Not a Strategy

Victims often recount examples where workplace leaders respond to an allegation of inappropriate behavior by physically separating the person aggrieved from the perpetrator by moving the victim's office. Not only does such a measure fail to change workplace dynamics overall, but it also frequently causes revictimization. Physical isolation may impact future work assignments available to a victim removed from the mainstream. It can also impede other career opportunities through decreased visibility to key leaders and loss of proximity to work colleagues and supportive peers.

In many cases, victims are not moved but simply advised to stay away from the offender. As a strategy, this form of avoidance is generally not even possible because of the underlying working relationship. For example, are young people in an organization supposed to steer clear of senior leaders who may have been abusive or have otherwise engaged in inappropriate behavior but who are an important source of work? What would prevent further negative career impacts? And why should the responsibility fall on the victim to make the required adjustments? Commenting on the implications of imposing restrictions on interactions that are essential to career development, former American Bar Association president Laurel Bellows stated, "Gender discrimination is not the solution to sexual harassment."[266]

In the study of female supervisors harassed at work, the researchers highlighted an example of a woman being groped by a client at a company dinner. As the only female in upper management, she stayed silent even as she tried to push the client's continually roving hands away. When male coworkers finally noticed the client's inappropriate conduct, they moved quickly to pay the bill for dinner so the female could have a comfortable excuse for extracting herself from the situation. The men, however, including her supportive coworkers, all stayed together for drinks after she went home.

As the study authors noted, the coworkers did not address the client engaging in the behavior but instead assumed a protective role toward their female colleague, helping her absent herself. In so doing, however, they also served to undermine her authority. Her colleagues chose to protect her by facilitating an end to the dinner so she could leave. Her harassing client was neither punished nor even reprimanded for his behavior, and she was deprived the professional and social benefits of the rest of the occasion. The result had no long-term benefit and diminished the role of the female supervisor: "Sexual harassment policies are put in place to protect workers, but organizational practice is often misaligned with formal policies or grievance procedures, calling into question fundamental assumptions many sociologists make regarding organizational constraint and agency . . ."[267]

Respondents to the Women's Bar Association of Massachusetts survey provided many examples of avoidance as a substitute for resolution. For example:

> *The first incident involved inappropriate behavior directed at me from a potential client, who was intoxicated and started making inappropriate/suggestive comments. I was the only woman in the group and the partners who were with me did not immediately intervene, although they ultimately did do so. The potential client emailed me directly the next day . . . I was uncomfortable responding to him directly, so I directed him to another partner at my office and never heard from him again. The second incident took place at a firm meeting. An intoxicated male partner . . . started making wildly inappropriate comments to me and another female associate. . . . I avoided him at the firm meeting this year.*

In each instance where a target of inappropriate behavior is removed from the circumstances, there is likely to be some career impact experienced as a result of the isolation. This burden should not fall on the victim.

Beware of "Death by a Thousand Cuts"

In the workplace, humor can be used both as a sword and a shield. Attempts at jokes that target gender, religion, race, ethnicity, LGBTQ status, or any characteristic that seeks to isolate one's differences inflicts damage. Such alleged jokes are cutting to those who are victimized by the comments, while offering the protective shield of "It's just a joke" to the perpetrators—who then accuse complainants of lacking a sense of humor.

This dynamic was described many times in the Women's Bar Association of Massachusetts survey. For example, a respondent described multiple instances of "conversations pushed too far," both in the office and during work social settings. Complaining about this was not an option:

> It would seem minor, "oh you misunderstood," and I'd be the one who comes out the other side of it looking bad. In a male-dominated practice I can't risk being the female without a sense of "humor" or who causes problems for "'everyone else."

Humor that denigrates others is not funny. Individuals should be free to go to work without facing offensive comments justified as jokes and then made to feel badly for not laughing.

It Takes a Village—and It Takes Courage

People generally seek to commiserate with each other when something bad happens. A sympathetic ear can feel like the only alternative when the workplace does not seem to offer viable paths to a solution. By sharing stories with supportive colleagues, targets of negative behavior can find comfort, validation, and affirmation that they did not deserve what they experienced.

While it is important to have trusted colleagues at work to whom one can speak confidentially about sensitive topics, this approach generally will not help the individual's circumstances and will certainly not bring about positive change. Those who hear stories of improper behavior in the workplace should have an opportunity to respond in a way that is not simply comforting to the victim's feelings but can result in corrective measures being taken.

The panel of the Harvard Business School faculty stated that "[c]ompanies should openly encourage people to speak up when they notice a problem. . . . By allowing everyone to feel safe about reporting bad behavior, the onus is taken off only women to step forward and encourages men to speak up, too."[268]

It is important to develop a process that finds a constructive way to move beyond shared stories with trusted colleagues and help pave the way for future employees to avoid the same pain. To do so requires the courage to speak up to help change culture.

There is good news for people who fear speaking up for positive change because they believe the risk is too great, that they will not succeed, or that they will be ostracized or worse. A professor of business administration who has researched positive examples of individuals exercising workplace courage and speaking up to express their ideas for improvement described action steps that can help ensure a successful resolution:

> *I've found many examples of people at all levels who created positive change without ruining their careers. Their success rested primarily on a set of attitudes and behaviors that can be learned, rather than on innate characteristics. I call people who exhibit these behaviors* competently courageous *because they create the right conditions for action by establishing a strong internal reputation and by improving their fallback options in case things go poorly; they carefully choose their battles, discerning whether a given opportunity to act makes sense in light of their values, the timing, and their broader objectives; they maximize the odds of in-the-moment success by managing the messaging and emotions; and they follow up to preserve relationships and marshal commitment. These steps are useful whether you're pushing for major change or trying to address a smaller or more local issue.*[269]

While interviewing people for this book, there were several examples given of positive results that occurred when people raised concerns within their own organization. In a number of instances, individuals did not accept that senior-level executives or leaders had actual knowledge of someone's bad behavior, notwithstanding admonishments from others in the workplace to the contrary. Their suppositions were correct, as was their belief in the underlying decency of the organization's leaders. Their intervention resulted in a swift response that left no doubt about leadership commitment to a culture in which people are treated respectfully.

Develop Training Techniques for and Encourage Implementation of Bystander Intervention

To ensure a culture that encourages reporting, organizations should consider the results of a study demonstrating the link between a strong sexual harassment policy and the likelihood that a bystander will report the behavior. This study revealed that noticeable and prominent policies are more likely to result in bystanders taking steps to formally report misconduct.[270]

The study showed that people will feel more comfortable reporting both severe and moderate forms of harassment if they believe the workplace firmly and explicitly articulates its lack of tolerance for harassing behaviors. The significance may be that when the workplace policy makes clear that harassment is taken seriously, it signals to bystanders that they are at low risk for retaliation if they report.

Bystanders who observe inappropriate behaviors have an important opportunity to give voice to someone who may feel voiceless or to amplify a rebuke to what is transpiring. Interventions can be as simple as a stern retort following an inappropriate comment, a humorous remark to redirect the behavior, or a private aside that lets the perpetrator know why the comment was offensive.

There are also circumstances when a more complex level of intervention may be warranted. There are many forms of bystander intervention that can help make a difference, and organizations should offer training to teach constructive strategies for knowing when—and when it may not—be safe to intervene.

A corporate employee spoke of her response to inappropriate emails that she described as:

> Multiple sexist, racist, obscene, and inappropriate "comics" supposedly meant to "cheer" employees.

She then described her proactive response, including an email sent to all emphasizing the inappropriateness of the communications. In addition, she privately followed up with the perpetrator. The leadership of the organization responded with the issuance of a policy to curb any future actions of a similar nature.

A young lawyer described an embarrassing incident that happened in court, when another counsel put his arm around her and joked in a demeaning way. She noted:

> It was witnessed by lead counsel on our side, also male; he [later] directly confronted opposing counsel . . . on the record.

Her story is an example of the myriad forms that bystander intervention can take. The situation may not have been appropriate for an immediate response, depending on other circumstances taking place in that courtroom. Her more senior colleague picked the moment he felt that he could be most effective and acted in a way that should give the perpetrator pause before ever displaying his form of demeaning humor again.

In another example, a Women's Bar Association of Massachusetts survey respondent noted that at a firm event where people were drinking and "tipsy," a male partner was overheard making "extremely offensive" comments to a female associate. The respondent followed up aggressively:

> [I] spoke directly [with the] female associate informing her that I saw the offense as very serious and would address it [with] my partners. Notified [the firm partner responsible for] employment issues. Notified all partners. The offending partner was spoken to.

The respondent did not know whether any direct punishment was imposed, but she stated that there was reputational damage to the offending partner from the incident.

Sometimes bystander intervention can be as simple as a quiet presence. A young employee described the discomfort she felt by the advances and suggestive comments she regularly endured at her organization's events. Because of the seniority of the offending individuals, there was not an official route of reporting available. She shared her experiences with a male colleague who, absent a structural path within the organization that would guide his response, offered a practical intervention:

> *[H]e would try to be standing next to me when a firm event ended so the [perpetrator] could not hug or kiss me.*

As the EEOC Task Force Report noted, bystander intervention training has its roots in violence prevention programs and has gained widespread acceptance on college **campuses** to help prevent sexual assault. According to the EEOC, bystander training could also be effective in the workplace:

> *Such training could help employees identify unwelcome and offensive behavior that is based on a co-workers' protected characteristic under employment non-discrimination laws; could create a sense of responsibility on the part of employees to "do something" and not simply stand by; could give employees the skills and confidence to intervene in some manner to stop harassment; and finally, could demonstrate the employer's commitment to empowering employees to act in this manner. Bystander training also affords employers an opportunity to underscore their commitment to non-retaliation by making clear that any employee who "steps up" to combat harassment will be protected from negative repercussions.*[271]

The EEOC Task Force Report recommended that bystander intervention training be constructed to meet four strategic goals. The first is to create awareness that will help people recognize problematic behaviors. Second, the training can create a collective responsibility that will help bystanders feel motivated to step up where appropriate. Third, an effective training program should empower bystanders, giving them a sense of confidence in their ability to intercede under certain circumstances. Finally, training should provide bystanders with the resources they need to be supported in an intervention.

By knowing when and how to intervene, bystanders have a special opportunity to keep negative conduct in the workplace from being normalized. As author Brigid Schulte wrote:

> *It's all about building a sense of community. . . . At the most fundamental level, bystander interventions could begin—long before an incident of harassment—with workers having non-threatening, informal conversations in unstressed moments about how to treat each other, how they can help each other do their jobs or make their days better, and practice giving positive feedback.*[272]

Resist Backlash

The emerging undercurrent of resistance to the focus on #MeToo threatens to undermine the movement's importance in providing a voice to those who have previously felt voiceless. In response, it is critical to consistently reiterate that this resistance is not based on facts.

At a public meeting of the EEOC, panelists consisting of federal regulators and experts discussed the lack of evidence to show that the focus on sexual harassment is harming men. Rather, the panelists noted the greater likelihood that women are bearing the brunt of the unintended consequences by being "left out of advancement opportunities, such as socializing with bosses or mentorships."[273] As one panelist noted, the #MeToo movement emerged not out of false complaints, but out of complaints never made.

In light of the overwhelming data demonstrating how difficult it is for women to come forward and report negative experiences, the #MeToo backlash should be treated for what it is—a decoy, directing attention away from the real and compelling need to bring improper workplace behaviors to light. We have seen overwhelming data and countless anecdotes demonstrating how difficult it is to speak up and report incidents of harassment. To now seek to denigrate the long-overdue focus on victims is simply another way to further victimize those who are the recipient of negative behavior.

The range of fears expressed as part of the #MeToo backlash seems to go beyond rational concerns. For example, backlash commentary includes men who claim they are fearful of complimenting someone on their outfit. The #MeToo movement, however, has nothing to do with whether someone tells another person in the office that her dress is pretty. It has everything, however, to do with leering remarks and comments specifically directed to a woman's chest or other parts of her body.

Nor are women complaining about positive relationships with men at work. In fact, the data shows that women lack the sponsorship that their male colleagues benefit from and that fuels career growth. Rather the objection is to men who seek mentoring meetings in bars or in hotel rooms while on work trips.

People being kind to and complimenting one another is not unacceptable behavior. Remarks, however, that are clearly sexual in nature or that, at their core, reinforce a power imbalance or otherwise seek to undermine a colleague in the workplace should not be acceptable.

Tolerating an overreaction that results in the avoidance of women is, as Professors Joan Williams and Suzanne Lebsock wrote, "unnecessary, unfair, and illegal: It deprives women of opportunities simply because they are women. You cannot refuse to have closed-door meetings with women unless you refuse to have closed-door meetings with men. Otherwise women will be denied access to all the sensitive information that's shared only behind closed doors, and that's a violation of federal law."[274]

The fact is that nothing will do more to create healthy relationships free of fear than measures that help normalize interactions. As recommended in the previously discussed *New York Times* article about the potential backlash to #MeToo:

> One way to encourage these relationships is to have more people at the top of companies who are not straight white men. In interviews, women in companies with many female or gay executives were more likely to say one-on-one relationships had never been an issue for them. Another way is for companies to explicitly support relationship-building meetings. Some companies, for instance, have designated a certain restaurant where senior leaders take protégées for breakfast or lunch. . . . It helps when leaders talk

about their families, introduce junior employees to their spouses or invite them to their homes. . . .[275]

The backlash must be resisted at every level. This requires leadership to be engaged in all aspects of creating a respectful workplace culture that includes monitoring for signs of backlash and the career disadvantages that can follow.

Consider Curbs on Social Drinking and Exclusionary Activities

Many reported anecdotes in various studies reveal a pattern of inappropriate behaviors that occurred at a holiday or other social gathering in which the perpetrators were clearly inebriated. Organizations should consider ways to curb excessive drinking at business-sponsored social events.

The fact is, social events infrequently take into account whether awkward conditions make it difficult to relax and enjoy the gathering. When liquor flows freely, the resultant lowered inhibitions can set an uncomfortable tone for many. Moreover, the nature of the activities chosen for outside events can also feel exclusionary.

Consider the observations of a female professional describing her own and others' experiences with summer social activities:

> *When striving for an inclusive environment for diverse employees, I wish companies would re-think the pool party and country-club experience. First off, in my experience it has been very clear that senior male executives looked forward to seeing the more youthful distaff members without their clothes on. They would often discuss this openly, at one time anyway.*
>
> *The other part is that certain kinds of country-club recreation, especially water sports, are unfamiliar to many who didn't grow up with privilege. The issues around swimming pools, etc. are still pretty apparent in the headlines.*
>
> *Making sure that there are activities that participants can do that don't involve disrobing, imbibing alcohol, or pool sports and*

boating would be helpful. Those activities could be offered, but no one should feel pressure to participate. (Not everyone can play tennis or golf, either.) In my opinion, pressure to participate in pool-related activities or hot-tub stuff is really bad and creates bad situations.

It also warrants noting the frequency with which young professionals mentioned that senior executives in their organization take their clients to strip clubs, either to celebrate a successful deal or in appreciation of their business. Employers who have to be told that strip clubs as a form of business entertainment are a bad idea likely have deeply embedded problems with their culture. It is a way of entertaining clients that shows no respect for current employees who attend but may be uncomfortable, as well as those who do not attend because they find it an offensive form of work entertainment. It also may undermine a client's respect for the organization's culture and the choices that it makes.

Imagine

Sorry Seems to Be the Hardest Word

Even with the best policies, robust reporting procedures, immediate and thorough investigations, and transparent responses, people will make mistakes. It is inevitable that someone will say something inappropriate, become upset when challenged, or otherwise act in a way that is hurtful to others. We are far from perfect, as are our systems. As a result, there are occasions where the correct response is to apologize.

Too often, however, we hear of apologies that completely miss the mark. There is nothing more hollow than the "I'm sorry if I offended anyone" apology. The words have no meaning and leave everyone involved generally feeling worse.

Massachusetts Rabbi Danny Burkeman gave a powerful sermon about these non-apology apologies. He identified several of the highly visible examples that have occurred in this #MeToo era, noting their significant omissions and efforts to appear as though the person apologizing is a victim as well:

> *Ohio State Football coach Urban Meyer was forced to apologize after taking no action and remaining silent when a coach on his staff was charged with physically abusing his wife, for the second time. Note that I said forced to apologize. This is not something that Meyer appeared willing or particularly eager to do. In Meyer's*

press conference, he apologized to his colleagues, his students and the whole Buckeye nation. But he failed to apologize to the woman who had been assaulted by her husband, failed to apologize for doing and saying nothing in the many years he knew about it, failed to apologize for his own wife encouraging her to stay with him. And when pressed about what he would say to the woman who had been assaulted, he responded: "Well, I have a message for everyone involved in this: I'm sorry that we're in this situation, and, I'm just sorry we're in this situation." It took a further three days for a statement to be released on his behalf including a direct apology to her. His punishment: a three-game suspension, because ultimately success on the football field and the revenue it brings is more important than a woman's, or the students', safety.

When Harvey Weinstein originally released a statement, it said: "I came of age in the 60's and 70's, when all the rules about behavior and workplaces were different. That was the culture then."

While I didn't grow up in that generation, I am 100% certain that assault was never part of the accepted culture; this is an offensive excuse for unacceptable behavior. In a similar vein, Charlie Rose included in his statement: "All of us, including me, are coming to a newer and deeper recognition of the pain caused by conduct in the past, and have come to a profound new respect for women and their lives." . . .

Urban Meyer, Harvey Weinstein, Charlie Rose and countless others . . . are apologizing not because they are remorseful for what they have done; they are apologizing for fear of the consequences if they do not.

Rabbi Burkeman then drew from the wisdom of an influential Jewish scholar from the Middle Ages to provide guidance on the elements of a truly meaningful apology:

Rabbi Moses Maimonides, arguably the greatest Jewish mind of the Middle Ages, suggested that there are primarily four stages to repentance. We need to confess what we've done, we must feel regret and remorse, we are obligated to offer reparation or restitution to the person we have wronged. And then finally there must be a resolution not to repeat the action; . . . complete repentance only happens when a person finds themselves in the same situation as they were previously in and behaves in a different way. . . .

A genuine, heartfelt apology has immense power to heal wounds. It is a shame that so many of our celebrities fail to fully confess their wrongdoings, exhibit no remorse for their actions, appear unwilling to say they're sorry to the people they've wronged, and focus on themselves rather than the people they hurt. . . . [W]e can learn from them what not to do as we seek to make amends and apologize to the people we have wronged.

Reflecting on these failures to meaningfully apologize in the context of those who have found their voice through the #MeToo movement, Rabbi Burkeman concluded his sermon with these extraordinary thoughts:

The #MeToo movement has forced a long overdue reckoning on the every day suffering and abuse that women experience in our society and culture. I have reflected on my past actions and those things that I have witnessed, and while I can say that I have not committed any of these abuses, I do bear responsibility. It has been a harsh reality to face that about 90% of the people who have committed these abuses look very similar to me.

So now it is time for my own confession.

I confess that there are times I have not recognized that I am receiving benefit from a societal structure that affords me every privilege and opportunity as a white male, at the cost of others.

I confess that there were times when my eyes were closed to the frequent suffering that women endure; blind to what was happening right in front of me.

I confess that as certain celebrities have apologized, my initial response was sadness at their fall, before I began to think about the victims they had hurt.

I confess that I have failed to understand the regular sexism and inappropriate attention and contact that are a part of many women's experience.

I confess that I have not done enough to address the inequalities that still exist in our society and the challenges that women face every day.

I confess that without the #MeToo movement I would have probably remained unaware and blind to what was happening in front of me.

To all of you, to those this behavior has hurt, and to God, I say I am truly sorry.

I commit to make amends.

I will do better.

We must do better.

I am sorry.[276]

These words serve as remarkable guidance for those who feel troubled by their own words or deeds and who seek to make amends. Words of repentance, when meaningfully offered, have a powerful ability to heal.

Of course, apologies are not a substitute for needed behavioral change. As Professor Sutton wrote, "[I]f you find yourself apologizing again and again, it's time to stop. It's probably a sign that you are using apologies as a substitute for learning and toning down your act."[277]

The School Recruitment Firewall

Many business and professional service organizations recruit on campus for their next generation of talent. Universities, business schools, law schools—all host recruiters searching for students who can bring the requisite skills into their work environment. For schools anxious to assist their students, and whose ranking may partially depend on the success of their students' post-graduate employment, relationships with workplace recruiters can be important to cultivate.

This creates a power dynamic that can be unhealthy if universities do not try to ensure that their students are safe in their internships and first jobs. A law school career counselor described steps her school had to take to remove individuals from on-campus recruiting because the school learned of their highly inappropriate behavior toward students. For example, one partner would only hire attractive females and would then send inappropriate texts after hours. He also reportedly had an affair with a new hire.

Another career counselor described recruiters whose conversations with students during the interview process included statements or behaviors that left them feeling uncomfortable. As the counselor noted, however, students try to normalize the conduct they encounter because of the potential career impact.

Universities have an important role to play by modeling ways to address inappropriate behaviors in the workplace. If they proactively monitor the experience of students, establish a process that encourages students to report, and then address problem behaviors with potential employees, universities would send a clear signal that conduct matters.

Such a process would also provide an opportunity for students to learn how to successfully address these issues in the workplace. If colleges set clear standards and remove recruiting privileges in response to reports of inappropriate behaviors, they will teach an important lesson to those beginning their career journeys.

Judges Should Level the Playing Field That They Made Uneven

As described previously, court rules and decisions have combined to create a judicial system where employees are at a disadvantage. The data demonstrating the frequency with which victims are unable to get past the barrage of hurdles that courts themselves created should be an embarrassment to the judicial system.

As Judge Gertner noted, it is important to remove these barriers in order to create the fair process that all parties deserve in the court system:

> *First, the problem has to be named: judges have made rules that have effectively gutted Title VII. These rules are not required by the statute, its legislative history, or the purposes of the Act. Second,*

the problem has to be addressed directly. Congress could, for example, amend Title VII to make its prohibitions more explicit. Alternatively, judicial education programs can train judges not on how to "get rid" of these cases, but rather on how to analyze the merits in a way that privileges jury decisionmaking and reminds the decisionmakers what the law was designed to reform in the first place. And finally, to address asymmetry, courts must write decisions if only to show what counts as discrimination, and not simply what does not.[278]

Hopefully, the courts will seek to remove the barriers they erected. Until then, unfortunately, victims who seek recourse through the courts must be prepared for the difficult road ahead. No victim should feel dissuaded from pursuing justice.

Change That Works

The development of a respectful and inclusive work environment requires hard work and commitment from all levels of the organization. If this were easy to do, we would have long ago had workplaces where harassment and demeaning behaviors were relics of a by-gone day and not a contemporary problem.

Even though implementing these recommended measures requires focus and involvement from the top levels of the organization, the reward is that behavioral shifts will follow. So, too, will greater engagement and productivity in the workplace.

Fortunately, there are many examples of strong leaders willing to respond to these challenges. Consider the experience of Joe, the CEO of a large organization who hired Raymond, a new member of his leadership team. Shortly after he began, Joe heard that Raymond was making lewd comments to women. Joe intervened and spoke to Raymond, but the behaviors and highly suggestive remarks continued. For several months, whenever Joe heard of an incident, he apologized on behalf of the company and similarly had Raymond personally apologize. He also had Raymond take classes and participate in counseling. Along with these progressive disciplinary steps, Joe informed Raymond that the company was implementing a zero tolerance approach going forward—any further incident would result in termination.

One night, while drunk at a work-related social event, Raymond made passes to female employees in attendance. The women did not report the behavior to Joe, but Joe did learn of it from a man in attendance.

When Joe later asked the women—who had positions of considerable leadership in the company—why they did not tell him what happened, they responded with the stoicism that can mark the behavior of victims of harassment, particularly those who may be more senior in the workplace. One indicated that this was just what women have to deal with, and the other passed it off as simply another example of being hit upon by a man. Underlying their response was a desire not to look like complainers or like employees who could not handle such circumstances.

Shortly after this event, Joe called Raymond into his office, along with the head of HR. Seeing both present, Raymond understood that he was experiencing his last day at work.

In addition to swiftly reacting to the episodes he learned about and implementing escalating responses, including apologies, counseling, training, and, ultimately, termination, Joe did something else of critical importance. He followed up within the company as transparently as possible so people in the workplace would understand that such behavior was not tolerated.

Joe understood that there were risks in remaining silent as well as risks in speaking up, but he was acutely aware of Raymond's reputation in the company and the likelihood that people were watching his response closely. As a protective measure that ensured Joe's own voice was not silenced in his interactions with employees, he took the step of crafting a separation agreement with Raymond that imposed restrictions on what Raymond could say about the company but did not restrict what the company could say about Raymond.

Joe chose to send a clear message within the workplace that such conduct was anathema to the company's culture and would not be tolerated. He explained publicly that the company tried to engage in a process to help Raymond better communicate but that he was not matching up to the organization's cultural values. Joe further stated that even though Raymond occupied a position of leadership, he still had to conform to the company's values. He noted that the organization will not tolerate people being treated the way Raymond treated others, that they tried to help him change, but ultimately it was not the right hire. Joe then again apologized on behalf of the company.

Joe's handling of the situation resulted in a positive response from others in the company, including several who thanked him for his honesty. Although HR professionals may differ regarding the degree of transparency a leader should demonstrate after taking steps to discipline someone for negative conduct, Joe's response was grounded in a recognition of the realities of life in a workplace. He knew that people communicated with one another all the time about these issues and understood that had he stayed silent, he would fuel further speculation about whether the company responded appropriately.

By claiming the narrative, Joe communicated the company's cultural values and his own willingness to be transparent.

Defying Gravity

A particularly confounding obstacle to changing workplace culture is the fear of the unknown. People adapt to their circumstances; changing past norms and patterns is complicated and feels risky. But it does not have to be this way. In fact, the changes that need to be made should be less fearful because they involve changing norms that no longer work for men or for women.

Mary Beard, a professor of classics at the University of Cambridge, traces the silencing of women's voices back more than 3,000 years to the days of ancient Greek and Roman antiquity. She wrote that the primary exceptions in the classical world against the public voices of women were either as victims and martyrs, or in defense of their own interests such as their homes, children, husbands, and other women.

Women, in other words, may in extreme circumstances publicly defend their own sectional interests, but not speak for men or the community as a whole. . . . [P]ublic speaking and oratory were not merely things that ancient women didn't do, *they were exclusive practices and skills that defined masculinity as a gender.*[279]

Professor Beard compares examples from the classics with the modern-day internet threats hurled at women who enter the public discourse. From threats of rape and death, to the simple admonishment of "Shut up, you bitch," she notes: "In its crude, aggressive way, this is about keeping, or getting, women out of man's talk."[280]

Professor Beard offers an important challenge, however, to the general advice that victims of internet trolls—or other outward efforts to silence women—receive:

> *Ironically, the well-meaning solution often recommended when women are on the receiving end of this stuff turns out to bring about the very result the abusers want: namely, their silence. "Don't call the abusers out. Don't give them any attention; that's what they want. Just keep mum and 'block' them" you're told. It is an uncanny reprise of the old advice to women of "put up and shut up," and it risks leaving the bullies in unchallenged occupation of the playground.*[281]

The answer is not, Professor Beard suggests, to engage in the old and failed practices of changing women to be more like men. Rather, she proposes a fundamental rethinking "about the rules of our rhetorical operations."[282]

That rethinking involves a willingness to ask questions about the purpose of speech itself and how and why the template for defining power remains male:

> *What we need is some old-fashioned consciousness-raising about what we mean by the "voice of authority" and how we've come to construct it. . . .*
>
> *How have we learned to look at those women who exercise power, or who try to? What are the cultural underpinnings of misogyny in politics or the workplace, and its forms . . .? How and why do the conventional definitions of "power" (or for that matter*

of "knowledge," "expertise" and "authority") that we carry round in our heads exclude women?[283]

As Professor Beard noted, phrases generally used to describe women accessing power suggest that they are taking something that perhaps they are not entitled to have: "smashing the glass ceiling" or "knocking on the door," for example. But by redefining power—reframing it so power is not simply conferred on the elite or as linked to prestige or celebrity—perhaps the word can evolve so it is no longer coded as male:

> *What I have in mind is the ability to be effective, to make a difference in the world, and the right to be taken seriously, together as much as individually. It is power in that sense that many women feel they don't have—and that they want.*[284]

Finally, Professor Beard also advocates for the right for women to avoid another double standard: the ability to make a mistake without undergoing the far harsher treatment they receive than their male counterparts who err. Women should not have to both find it more difficult to succeed and be treated more harshly when they fail.

Women have long faced barriers to the exercise of power that will require focused attention by both men and women in the workplace to remove. The Center for Women in Law at the University of Texas School of Law has held several Women's Power Summits to analyze the complex relationship between women and power, with a specific focus on how women can best attain and exercise power: "It is not always easy to talk about power and it can be even less comfortable to talk about acquiring power. A critical first step to building power, therefore, is to understand the source of that discomfort."[285] Research tells us that much of that discomfort arises from the judgments women face as they find their voice and exercise their power.

The Future Feels Close

For much of my adult life, when I have interacted professionally with those who are arrogant, or mean, or who act like bullies, or who exhibit inappropriate behaviors in the workplace that diminish or demean others, I think about what these people will be like when they are old, or infirm, or develop a weakness or face other challenges that leave them vulnerable. These are conditions that they cannot imagine, and their behaviors often attest to the invincible shield they believe surrounds them wherever they go.

But no one is invincible. And few have the requisite long view to recognize that there will be a time when they may need the relationships they have been burning through or seek the kindnesses they are unwilling to offer. A suggested way for CEOs to eliminate their worst personality tendencies, suggested Professor Sutton, is to do "time travel":

> *This mind trick . . . entails deciding what to do today based on how you want to feel about yourself when you look back from the future. As one of my correspondents noted, "When they are on their deathbed, no one ever says, 'I wish I had been meaner.'"*[286]

The Answer Was Here All the Time

As the myriad recommendations and research examples indicate, there is a roadmap for eliminating harassment and other negative behaviors in the workplace, and it starts with changing workplace culture. The specific ways to accomplish this change may vary from workplace to workplace, but the answers exist and are accessible to any organization with engaged leaders willing to commit to the effort.

As was noted in the final report issued by the National Academies of Sciences, Engineering, and Medicine, the elimination of sexual harassment from the workplace will ultimately be dependent on a commitment to a diverse, inclusive, and respectful culture. The Academies' definition of what that type of environment would look like in actual operation is instructive:

> *Diverse, inclusive, and respectful academic environments are environments where careers flourish, but sexual harassment does not. Such environments have a culture that values diversity,*

inclusion, and respect, but they also need to have a climate that demonstrates that these values are put into action. Diverse and inclusive environments are ones where cultural values around gender and racial equity align with a climate where policies and practices do not disadvantage groups of people, and thereby making them incompatible with sexually harassing behavior. Similarly, a respectful environment is one where civility and respectful work behavior are not just valued but also evaluated and rewarded, and this is reflected in policies and procedures. Respectful behavior is particularly important in preventing sexual harassment because sexual harassment often takes place against a backdrop of incivility or in other words, in an environment of generalized disrespect. This is especially true for gender harassment, because when it occurs, it is virtually always in environments with high rates of uncivil conduct. . . . Thus, promoting and establishing a culture of respect is a key component to preventing sexual harassment.[287]

History provides many lessons for the ways in which rights and opportunities have been fought for and obtained in a variety of fields. An article exploring what can be learned from the efforts by women lawyers to be hired at law firms is instructive (recall that the first female Supreme Court justice, Sandra Day O'Connor, was offered a position as legal secretary upon her graduation at the top of her class from Stanford Law School). The impact described extends far beyond the practice of law and touches issues of diversity and inclusion throughout the workplace:

Most important of all, the lawsuits and breakthroughs of the 1970s and 1980s would not have happened without the reawakening of the women's movement in the 1960s and the activism and feminist lawmaking of the 1970s. Without the revival of feminist consciousness, Title VII's promise would not have been fulfilled. It required pressure on the EEOC as well as individual lawsuits to convey that women really must be treated as equals in employment, including in law firms. Activist women lawyers carried out litigation campaigns that not only brought more women into the profession but also changed the definition of equality for all women. Moreover, without changing social norms, male lawyers might not have begun to suggest to their older partners that firms needed to hire women lawyers even before they were forced to do so by litigation. . . . The role of the media in bringing about some of the pressure to change should also be noted. . . .

Another lesson to be drawn is that intergenerational connections among women are centrally important to social change with respect to women's rights. . . .

The importance of building relationships with supportive men also emerges from these stories. . . .

Another lesson that leaps out from these stories is the importance of never forgetting the interconnections among sex, race, class, and sexual orientation.[288]

One year after they first reported on the allegations against Harvey Weinstein, *New York Times* writers Jodi Kantor and Megan Twohey reflected on the revelations and events that followed and what is likely to happen going forward. They noted:

All of us have long been told that the key to gender equality is looking to the future. Study and work hard. Lean in. Build the pipeline. Look to our daughters. The past year has shown that this wisdom is incomplete. To move forward, we have to excavate the past. . . .

For men (and women) who are accused, a general lack of accountability has given way to a lack of consensus over what kind of behavior merits warning, a firing, or career obliteration. . . .

And though organizations have formed and mobilized, money has been raised, and meetings have been held, it's not yet clear whether they will lead to an ambitious, disciplined, long-term strategy to reach once seemingly impossible goals.[289]

The issues raised by the reignited #MeToo movement are indeed complex. But even as we grapple with the proper way to respond to differing levels of misconduct, it may be easier to agree that no one should be objectified in the workplace. Sexual harassment must be aggressively thwarted. Jokes that insult, leers that are fleeting, hurtful albeit offhand comments about one's religion or sexual orientation or any characteristic that singles out one's status as different from the workplace majority all cause harm in some form and isolate victims from needed relationships with coworkers.

Our collective goals should be to create a respectful and inclusive workplace culture where it is clear that negative behaviors and hurtful conduct are not tolerated and where victims and bystanders are encouraged to report misconduct and are protected when they do. Everyone deserves the right to feel safe and respected at work. And every workplace will benefit from providing that environment.

These are goals that can only be achieved when the silence that nourishes misconduct is shattered. Victims have a voice. It is up to workplace leaders to ensure those voices are heard.

Appendix

A Detailed Glimpse into the Legal Profession from the Women's Bar Association of Massachusetts

As we have seen, no sector is immune from workplace misconduct and inappropriate behaviors. Survey data, where it exists, can be instructive in helping to provide a more nuanced perspective, particularly with respect to victim impacts.

In 2018, the Women's Bar Association of Massachusetts undertook a survey of conduct in law firms to understand better both the types of negative behaviors that may be prevalent in that environment as well as how targets of such behaviors responded. In particular, the survey sought to explore whether victims and bystanders reported such behaviors and, if not, why not.

The study is instructive in offering a nuanced look at these issues.[290] The Overview, Methodology, and Analysis from the Women's Bar Association of Massachusetts study are fully reprinted below to (1) provide a more specific view of direct data in a particular sector, and (2) encourage others to undertake similar fact-finding in their own workplaces. The report was written by Lauren Stiller Rikleen, and its recommendations have been incorporated into and expanded upon in Chapter 8.

Overview

In the wake of the #MeToo movement and the enormous focus on workplace behaviors that profoundly impact careers, the Women's Bar Association of Massachusetts ("WBA"), in partnership with the Rikleen Institute for Strategic Leadership ("Rikleen Institute"), developed and distributed a detailed survey to: provide a more nuanced understanding of behaviors that take place in the law firm environment; identify steps that have been taken to address behaviors of concern; and offer recommendations to help law firms provide a safe, respectful and inclusive workplace for all employees.

This survey comes at an important moment, following a deluge of media coverage reporting allegations of workplace sexual harassment. This media coverage, however, should drive every organization to look both at and beyond sexual harassment, and to analyze its own workplace culture with the goal of providing a safe and respectful environment for employees every day.

Understanding whether incidents of sexual harassment occur is one component of that goal. It is also critical to know whether other behaviors that negatively impact workplace culture are prevalent. Every organization should provide a workplace free of fear, intimidation, and any behaviors that diminish or disparage individuals or groups, even where such instances may not meet a legal definition of harassment.

The WBA is proud to be addressing these issues in the legal profession - a high stress environment for everyone. People go to work each day, committed to doing their best work on behalf of their firm's clients, often against a backdrop of long hours, crushing deadlines, complex legal issues, and a host of other considerations, including an ego and emotional investment in the outcome.

This engagement can come at a price. People manifest their stress responses in a variety of ways that can deeply impact those around them. Left unchecked, these behaviors can further facilitate a cycle of negativity that imbues the entire workplace, resulting in a culture that inhibits high performance and employee engagement.

The goal of this survey is to develop a better understanding of whether behaviors exist in the law firm environment that negatively impact lawyers, paralegals, firm administrators, support staff, interns, and law students. In addition, the survey provides specific recommendations for positive change that can be of benefit in any workplace environment.

Methodology and Limitations

Survey questions were developed to provide insight into the possible existence of a range of behaviors that are unwelcome, inappropriate, offensive, or otherwise contribute to an environment that negatively impacts one's workplace experiences. It is important to emphasize that the questions purposefully did not focus solely on behaviors that would meet a legal definition of harassment or that were otherwise legally actionable.

Rather, the WBA was seeking to understand the day-to-day experiences that people may have in the law firm environment and determine whether there are patterns of behaviors that negatively impact an individual's performance and sense of well-being.

The survey was open between February 5, 2018 and April 2, 2018. Responses were sought from individuals who work or had worked in a law office in Massachusetts, whether or not the firm had offices in other locations outside of the Commonwealth.

The survey was distributed in a variety of ways to ensure widespread distribution within the Massachusetts legal community:

1. The WBA posted a description of and link to the study on its website.
2. The WBA distributed 6 email blasts to its 1,500 members, as well as included the survey link in its weekly e-newsletter throughout the time the survey was live. In each communication, the WBA highlighted the importance of and provided a link to the survey.
3. The WBA sent 5 separate emails to the managing Partners of the top 100 law firms in Massachusetts, reaching firms ranging in size

from approximately 20 lawyers to more than 500 lawyers, requesting their support distributing the survey link within their firm.
4. Massachusetts Lawyers Weekly, as a sponsoring partner of this
research project, ran a story in advance of the survey and then promoted it extensively over several weeks via print, web and email.
5. The Massachusetts Bar Association posted a link to the survey
on its website.
6. The WBA and Women's Bar Foundation Board members distributed links to the survey to their own networks, as did many others
who knew of the survey and offered to help reach a wide audience.
7. The WBA reached out to many affinity bar associations in the
state to enlist their assistance in distributing the survey link to
their respective membership.
8. Several allied organizations also distributed the survey link to
their members.

Each time the survey was distributed, the link was preceded by
language stating that all responses would be confidential and no
individuals or firms would be identified. The survey was open to
both men and women.

In total, 1,243 individuals responded to the survey. As is normal with
surveys of this nature, not all respondents answered every question.

At the outset, the WBA anticipated that law firms—either through
firm management or via women's affinity groups—would be willing to distribute the survey internally, particularly in light of the fact
that no firms or individuals would be identified. Based on anecdotal
responses, firm-wide distribution appears to have occurred only on a
limited basis. Although a number of firms made survey links internally
available, there were also firms that responded to the WBA's request by
stating they were not willing to distribute the survey, notwithstanding
the commitment of confidentiality. As a result, that avenue of outreach
was less available than had been expected. This proved to be a similar
constraint with respect to the WBA's hope that there would be wider
distribution through other bar association networks or website access.

The WBA is pleased that, notwithstanding these constraints, the
results showed widespread interest and a desire by many to share their
stories. The constraints, however, also indicate the sensitivity of the

topic and the reluctance that some feel about directly addressing these issues in a survey of this nature.

Numerous respondents gave examples of behaviors responsive to each question. The anecdotes that are included give voice to the experiences described. Only quotes that ensure the protection of the respondent's confidentiality were selected (and in a few instances, potentially identifying details that the respondent may have included has been omitted for that same reason). Moreover, quotes that are included are representative of other quotes detailing similar experiences. Quotes that describe unique experiences are also not included for reasons of confidentiality.

Of the respondents who answered the demographic question regarding gender, approximately 80% were women and approximately 17% were male; most of the remaining 3% chose not to specify.

Respondents were also asked to identify their age range to provide insights into which generations were responding to the survey. The distribution was relatively even among the three major generations in the workplace. Of those who answered this question: 36% were Millennials; 30% were in Gen X; and 33% were Boomers. Only 2% were born in the generation prior to the Boomers (Traditionalists).

For each question, respondents were asked if there had been a woman on the firm's highest governing committee at the time of the incident(s); however, because only a very small number responded to this subpart in each of the questions, there is insufficient information to report this data.

Respondents were asked to identify approximately when the behaviors identified in this survey occurred. The purpose was to determine whether the preponderance of the behaviors happened in past decades, as compared to more recent years, to see whether such behaviors were diminishing over time. The time periods that respondents could select were by decade, beginning with 1980–1989.

For each question, a significant percentage of the respondents stated that the incidents occurred between 2010 and 2018. This makes clear that these behaviors are not relics of a past era but are contemporary concerns.

The highest percentage of affirmative responses in that 2010–2018 time-frame was for question 11, regarding whether others in the firm had spoken with the respondent about workplace behaviors that made them uncomfortable. This response is interesting on two levels. First, it is another indication that negative workplace behaviors remain a challenge. Second, it may also demonstrate that people are more willing to identify and discuss—at least among themselves—concerns about behaviors that, decades ago, were buried in silence.

There are inherent limitations in any method of inquiry. Accordingly, these survey results should not be viewed as offering definitive conclusions about the legal profession overall. Rather, the results offer a snapshot in time that provides a more nuanced understanding of the experiences of individuals in law firms.

As noted above, this survey was not designed to define sexual harassment or otherwise focus only on behaviors that might be considered to fall within a legally actionable definition. It is intended to seek information about the possible presence of a broad range of behaviors that can inhibit employee engagement and diminish an individual's self-worth or ability to perform at work without fear or discomfort, notwithstanding whether such behaviors are technically legal.

The responses to this survey suggest that much work needs to be done to ensure that law firms are providing a workplace culture where negative behaviors are not tolerated and where people can work without fear. The analysis and recommendations that follow are in the spirit of facilitating conversations that can help the legal profession serve as a model for self-reflection and, ultimately, the implementation of practices that allow all personnel to thrive in a safe, respectful, and inclusive environment.

The WBA and the Rikleen Institute for Strategic Leadership are deeply grateful to the women and men who took the time to respond to this important survey. We are confident that their efforts have made a positive contribution to improving the workplace.

Executive Summary

It is critical to highlight at the outset that, although many of the details provided by the respondents are disturbing, they are examples of behaviors that occur in other workplace settings

across the country. One need only follow the numerous and comprehensive media accounts covering multiple industries to recognize that too many people face seriously flawed workplace cultures that impact workers on a frequent basis. The legal profession is not alone in facing these challenges.

Lawyers have an opportunity to serve as leaders by addressing these issues in their individual workplace and putting in place mechanisms across the profession that ensure the highest standards are met. Lawyers are the gatekeepers to our justice system; accordingly, they have a unique opportunity to serve as role models to other professions and businesses, to our clients, and to our employees.

Unchecked power imbalance serves as the foundation for and perpetuation of negative and inappropriate behaviors in the workplace. This is a clear theme that emerged from the responses to each question. In the vast majority of responses, the incidents described happened to individuals in the age range of associates, or to others in the firm who were young or were otherwise in a subordinate role.

Power imbalances also emerged in the ways in which negative behaviors were or were not addressed. For example, many of the experiences described by the respondents were perpetrated by partners and, frequently, important rainmakers or senior leaders in the firm. Because of their status, respondents did not report the behaviors, often because they feared retribution or because the people they would report to were involved in the incidents described. Respondents pointed to examples where firms ignored negative behaviors of key partners, or where retribution was taken against those who did report. This was particularly the case where firms did not seem to have a process in place to protect those who reported or felt victimized by alleged negative behaviors.

A number of respondents stated that they discussed the offending incidents with a female partner. In most such cases, the respondent also noted that there was no follow up and that no action was taken. There was generally no indication that the women who were told had a position of authority within the firm or otherwise had any power to follow up without repercussions. Yet we know from the extensive body of research regarding women in the profession that women are under-represented in law firm leadership roles, particularly at the management or executive committee level. It is possible that some of the senior women may themselves have felt vulnerable and without power to act on inappropriate situations brought to their attention. In firms with relatively few, if any, women equity partners and where women may not be serving in key firm management roles, it is difficult to place the expectations for addressing these behaviors on a woman partner, if that partner does not have the authority to take the necessary steps to follow up.

Reporting is also inhibited by the pressure to "go along with" or otherwise accept inappropriate comments as "just a joke". Respondents reported numerous incidents of office conversations that were racist, sexist, homophobic, xenophobic, and offensive to individuals and groups. Too often, however, there was clear pressure in the workplace to avoid being viewed as humorless or as not a team player.

Analysis

1. Have you ever been the recipient of or copied on unwelcome emails, texts, or instant messages of a personal or sexual nature at work?

Nearly 38% of the respondents to this question stated that they had been the recipient of or copied on an unwelcome email, text, or instant message of a personal or sexual nature at work. Nearly half stated that the incident occurred between 2010 and 2018.

Question 1	Percentage
Yes	37.50%
No	62.50%

More than two-thirds of those responding to this question were Associates at the time of the incident, 10% were Partners, and approximately 18% were in Administrative, Paralegal, and Support Personnel roles.

Approximately three-quarters of the respondents who provided information about the size of their firm at the time of the incident were in offices with fewer than 50 lawyers.

More than 66% of those responding to this question stated that they did not report the incident.

Reported	Percentage
No	66.67%
Yes	33.33%

Examples of Behaviors Included in Survey Responses to Question 1

Examples of behaviors described in the responses included:

- Numerous examples of sharing images of sexually explicit photos (some photo-shopped to look as though it were a colleague). Many described the distribution of graphic images such as adult porn or links to videos that respondents described as "vulgar" and "inappropriate." In some examples, images seemed meant to ridicule same-sex relationships.
- Numerous examples of emails that included offensive jokes of a sexual nature, or included inappropriate and demeaning remarks about race and gender. Some described emails that ridiculed others or that made the recipients uncomfortable, such as negatively commenting on maternity leaves and commentary defending individuals in the news accused of sexual harassment.
- Partners and senior colleagues (some married or engaged) sending cards or emails expressing romantic interest in younger colleagues. Some respondents described persistent communications that felt as though the senior colleague was exerting pressure.
- Partners, senior colleagues, and clients sending comments of a sexual nature either via email or text.
- Inappropriate text messages from lawyers in supervisory roles, commenting on the physical appearance of young female lawyers.

- Sexually-charged telephone calls, or instant messages, including from inebriated colleagues.
- Senior colleagues sharing details of marital problems.
- Senior colleagues expressing anger in emails through graphic descriptions.

Respondents' Perspectives on Reporting Behaviors

The respondents provided detailed insights into their reasons for not reporting behaviors to others in the firm. In many instances, the offending behavior came from someone in a position of direct authority or power over the victim. As a respondent in a small firm who felt there was nowhere to turn described:

> As far as I know nothing was said or done because it was the owning attorney who made the comment who was known to be offensive to women and all kinds of different subcultures. It was an employee-at-will office and he was known to dismiss/fire/lay people off on a whim. It was a terrible office to work for.

Many stated that they based their decision not to report on the experiences of others who reported in the past. One respondent best summarized this line of comments:

> People who had been subjected to their advances and reported the issues were no longer employed there and these men were. Is there anything more to be said?

Some respondents tolerated frequent advances received via both email and directly because they feared even more negative repercussions from reporting. For example, a lawyer described why she did not report recurrent romantic overtures from a married partner:

> I was young and naïve, hoping that it had been a one-time indiscretion on his part and that this was not a pattern of activity. I didn't want to ruin his career and family . . . but he certainly derailed mine for a period of time.

Another stated:

> *Would have impacted my review and ability to remain on partner track. Would not have been viewed as a team player.*

Similarly, a respondent who was the recipient of vulgar and inappropriate emails noted:

> *It's my boss, an equity partner, and our HR dept. is useless. It would only jeopardize my job.*

Still another did not report suggestive texts and inappropriate touching because of:

> *Concern for repercussions in ability to get billable work.*

Some who did share their concerns with others in a more senior role stated that the behaviors were dismissed as in keeping with the offender's personality. For example, a respondent described the inappropriate texts and uninvited touching she'd experienced from others, including a partner, and noted:

> *Told multiple supervisors . . . and was told the comments I was receiving were typical from the individual so don't worry about it. I told one female supervisor when it got to be unbearable and she did report it. I told a male supervisor (of another instance) and it was immediately reported. However, once it was reported, I was told this individual is notoriously inappropriate so . . . just move on.*

A respondent describing sexual comments received from partners similarly stated:

> *It was firm culture. When discussed, it was dismissed.*

Numerous respondents described negative consequences that followed from discussing their concerns internally. For example, a respondent described the retaliation she experienced after reporting emails that denigrated women:

> *[One of the partners who wrote the emails] retaliated with a false, critical performance review.*

A respondent who was the recipient of many unsolicited romantic emails from a senior lawyer stated:

> *Spoke to female coworker and friend. No follow up actions took place. Eventually I was asked to leave the firm.*

In some instances, respondents noted that, although no steps were taken within the firm to officially address the behaviors, they did receive an apology. Another stated that after an attorney inadvertently sent an inappropriate email to the entire firm:

> *HR followed up within the firm with some mandatory training.*

2. Have you ever been the recipient of or witnessed unwelcome physical contact at work?

More than 21% of the respondents to this question stated that they had been the recipient of or witnessed unwelcome physical contact at work. Of these, 36% stated that the incident occurred between 2010 and 2018.

Question 2	Percentage
Yes	21.56%
No	78.44%

Nearly 51% of the respondents to this question were Associates at the time of the incident, 9% were Partners, and the Administrative, Paralegal, and Support Personnel categories exceeded 33%.

Approximately 47% of the respondents who provided information about the size of their firm at the time of the incident were in offices with fewer than 50 lawyers; 40% were in offices of 100 lawyers or greater.

More than two-thirds of those responding to this question stated that they did not report the incident.

Reported	Percentage
No	68.02%
Yes	31.97%

Examples of Behaviors Included in Survey Responses to Question 2

Examples of behaviors described in the responses included:

- Nearly all of the respondents who provided anecdotes reported examples of unwanted and unsolicited hugging, back-rubbing, groping, shoulder rubs, kissing, and lewd comments.
- Numerous respondents described inappropriate groping and other forms of unwanted physical contact during holiday parties and at other social gatherings where there was alcohol.
- Many respondents reported witnessing inappropriate behavior by male colleagues towards younger female associates or staff members.
- Several respondents identified examples of men leering, staring at various parts of a female's anatomy, and standing or walking or "brushing by" inappropriately close.
- Several respondents described incidents early in their career where their boss would proposition them or offer suggestions for ways to dress that would appeal to clients, or otherwise flirt with them.

One respondent, describing numerous examples of "virtually on a daily basis" being propositioned, then bullied when those advances were resisted, stated:

> It created emotional, financial and professional turmoil in my life which continues . . . I hope that this survey demonstrates how much even lawyers feel hopeless and incapable of standing up to sexual harassment in a law firm.

Respondents' Perspectives on Reporting Behaviors

In so many responses to this question, respondents were more likely to stay silent than report offensive or unwanted contact. Most of the respondents who provided anecdotes of unwelcome physical contact focused on the power imbalance as the reason for not reporting concerns about more senior and often powerful colleagues. In particular, they frequently expressed concern about damaging their career opportunities, for example:

> *I was an intern, I wanted a job or good recommendations for future jobs.*

A respondent described a married partner's persistent physical contact when they would be working together. She explained her reason for remaining silent:

> *I was an associate close to partnership. He would vote on my partnership.*

A respondent described inappropriate touching by a colleague and stated her concern about the possible repercussion to her young career:

> *I believed that reporting my male colleague would result in my termination.*

Another respondent who described an incident of inappropriate touching stated:

> *Partner who did this was very popular/made lots of money for the firm and if one of us had to go it would have been me.*

One respondent in a small firm noted:

> *Firm had culture of demanding compliance with inappropriate behavior to "belong," the firm's small size meant that the*

*management committee was overly concerned with protecting
partners at all costs.*

Others observed that no actions had been taken with respect to past
allegations, so there was no reason to expect a different result in the
future. For example, a respondent stated:

> *Prior complaints about male partner behavior were not heeded.
> Firm prioritized workplace experience of partners over associates.
> Size of firm and power dynamic . . . rendered associates without
> power and required compliant behavior to keep employment.*

Another respondent who also described multiple incidents of inappropriate contact and comments by both a male partner and a senior
associate stated:

> *I spoke to friends and peers. . . . given the treatment of senior
> people who committed far more egregious acts, what would be the
> point in raising the issue?*

Another described incidents of partners trying to date associates
and noted:

> *The firm was aware of the behavior already and did nothing.
> Firms care about rainmaking more than associates.*

A number of respondents informally shared information with lawyers in their firms who were more senior, but were told to treat the
remarks or behaviors as a joke. This type of response was recurrent.
A respondent who reported unsolicited touching stated:

> *It was treated as a joke and we just had to put up with it.*

A respondent described being inappropriately touched with regu-
larity and stated:

> *Told senior partners and it became a joke. Not taken seriously.*

Similarly, a respondent described a senior partner who frequently engaged in unwelcome physical contact, noting:

> *The senior partner was enormously powerful and popular, and furthermore his conduct was well-known and done in front of other partners and the senior managing partner - and the employment partner - on a regular basis. People who complained about this and other forms of harassment were told they had no sense of humor. . . . What's the point?*

In other instances, people shared a warning system to alert others:

> *This man's behavior was so well-known that a male partner once asked me to warn a new female . . . associate about him.*

Another described her efforts to warn:

> *That individual had a reputation for hitting on young women, whether paralegals, summer clerks or associates and I did my best to warn those coming in to the firm to stay clear of him.*

Others shared examples of where efforts to inform others more senior in the firm were unheeded. One respondent noted:

> *I told multiple people including partners. I did not want to make a formal report. No follow up actions took place.*

Another respondent described multiple incidents of unwanted physical contact, stating:

> *Told head of HR . . . but asked that it be off the record. Also told male colleagues, venting. Nothing ever happened to my knowledge.*

In many of the responses provided, fears of retaliation appeared warranted. Respondents who did report told of circumstances in which they were the target of retaliation. For example, one respondent described her response to a partner's groping and other unwanted physical contact:

> I was nervous about mentioning it to HR, so I first told co-workers and some of the younger attorneys. They were . . . unsure of the repercussions of reporting an equity partner of the firm. [Described process by which another equity partner assisted with follow up.] The situation was handled but some of the long-term attorneys blamed me.

Respondents described a variety of retaliatory actions, but all had career impacts. Stated one:

> Ultimately I was given less and less work after that until I left the firm.

Some respondents told of providing information confidentially to a more senior lawyer, to help others identify patterns in the future, for example:

> [I] told a female senior partner, said I didn't want to make a formal complaint but wanted someone to know in case things escalated.

Several respondents noted specific examples where bystander intervention—usually by male colleagues—immediately halted the improper behavior. For example, an attorney who witnessed offensive comments being made by a partner to an associate at a social event where people were drinking stated:

> Spoke directly [with the] female associate informing her that I saw the offense as very serious and would address it [with] my partners. Notified [person who handles employment issues within the firm]. Notified all partners. The offending partner was spoken to. No direct punishment but I think damage to his reputation.

In another instance where a male was inappropriately touching and making suggestive comments to female law clerks, bystander intervention helped when male coworkers collectively told the offending lawyer his behavior was unacceptable.

Several noted that they cut off contact with the individual involved by moving to a different location in the firm or changing practice groups.

3. Have you ever felt that someone was trying to engage you in unwelcome discussions (including through comments or actions) of a sexual nature?

More than 25% of the respondents to this question stated they felt someone had tried to engage them in unwelcome discussions of a sexual nature. Of these, approximately 35% stated that the incident occurred between 2010 and 2018.

Question 3	Percentage
Yes	25.38%
No	74.62%

Of those who responded to this question, nearly 70% were Associates at the time of the incident, slightly more than 6% were Partners, and the Administrative, Paralegal, and Support Personnel categories comprised 21%.

Nearly 56% of the respondents who provided information about the size of their firm at the time of the incident were in offices with fewer than 50 lawyers, 21% were in offices with between 50 and 99 lawyers, and 23% were in offices of 100 lawyers or more.

Nearly 75% of those who responded to this question did not report the behavior.

Reported	Percentage
No	73.91%
Yes	26.08%

Examples of Behaviors Included in Survey Responses to Question 3

Examples of behaviors described in the responses included:

- Male lawyers demeaning young women in front of male colleagues or clients through sexual references.
- Discussions of extra-marital affairs, sexual escapades, or sexual fantasies.
- Senior male colleagues moving conversations from the professional to personal issues.
- Frequent vulgar or sexualized jokes and remarks that objectify women.
- Prying into the personal and sex lives of women in the firm.
- Direct sexualized and objectifying comments to women about their physical appearance or the physical appearance of others.
- Sexualized comments, innuendos, or propositions made at or after firm social events at which alcohol was served.
- Leering and comments directed at summer associates by partners and senior associates.
- Inappropriate comments, unsolicited touching, and prying questions to LGBT lawyers, prying into their sexual life.

Respondents' Perspectives on Reporting Behaviors

Many respondents expressed an unwillingness to report these behaviors. Reasons centered on the lack of a clear avenue for reporting, the involvement of senior leaders in the behaviors, and concerns about negative repercussions. For example, one respondent observed:

> *I didn't have a supervisor. There was no person or process for reporting. [I]f I had tried to make an issue of it I would have lost my job.*

A respondent who did not report a partner's highly sexualized comments noted:

> *It's my boss, an equity partner, and our HR is useless. It would only negatively impact my job.*

Another respondent discussing a culture of vulgar or sexualized jokes stated:

> *I was a young associate in a virtually all-male department and afraid I would be perceived as not "fitting in."*

Similarly, a respondent observed:

> *It was expected and accepted behavior by other partners and staff.*

Long-term career impacts loomed large in the calculation many respondents made in deciding whether they had any place to turn within the firm. A respondent who was the recipient of frequent lewd comments and behaviors stated:

> *Fear of retribution, fear of rocking the boat as a brand new attorney with no status in the firm yet, desire to be seen as a "chill", non-dramatic team member . . . My career was directly in these partners hands, since even first year associates were beholden to partners for feeding them work in a vassal/feudal sort of structure the firm insisted on maintaining.*

Another respondent who endured frequent comments about her body and sexual innuendos noted she did nothing because the behaviors were:

> *Part of the . . . culture; the comments came from senior partners; and there was no one to report to whom I considered to be sympathetic to the issues. Also, fear of retaliation.*

A respondent described explicit overtures that were made and stated:

> *The transgressor was the managing partner and there was no one else to go to.*

Many respondents described sharing their stories with others, but not reporting to anyone with authority within the firm. A respondent who was the frequent recipient of improper comments explained why she spoke only to friends and peers:

> *No sense in reporting. These individuals had had indiscretions and improper conduct with subordinates that had been reported and known . . .*

Some respondents noted that they shared information with a woman partner, for example:

> *I reported [the behaviors] to a female partner. No follow-up.*

A respondent who did not report an uncomfortable proposition from a married partner while she was an intern also revealed how continued silence fuels ongoing inappropriate behaviors:

> *Later on, I did [speak] with a female partner and I did tell her, and she said she was not surprised to hear the story.*

A respondent who did not report a partner's frequent sexualized comments and demeaning remarks noted a satisfactory result when the behavior was finally reported:

> *At the time, I just ignored it. Eventually someone else reported it and this person was asked to leave the firm due to other inappropriate behavior.*

Several respondents reported that they handled the situations by confronting the offending lawyer directly, sometimes with positive results:

> *I dealt with it myself. I also think the person who engaged in the conduct would not do it again to me or anyone else at work.*

Similarly, another respondent reported a successful result when direct action was finally taken:

It finally stopped when I confronted the people involved about it and explained why I thought their actions were a problem. It took me a couple of years to do that.

4. Have you ever witnessed materials or items of a sexual or disparaging nature, including sexual images, displayed in your workplace?

Slightly more than 10% of those who responded to this question stated that they had witnessed materials or items of a sexual or disparaging nature displayed in the workplace. Of these, 36% stated that the incident occurred between 2010 and 2018.

Question 4	Percentage
Yes	10.22%
No	89.78%

Nearly 54% of those responding were Associates at the time of the incident, almost 17% were Partners, and the combined categories of Administrative, Paralegal, and Support Personnel comprised approximately 22%.

Approximately 75% of the respondents who provided information about the size of their firm at the time of the incident were in offices of fewer than 50 lawyers.

More than 72% of those responding did not report the incident.

Reported	Percentage
No	72.83%
Yes	27.16%

Examples of Behaviors Included in Survey Responses to Question 4

Examples of behaviors described in the responses included:

- Content displayed on a computer, including inappropriate screen-saver images as well as watching porn.

- Sexual posters or other images in restrooms and office areas.
- Attorneys sending or sharing pornographic emails or images.

Respondents' Perspectives on Reporting Behaviors

Respondents generally did not report these behaviors, stating that, in most instances, it was already known and, in other instances, they did not want to risk retaliation. For example, one respondent said:

> ... perhaps cowardice; but more likely a strong desire to remain employed and meaningfully engaged within my practice, without imaginable retaliation.

Another described her reluctance to report attorneys who shared sexual images:

> I feared that I would be ostracized/retaliated against.

Several respondents stated that their supervisors were involved in the offending conduct, rendering reporting futile. Others stated that they just ignored the images or put it out of their mind.

Some respondents reported instances of pornography with mixed results. One respondent noted that inappropriate graphic imagery was reported to two partners, including the Managing Partner:

> I expected that the individual who was engaged in the action I reported would be spoken to but I learned that did not take place.

One respondent took an effective route by reporting pornography on another lawyer's computer to the IT department:

> Notified our IT department and personnel to make sure the computer was purged and blocked.

A respondent who did not report a co-worker's excessive watching of porn stated that, after the behavior was reported by someone else, the individual was terminated.

5. Have you ever witnessed any incidents of disparagement of other people or groups in the workplace that made you feel uncomfortable?

More than a third of those responding to this question stated that they had witnessed incidents of disparagement of others at work in a way that made them feel uncomfortable. Of these, more than 50% stated that the incident occurred between 2010 and 2018.

Question 5	Percentage
Yes	35.31%
No	64.69%

Approximately 69% of those responding to this question were Associates, 10% were Partners, and the combined categories of Administrative, Paralegals, and Support Personnel comprised more than 17%.

More than 60% of the respondents were in offices of fewer than 50 lawyers, and nearly 25% were in offices of 100 lawyers or more.

Nearly 75% did not report the incident to a coworker or supervisor.

Reported	Percentage
No	74.24%
Yes	25.75%

Examples of Behaviors Included in Survey Responses to Question 5

Examples of behaviors described in the responses included:

- Slurs and demeaning comments about race, gender, religion, and sexual orientation.
- Disparaging or inappropriate comments about pregnancy, maternity leaves, or status as a mother.
- Negative behaviors toward minorities, women, and older workers.
- Women partners dismissive of experiences of younger female lawyers with respect to work-life choices.
- Anti-immigrant comments.
- Ageist comments.

One respondent commented on her three decades in the profession, including multiple workplaces:

> *Many, many, many, many, many (seems like countless) deroga-*
> *tory remarks about people of color, people of different ethnicity, gay*
> *bashing, transgender bashing from all levels (clients, coworkers,*
> *management) in every single position, every single firm I have held/*
> *worked for throughout my 30 year career. I wish I could say I was*
> *exaggerating but, alas, I am not. . . . Believe me when I say all kinds*
> *of 'isms in Massachusetts are alive, well and thriving throughout*
> *all different kinds of law firms, throughout all different levels.*

Respondents' Perspectives on Reporting Behaviors

Respondents who did not report disparaging comments that they witnessed or that were made directly to them offered reasons similar to the responses in prior questions for remaining silent: no expectation that anything would be done; the engagement of senior leadership in the behaviors; and the belief that, by reporting, the respondent would be labeled as humorless.

One respondent described the frustration of seeing behaviors continue unchecked across the span of the respondent's career, which included multiple law firms:

> *Many comments were made by management which does not*
> *encourage one to report anything. The comments that were made*
> *by co-workers I tried to address myself to no avail. The few times*
> *I have mentioned things to management they were swept under the*
> *rug as a non-issue. When this happens more times than not, you*
> *just stop reporting the micro-aggressions and learn how to live/*
> *deal with it to the best of your ability.*

Many respondents noted the power imbalance that enabled lawyers to act with impunity. One such respondent noted:

> *He was one of the controlling rainmakers in the firm. No one*
> *said no to him or could control him.*

Another respondent commented on the power imbalance that prevented a response to a culture of "demeaning racial/ethnic jokes":

> *I was a young associate in a predominately male department afraid of being perceived as not fitting in.*

A respondent who did not report what she saw as anti-immigrant and misogynistic comments observed:

> *They mostly knew and did nothing about it, so the expectation was that even if they were told of something new they would still not do anything about it.*

Another respondent described a culture of "innumerable sexist, homophobic, racist, anti-Semitic comments," noting:

> *[I] did not feel empowered to do so as associate who needed job to pay student loans and support young family,* etc.

One respondent did not report frequent observations of disparaging treatment of support staff by partners:

> *Because I had no power. Instead, I looked for a new job.*

An LGBT attorney described a culture of frequent disparaging jokes against multiple targets and that such comments were "never aggressively offensive, but deniable in the just-joking-around context." The respondent stated why reporting did not feel like an option:

> *Culturally accepted in the firm. Had no faith in ability to change the culture.*

A young lawyer who did not report shared the pain experienced from hearing disparaging comments about immigrants:

> *I was a diverse scholarship winner at the time and I didn't know how to even begin to explain how hurtful it was to hear people in*

the firm make jokes about immigrants and other minorities. I had higher expectations for the firm.

Respondents frequently described a culture where the comments were expected to be viewed as humorous. As one respondent stated:

There was no point - such remarks and commentary were routinely tolerated and brushed aside as "jokes." Reporting would only jeopardize my position. I would be viewed as someone who "can't take a joke." Reporting would not have brought about a positive change.

Another, describing ongoing crude commentary, noted that a:

. . . toxic culture of inappropriate behavior was tolerated and laughed off. There was a feeling that there was no point in reporting.

Numerous respondents stated that there was no one to report to, as those in charge were part of the problem, for example:

The comments were made by or to the person to whom I would have reported.

Similarly, another noted:

Everyone I would report the conduct to is always in the room when it happens.

A few respondents gave examples of an HR structure that declined to get involved. For example, one respondent who reached out to HR with concerns about discriminatory behaviors against women stated:

I informed the HR manager, who said the Partners were "out of touch" and told me to ignore them.

Another stated:

HR was present when senior partner made disparaging comments and did nothing.

In some cases, reports of disparaging comments were made, but no follow-up feedback was provided. For example, a respondent described a senior attorney's disparaging treatment of support staff and noted:

> *I informed the managing partner. To my knowledge, no steps were taken to resolve the issue.*

In other instances, respondents who tried to report were told to figure out how to avoid the individual or improve the relationship. For example, one respondent described her effort to report a female partner's disparagement of her pregnancy and status as a mother (a situation described by several respondents):

> *I told an equity partner. . . . He told me that if I wanted to become a partner, I had to get this female partner to like me more.*

Some stated they tried to shut down the conversation when offensive stereotyped comments were made, as this respondent indicated:

> *Most of the time, I just told them to stop.*

A partner in a leadership role described responding to a lawyer who openly expressed bigoted views:

> *I . . . immediately addressed this issue with the person and it never happened again and nobody ever told me that they had heard any derogatory remarks or discriminatory remarks from him after this.*

A few respondents described a reporting process that worked. One respondent noted:

> *In fact, we have reporting systems in place at my current office. I know of incidents witnessed by co-workers that have been reported and are being addressed by HR/management.*

One respondent described the eventual termination of an equity partner who continued to make disparaging comments, notwithstanding efforts to coach and monitor his behavior:

> *I told our local managing partner and the firm's managing partner . . . After attempting coaching, sensitivity training, and months of supervising his behavior, the firm eventually fired him.*

A respondent described responses to several incidents of disparaging comments and behavior, including at a social event and another in the office:

> *As to the misbehavior [at the social event], it was widely reported, and the firm disciplined the partners involved and held trainings throughout the firm. As to the other one, the . . . department investigated and reprimanded the person.*

6. Have you been present when comments or jokes were made that were sexual in nature or disparaging of other people or groups?

This question garnered the highest percentage of affirmative responses, with 40% of those responding to this question stating that they had been present when comments or jokes were made that were sexual in nature or disparaging of other people or groups. Of these, approximately 40% stated that the incident occurred between 2010 and 2018.

Question 6	Percentage
Yes	40.23%
No	59.77%

More than 65% of those who responded to this question were Associates at the time of the incident, 11% were Partners, and the combined categories of Administrative, Paralegal, and Support Personnel comprised 21%.

Approximately 58% of those responding to this question were working in offices of fewer than 50 lawyers and approximately 28% were in offices with 100 lawyers or more.

Nearly 87% stated that they did not report the information to a coworker or someone in a supervisory role, the question with the highest percentage of non-reporting respondents in the survey.

Reported	Percentage
No	86.66%
Yes	13.33%

Examples of Behaviors Included in Survey Responses to Question 6

Examples of behaviors described in the responses included:

- Frequent gender-based jokes and efforts at humorous commentary focusing on women's bodies, specifically relating to breasts, sexuality, weight, and maternal status.
- Frequent jokes and commentary by men referencing their sexual fantasies or joking about sexual exploits.
- Frequent jokes that involve race, religion, sexual orientation, and gender.
- Inappropriate jokes told at events where alcohol was served; sometimes the jokes were told publicly, as part of a lawyer's official remarks, and sometimes privately within social groups.

Respondents' Perspectives on Reporting Behaviors

Many respondents to this question described off-color or disparaging humor as "pervasive" or "too many incidents to describe." Most did not report the incidents. Consistent with the reasons provided in other questions, many felt fearful of retaliation or that there was no one to report to, particularly because of the status of the offending individual. In many instances, these types of remarks felt like part of the firm culture.

Several respondents described the conflict between the danger of appearing humorless compared to the sense of being worn down by the continued stream of insulting remarks. A respondent commented on her reaction to frequent disparaging jokes about women:

This kind of commentary was tolerated and accepted as part of the culture. Reporting would not bring about a change and would only negatively impact my career. Additionally, a single comment can easily be brushed aside as a joke - one almost feels silly/doesn't want to be viewed as being too serious about any one offhand comment.

Similarly, a respondent observed:

It seemed like it was expected and "normal," and I was too junior to complain.

Another noted that jokes about females were "pervasive":

People in highest positions do it. It's a "joke."

Again, the status of the individuals making the comments seemed to serve as an inoculation against a negative response; for example:

Such behavior and statements are typical of this senior partner, and after repeated instances of such, there is an understanding that there are no repercussions for this person, so there is no reason or person to report this to.

Another respondent stated why she did not report graphic joking from a partner:

The firm had a history of ousting women who reported issues. He was a practice group co-leader at the point. We were junior associates. We preferred to stay employed.

A respondent further highlighted this point:

> *I reported this to a female partner. She agreed this was despi-*
> *cable but nothing was ever done because the partner who made the*
> *comments was a big rainmaker.*

One respondent observed how the power imbalance can shift over time, depending on one's status within the firm:

> *On most occasions, I was in a position to tell them to stop. When*
> *I wasn't a partner, I felt my job would be in jeopardy.*

Several respondents described sexually charged jokes at firm social events. One noted:

> *Those were the guys in power. No good would have come from*
> *reporting these incidents. I would have been ostracized.*

In a few instances, respondents spoke of off-color jokes as "locker room talk" or "banter" that was not harmful, so they did not feel a need to report the remarks.

One respondent highlighted senior partner support that stands as an example of a useful intervention. Describing graphic stories being told to a group during a break in a meeting, the senior partner left the room with the associate and further made it clear that the associate should never feel pressured to remain in such a situation.

In another positive example, a respondent described disparaging jokes made by a more senior lawyer and then noted the follow up:

> *I spoke with a[n] attorney, who brought me to a very senior*
> *female attorney. . . . She talked with me about options for what*
> *could be done, and let me choose. She did what I asked (which was*
> *for her to speak with this guy). She spoke with him, and he apolo-*
> *gized (it seemed sincere).*

A respondent who very directly "let offenders know this was verboten" noted her valid reason for doing so without worry about retribution:

I am the boss.

7. Have you ever been asked personal questions or questions of a sexual nature that made you feel uncomfortable?

Nearly 16% of those responding to this question noted that they had been asked personal questions or questions of a sexual nature that made them uncomfortable. Of these, approximately 41% stated that the incident occurred between 2010 and 2018.

Question 7	Percentage
Yes	15.80%
No	84.20%

Sixty-seven percent of those who responded affirmatively were Associates at the time of the incident and less than 5% were Partners. The combined categories of Administrative, Paralegal, and Support Personnel exceeded 22%.

Nearly two-thirds of the respondents were in offices of fewer than 50 lawyers; more than 28% reported being in offices of 100 lawyers or more.

More than 78% said they did not report the incidents to a coworker or supervisor.

Reported	Percentage
No	78.57%
Yes	21.42%

Examples of Behaviors Included in Survey Responses to Question 7

Examples of behaviors described in the responses included:

- Male lawyers asking pregnant women detailed questions about their physical condition, including questions about their breasts.

- New mothers being asked detailed questions about breastfeeding.
- Women asked questions about their age and their personal life such as whether they were married or engaged, and when they planned to have children.
- Men commenting on specific physical aspects of a woman (as distinct from a generic compliment).
- People being asked about their sexual orientation.
- People being asked questions about their sexual relationships.
- Clients asking questions of a sexual nature.

Respondents' Perspectives on Reporting Behaviors

Fear of retribution and concern about one's internal reputation again emerged as primary reasons for not reporting. Both of these concerns were highlighted in a respondent's explanation of why she did not report a male lawyer's prying comments:

> *This person was notorious for his treatment of females - it was already known from the top down. Reporting would not have made a difference. Also you worry what reporting would do to your own career. It wasn't worth the risk.*

A number of respondents stated that they did not report because they feared a diminished reputation in the firm. For example, a respondent who was asked highly inappropriate questions on multiple occasions noted:

> *[The concerns were] uncomfortable to talk about, not the only one who has experienced this and nothing is done about it. If something was done it would likely hurt my professional relationship with the attorney(s) involved as well as others at the firm.*

Similarly, another respondent who described her personal discomfort with sexualized questions stated:

> *Who wants to be known as the person who complained about something, rather than known for my skills?*

In many of the examples provided, and similar to the responses in other questions, respondents stated that they did not report the behaviors because the person to whom they would report was the person making the comments; for example:

> *The supervisor was the perpetrator. [I]t was either my career or report the comment(s). I was not going to let his actions hinder my career.*

Another respondent who described uncomfortable comments made to her about her sexual orientation succinctly stated why she did not report:

> *He was one of the managing attorneys.*

A respondent who described being asked inappropriate personal questions noted:

> *Perpetrator protected by management.*

Other respondents offered similar reasons:

> *The comments/questions came from the managing partner.*

Some respondents indicated they found solace by commiserating with others in the firm. For example, a respondent stated that female associates who found themselves the object of inappropriate questions and prying by another lawyer formed their own support network:

> *We both decided to be a support system for each other, and we discussed ways to avoid being alone with that attorney.*

Respondents also described informally sharing information with those more senior. One respondent gave examples of behaviors from someone she described as known to be a "serial harasser" and noted:

> *I reported him several times to a female partner.*

In a number of instances, respondents were the recipient of inappropriate questions and comments from clients. In those examples, the respondents generally spoke with a more senior person in the firm but often specifically asked that nothing further be done.

8. Have you ever been made to feel that you needed to engage in sexual behavior or develop a personal relationship with someone at work to advance?

This question had the smallest number of respondents. Of those who did respond, more than 28% answered affirmatively. Of these, nearly 35% stated that the incident occurred between 2010 and 2018.

Question 8	Percentage
Yes	28.57%
No	71.43%

Approximately 60% of those who responded to this question were Associates at the time of the incident, 8% were Partners, and the combined categories of Administrative, Paralegal, and Support Personnel comprised 16%.

More than 56% were in offices of fewer than 50 lawyers; approximately 30% worked in offices of 100 lawyers or more.

For this question, the percentage of those who reported the behavior was higher than the other questions (although the number of respondents overall was much smaller): more than 57% reported the behavior to someone else.

Reported	Percentage
No	42.86%
Yes	57.14%

Examples of Behaviors Included in Survey Responses to Question 8

Examples of behaviors described in the responses included:

- Lawyers describing sexualized behaviors and implying that such behaviors can help career advancement.

- Proposing to have "mentoring conversations" in a non-professional atmosphere such as a bar or hotel.
- Inappropriate advances toward summer associates.

Respondents' Perspectives on Reporting Behaviors

Respondents who provided information for this question generally did not feel they had any place to turn. Most simply expressed their frustration, for example:

> *It was clear that the only way to assure a good salary and a promotion was to sleep with the boss. He had the power and he made the decisions. The . . . only action we could take was to leave.*

Another, observing that firm partners revealed clear preferences for how they expected females to behave, noted:

> *I was unwilling to flirt or act like this, and felt I was ignored and even berated by certain male partners. The offending male partners were too powerful . . . Plus, I don't even think they were consciously aware of their bias.*

Some respondents said they felt unable to advance because they refused to be part of a culture where success seemed linked to social expectations. One respondent described how social interactions served as a gatekeeper to success:

> *Advancement within the firm/access to more sophisticated work was largely driven by personal relationships. . . . Despite . . . disparaging comments about the quality of a colleague's work, such colleague was given more opportunities because he played the game of drinking/going out/wing-manning with/for the young-ish partners.*

Another respondent described how reporting uncomfortable and inappropriate experiences as a summer associate backfired:

> *Reported it to [the] male . . . in charge of summer associate program and some hiring. It ended up becoming a mess because I was*

pressured to let him tell partners and ultimately the person who I reported found out I had done so and basically it made the work environment hostile.

9. Have you ever felt you were the recipient of or have witnessed bullying behavior in the workplace?

Nearly 40% of those responding to this question stated that they had been the recipient of or had witnessed bullying behavior in the workplace. Of these, approximately 44% stated that the incident occurred between 2010 and 2018.

Question 9	Percentage
Yes	39.45%
No	60.55%

More than 69% of those who responded affirmatively to this question were Associates at the time of the incident, nearly 10% were Partners, and the categories of Administrative, Paralegal, and Support Personnel comprised nearly 16%.

Approximately 56% were in offices of fewer than 50 lawyers; nearly 27% were in offices with 100 lawyers or greater.

As with all questions, the majority of the respondents did not report the behaviors, although the percentage of those who did not report the behaviors was less than in most other questions.

Reported	Percentage
No	54.05%
Yes	45.94%

Examples of Behaviors Included in Survey Responses to Question 9

Examples of behaviors described in the responses included:

- Partners screaming at or otherwise humiliating others (at all levels) in the firm.
- Bullying that escalated to physical abuse or throwing of objects.
- Feigning deadlines or other hazing behaviors.
- Feeling punished by more senior women.

Respondents' Perspectives on Reporting Behaviors

Respondents described a range of behaviors, including those that induced physical stress reactions in both the victims of bullying and the witnesses—who reasonably may have been fearful as to whether they were next. One respondent described negative physical consequences experienced by others in the firm, then explained why no action was taken:

> . . . *senior partner and head of the . . . department would routinely humiliate anyone who crossed him. . . . This would include his fellow partners as well as outside counsel. For example . . . he would make . . . snide personal comments . . . about [people's] height, weight, or looks. In general, he did this when he was about to be challenged on an issue. . . . This was a senior partner and decision maker. Raising the issue would just result in more humiliation.*

Another described bullying tactics she endured and offered similar reasons for not reporting:

> *My boss was a jerk, unnecessarily. His teaching style was to make me feel like I had done something egregiously wrong when it was a minor issue. He seemed purposefully to start a discussion by suggesting I had really screwed up when I hadn't. Every time I saw a note from him to see him, or I got a call from him, I would get very nervous. It was very stressful. . . . I did not report it for several reasons. First, he was the managing partner. Second, everyone knew that was just the way this partner operated. Indeed, it tends to be a revolving door of associates who work with this partner.*

Many respondents who specifically described bullying of associates that took place also reinforced, similar to responses in other questions, that the apparent common knowledge of the perpetrators' behaviors rendered reporting not an option; for example:

> *Some senior partners and associates would use demeaning language and actions directed at younger associates as part of their management style. It was common knowledge at the firm.*

Similarly, some respondents described extreme behaviors that went beyond verbal abuse and explained that the behaviors were not reported because the perpetrators were powerful partners:

> *Certain partners, mostly male, were extremely bullying and nasty to the staff and associates. [More than one] of them threw objects around the office. [Anecdote described an incident where someone was physically targeted.] No need to report it. Other partners were aware but powerless to rein in the powerful male partners, who also happened to be rainmakers.*

A number of respondents gave examples of escalating behaviors, with a similar reason for not reporting:

> *Partners regularly bullied associates by calling them out publicly on assignments, yelling and screaming at them, throwing files, dumping files, and if the partners knew associates had vacation coming, assigning new and/or additional cases so that the associate could not go on his or her trip. This was to ensure that associates knew who was in charge. This was the firm culture. It was well known that it would get worse if you started to complain to HR about it.*

Another respondent noted an atmosphere of intimidation with no recourse because of the status of the perpetrator:

> *Files . . . being thrown across room, staff being yelled at, staff members being pitted against one another, staff being belittled . . .*

Similarly, a respondent described intimidating behaviors that also included the throwing of objects:

> *Objects thrown around office. Screaming. Yelling. Slamming doors. Verbal threats.*

In many cases, the respondents highlighted behaviors that they said felt more like hazing than being part of a legal team. In such circumstances, the general view was that there was no point in reporting. One respondent typified many of the comments:

Insecure men bully to make themselves feel better. For example making associates pull all nighters in the office to haze them, knowing it was not necessary to meet client needs. Yelling. Screaming. Culture was to toughen up and take whatever a partner dishes out. Partner is always right.

Another respondent observed the hazing aspect with no opportunity for redress:

Senior partners frequently bullied associates as an intimidation and motivation technique - this was part of one's initiation in the world of large law firms. The persons conducting the bullying were senior members of the firm. They were the supervisors and everyone was aware this type of conduct was expected.

Similarly, a respondent noted:

Requests aren't made in civil tones, but in harsh tones, coupled with negative comments re: quality of associate's work or associate's commitment - especially if associate has family obligations. Felt like putting up with this conduct was a job requirement.

A few respondents described bullying behaviors from women; for example:

Women constantly knocked women. . . . The women in power did not have children, and seemed to not be able to relate to me or like me. I was a threat and was punished. What was the point - I needed to advance.

Another respondent similarly described bullying by female partners and the failure of the firm to follow up after reporting the behaviors:

> *My two supervisors, both of whom were women, were horrible bullies. One in particular never took personal responsibility for anything and always laid blame at the feet of others. It was truly a toxic environment. I told HR . . ., the CFO . . ., and the managing partner. . . . The entire firm was aware of the behavior, which was a pattern, and . . . no one has done anything about it because [they] bring in money. . . . The firm simply does not care.*

On the other hand, many respondents described women as receiving the brunt of verbally abusive tactics, yet few saw any hope for change. Noted one respondent:

> *Bullying and intimidation of women when older men felt threatened by their greater competence and social abilities. Fear of reprisal and negative impact on career [are reasons for not reporting].*

One respondent described the negative results following efforts to intervene:

> *I worked with a senior partner who bullied everyone around him. . . . He would make derogatory remarks as a matter of course to everyone. Because he was the principal rainmaker at the firm. When I did finally cross this individual in an attempt to protect a more junior attorney, I ultimately lost his good opinion, and left the firm.*

Several respondents who described an abusive culture noted that efforts to report proved futile; for example:

> *Been through countless meetings and encounters - senior partner(s) scream and yell and throw things because they are unable to properly express their frustrations. This is the hardest*

part of my work environment. I have developed a fear response, which is ridiculous. [Reporting has usually been done to] HR or close male colleagues. Nothing is ever done.

In another example, a respondent described the lack of follow-through after behavior was reported:

At my firm, I am aware of two partners who have bullied subordinate attorneys and staff. In relation to the local partner . . . who engaged in bullying, I talked with the Partner in charge of our office . . . and the Practice group leader. . . . Further management training for the offending partner was discussed, but has not yet been implemented.

One respondent noted that an internal process may have been triggered, yet no specific information about follow up was available:

I witnessed numerous incidents of male partners screaming at and bullying younger associates - mostly female but some male. It was already under investigation.

Based on some of the comments, it appeared that there was greater follow-up when an associate engaged in wrongful behavior, rather than a partner. One respondent described being frequently bullied by an associate and how it was ultimately handled:

I spoke with [particular person within the firm who raised the issue] and it was nipped in the bud. They spoke with him and it was done in an appropriate way and the behavior changed.

A respondent provided an example of a firm taking action against a partner when it learned of the extent of that partner's behaviors, including physical intimidation and sexual harassment of female associates. The respondent spoke with the managing partner and other partners, and subsequently the offending partner was forced out of the firm.

Other respondents also provided positive examples of reporting that led to a satisfactory result. For example, one respondent told another lawyer of a partner's verbally abusive behavior and later received a phone call in which the partner apologized. In another instance, a respondent described an atmosphere of rudeness and disrespect by the managing partners. When a female partner addressed this directly, one of the managing partners called the respondent to apologize, and his behavior improved.

Another respondent reported on a successful self-help measure:

> I was berated and yelled at by senior attorneys for reasons that had nothing to do with my work. . . . The whole experience was absolutely horrible. I have since changed jobs and currently work for an absolutely incredible, very supportive firm where I truly feel that I have the tools that I need to succeed.

10. Have you ever felt threatened, embarrassed or humiliated, or witnessed someone being threatened, embarrassed or humiliated, by someone in the workplace?

Nearly a third of those who responded to this question reported feeling, or witnessed someone being, threatened, embarrassed, or humiliated by someone in the workplace. Of these, 44% stated that the incident occurred between 2010 and 2018.

Question 10	Percentage
Yes	31.69%
No	68.31%

Nearly three-quarters of those responding were Associates at the time of the incident, approximately 12% were Partners, and the combined categories of Administrative, Paralegal, and Support Staff comprised nearly 15%.

Approximately half of the respondents worked in offices of fewer than 50 fifty lawyers and nearly 40% were in offices of 100 lawyers or more.

Sixty percent of those responding affirmatively to this question did not report the behaviors.

Reported	Percentage
No	60.18%
Yes	39.81%

Examples of Behaviors Included in Survey Responses to Question 10

Examples of behaviors described in the responses included:

- Partners expressing anger by openly berating lawyers, yelling in public, or otherwise demeaning a younger colleague.
- Being directly asked to engage in sexual activity.
- Criticisms and insults designed to diminish the confidence of associates.
- Criticizing people in public for personal behaviors relating to what they eat, whether they exercise, their weight, etc.
- Sexualized behaviors and comments.
- Demeaning the skills of female lawyers by saying they were only being included (e.g., in a meeting, or assigned to a particular matter) because of their looks or because they needed to add a woman to the team.

Respondents' Perspectives on Reporting Behaviors

Many of the anecdotes described in response to question 10 were similar to the types of behaviors reported in question 9. Respondents described situations in which they felt intimidated and humiliated, with no recourse available.

A few respondents who were more senior in their career described earlier experiences where they endured humiliating behaviors from other lawyers. For example, one stated:

I have found in my career many lawyers with large egos who have taken upon themselves to humiliate me and others in order to make them feel large. There has been so many incidents that it would take a volume of pages to write them all. If you had reported any humiliating incidents, especially when it was in response to lawyers, you were seen as a troublemaker and run the risk of a bad annual review and possible termination.

Some respondents described behaviors that combined humiliation and actual physical assault:

One . . . partner would swear, berate and humiliate associates in public areas. . . . He also threw . . . desk items at associates. The incidents didn't happen to me, and it was already common knowledge to management.

A respondent who witnessed partners screaming at and insulting more junior lawyers did not see reporting as a productive option:

Did not want to hurt partner's reputation or damage my professional relationship with the partner or other professionals at the firm.

Another respondent noted a lawyer's humiliating tactics that were not reported:

A senior associate consistently humiliated me in front of co-workers and opposing counsel. I did not report it because I did not believe it would change the senior associate's behavior. I also thought that it would have negative consequences on my career.

As noted in responses to other questions, being a rainmaker served to inoculate many partners from being held accountable. One respondent, describing a senior partner who frequently yelled at and belittled others in the firm, stated why the behaviors were not reported:

Because everyone tolerated him because his book of business was really big and he was a good . . . lawyer.

Another respondent stated:

> *As a rule, many of the attorneys I worked for or with did not have good leadership or training skills and would make associates or others miserable while trying to train them. Just accepted that was the way it was.*

Some respondents described senior partners who seemed to use the humiliation of others as a tactic, observing that even where managing partners spoke to the offending lawyers, nothing changed.

Several female respondents noted incidents of sexualized behaviors. One respondent described having to continually ignore a partner's "intense" behaviors:

> *Partner was basically a good person who looked at my chest, not my eyes, a little too often.*

In another example of a male partner treating women in a demeaning way, the respondent described reaching out to a member of the large firm's leadership as well as the HR Department. The firm leader dismissed the concerns and HR did not follow up.

Humiliating behaviors sometimes took the form of publicly undermining the skills or capabilities of another attorney. For a number of female survey respondents, this happened when they were told that they were only being included in a meeting or assigned to a case because of their looks or because they needed a woman on the team. In one example, such a statement was overheard by a male partner who then reported the incident to the managing partner. The firm followed up with a clear reprimand that included the actions that would be taken if such an incident happened again.

Not all of the offending behaviors came from men. Some respondents described incidents where women partners humiliated others in the firm. In one such incident, the recipient of the berating behaviors was assigned to other partners; in another instance, efforts to speak to the partner failed to result in changed behaviors. Another respondent reported a successful resolution to a female partner's efforts to humiliate others:

> *I had a supervising attorney who would humiliate the other female attorneys; in retrospect she saw other females as threats. I confronted her about it, and she stopped.*

It is interesting to note that a few respondents challenged the notion that there might be something wrong with using humiliation as a tactic to address someone's mistakes. For example, one respondent stated:

> *It is not uncommon to be humiliated in the practice of law when things go wrong, and you have made a mistake on the part of a client. We should be humiliated when we screw up.*

Another observed:

> *Isn't the culture of a law firm to be highly critical and demanding? It's the culture—sink or swim.*

A few others seemed resigned to the idea that being a lawyer meant being part of a harsh culture. One respondent stated:

> *One of the senior partners would yell at me and at others as part of his "management style." It was not necessary to report it because it was widely witnessed and experienced by many people in the firm.*

11. Has anyone ever spoken with you about their concerns regarding workplace behavior that made them feel uncomfortable?

Of those who responded to this question, nearly a third said others had spoken to them about workplace behaviors that made them feel uncomfortable. Of these, approximately 62% stated that these conversations occurred between 2010 and 2018.

Question 11	Percentage
Yes	31.37%
No	68.63%

As with most other questions, the highest percentage of the respondents were Associates (approximately 44%). It is interesting to note that 20% of the Partners responded affirmatively—more than in any other question. This suggests that people in the workplace who share their stories may be seeking support from more senior level individuals.

Nearly 38% of the respondents who provided information about the size of their firm at the time of the incident were in firms of fewer than 50 lawyers. Approximately half were in firms of 100 lawyers or more, somewhat higher than the percentage reported in response to other questions.

Among those responding to this question, the percentage of respondents who reported was similar to the percentage of respondents who did not.

Reported	Percentage
No	50.44%
Yes	49.56%

Examples of Behaviors Included in Survey Responses to Question 11

Examples of behaviors described in the responses included:

- Colleagues sharing examples of being sexually harassed, sexually assaulted, or propositioned by partners in the firm (including incidents involving partners and summer associates).
- Colleagues sharing examples of experiencing homophobia.
- Colleagues sharing negative comments made about women becoming pregnant and having children.
- Colleagues sharing stories among each other about which partners to avoid.
- Summer associates sharing examples of inappropriate behaviors they experienced.

Respondents' Perspectives on Reporting Behaviors

Generally, respondents stated that they did not further report information shared by colleagues. For example, a respondent noted that a colleague had been the frequent target of sexual harassment by a partner, but the respondent did not report the behavior:

> *I feared being retaliated against, and I thought the colleague would also be retaliated against.*

A respondent stated that female colleagues shared their discomfort with having to thwart explicit advances from senior colleagues, then noted why the respondent did not further report these incidents:

> *It was not my story to tell.*

Several stated that anecdotes were shared in confidence. For example, a respondent honored the request of a colleague to not report that person's uncomfortable experiences with homophobic comments in the workplace:

> *My colleague asked me not to report it for personal reasons.*

The sharing of information among colleagues, in many instances, seemed to be part of the workaround, as this response exemplified:

> *Associates talked among ourselves; "whisper network" regarding specific partners to avoid or be careful around. Was culture of large law firm life.*

Another reported:

> *Associates would talk amongst themselves about which partners were the ones that were desirable to work for and which ones you wanted to avoid working for because of the poor treatment you would receive. It was known behavior in the firm from everyone else that had advanced through the partnership.*

A respondent commented on the many stories shared by colleagues about their uncomfortable situations:

> *I mainly played a listening role as my colleagues just wanted someone to talk to because they feared retaliation if they reported anything.*

When attorneys exhibited patterns of negative behavior, it frequently became common knowledge within the firm. Yet respondents often noted that no steps were taken to address the concerns; for example:

> *Other associates were afraid of working with the same person who had bullied me. Everyone already knew this person was a problem and firm had chosen not to do anything about it.*

Another respondent described the importance of shared behaviors in an atmosphere where reporting was not an option:

> *All of the women in the office knew that certain departments were a minefield and we all tried to work around it. . . . When does the firm become responsible for its persistent problems in not properly addressing the behavior?*

In some instances, respondent stated that friends at work discussed being bullied or propositioned, but did not report the behaviors:

> *The incidents weren't disturbing enough to report.*

A respondent commented on involvement in an investigation of a senior partner who made sexual overtures to young women:

> *There was a formal investigation. Senior partner-man—had clearly engaged in alleged behavior. The firm did more to keep young women away from him but there was no loss of stature for this person.*

One respondent offered a glimpse into the behaviors that colleagues endure and the varied responses:

> *Stressed, overworked, and/or unhappy partners demeaning others, not privately. I console and counsel them, sometimes report to HR, sometimes confront perpetrator.*

Another respondent followed up after young women expressed annoyance with the leering behaviors of male partners:

> *I spoke with a female partner on the firm's management committee. Not sure if anything happened but tend to doubt it.*

Some respondents intervened and described positive results. One explained the follow-up after a female associate shared comments made to her by a partner about her appearance:

> *I went to the senior partner, who was the offender, and told him that his behavior and comments were inappropriate and offensive, that he was not to make any further comments of that nature, and that he was to apologize to the associate.*

A respondent was told by an intern of a partner's sexual comments. The respondent spoke with the managing partner, who took immediate action against the partner. Another sought and received permission to report a colleague's experiences of being bullied.

One respondent offered an example of a reporting process that worked in response to a partner's inappropriate joking:

> *As a member of the firm's Management Committee I responded to the associate's complaint, reached out to the Partner in charge . . . and confirmed that the firm's sexual harassment committee would address the complaint. I received confirmation that the associate was satisfied with the committee's response and did not want to further pursue the complaint.*

In another example, a respondent stated that a colleague expressed concern about someone in the office making a racially discriminatory comment. The respondent noted:

I reported this to HR . . . and to a member of the firm's Diversity Committee. HR and the member of the Diversity Committee had follow-up conversations with the [person who raised the concerns].

One respondent described supporting a colleague who reported inappropriate comments made by men in the firm:

She reported it, I supported her, and we addressed this generally in anti-harassment training at the firm.

A respondent highlighted a number of ways of responding to concerns:

Our firm has a code of conduct - mostly unwritten originally, but more formal now. We have also mentors for attorneys and supervisors for staff, as well as currently formal HR procedures. On an irregular basis, associates, partners, paralegals, and support staff speak to me about concerns. I counsel them on how to deal with the concerns. Sometimes I intercede. Sometimes I initiate involvement by our HR folks. In egregious situations, or repeated situations, I go to HR. . . . In some situations, I raise the issue during evaluations. In some situations, I discuss the situation with another colleague. In some situations, I have a one-on-one meeting with the individual who caused the situation.

12. At the time of any incident(s) described above, did the firm have a process for reporting behaviors of concern?

The respondents provided a range of responses that lend greater insight to the challenges that firms face in addressing the issues identified in this survey. Only slightly more than one-third of the respondents to this question said that, at the time of incidents described in other responses to this survey, their firm had a process for reporting behaviors; approximately 20% said their firms did not. Of particular interest, close to half did not know whether the firm did or did not have a reporting process at the time.

Question 12	Percentage
Yes	35.14%
No	19.2%
Don't Know	45.65%

Many respondents reported that they had a sexual harassment policy made available to all, but did not further describe a process for resolving complaints. Others, as noted below, highlighted a variety of initial reporting mechanisms, but did not provide a description of the subsequent steps that would be taken after the report is made. It is, however, understandable that respondents to a survey would only provide minimal detail in response to an open-ended question.

For example, many said the firm had a committee to which complaints about inappropriate workplace conduct can be reported. Others stated that the firm had in place a rapid response team for such matters, and a few said the firm had an ombudsman to whom any type of matter could be reported.

Several said that complaints were to be directed to specific named supervisors or to the Human Resources Department. Some respondents noted that they had designated partners to address complaints. Others required reports to be made to practice group leaders or to the managing partner. A few respondents said that reports could be made to anyone in the firm with whom the complainant felt comfortable.

Some respondents indicated that the firm offered a number of different avenues for bringing concerns forward, for example:

We have always had a process for reporting violations of firm policy, including anti-discrimination and anti-harassment policies, which provided multiple routes for reporting. Also there has always been a strict anti-retaliation policy.

Another respondent created an alternative where the firm's process did not provide a point of contact that felt comfortable:

The process was to speak to the Managing Partner or another designated partner at the time. I was new to the firm and did not feel comfortable with either partner, so I went to a partner who I felt more comfortable with.

One respondent observed a discrepancy between firm policy and practice that should be cautionary to others:

It's on paper, but in reality . . . we know what the reality was. Partners would go for "sensitivity training." After they came back, they were deemed "cleaned up" until they did it again. It created a laissez faire top down culture.

13. If you are currently working in a law firm, does the firm have an internal process for reporting behaviors of concern?

As with responses to question 12, a significant number of respondents did not know if their firm has an internal process for reporting.

Question 13	Percentage
Yes	47.62%
No	13.16%
Don't know	39.2%

The responses to question 13 were similar to the responses to question 12. Respondents described a variety of reporting avenues within the firm that included one or a combination of: managing partners, management committees, standing committees or other designated groups for addressing complaints, HR departments, practice group leaders, firm administrators, specific partners, and office managers. In a few instances, respondents stated that a reporting mechanism was through partner mentors or other trusted partners.

Few respondents provided information about what happens after a complaint is made. In one instance, the respondent expressed concern about the designated individual:

> *The process involves speaking to the head of the non-attorney staff. However, I am not aware that she ever did anything to address any of the ... behaviors, and her judgment is suspect.*

In a couple of other examples, however, the respondent expressed a more positive view of the process; for example:

> *The behavior would be reported to HR who would then handle the situation. We have a zero tolerance policy so presumably, that person would be fired if found true.*

Another stated:

> *There is a standing committee with a variety of individuals (different genders, sexual orientations, positions in firm, etc.) who you can report any incident to. A discussion is held as to consequences. Any concerns are raised to the executive committee. Then actions are considered based on the victims' wishes and the firm's policies.*

Recommendations

Consistent with what is reported in the media about other workplace settings, inappropriate behaviors remain an ongoing challenge in law firms as well. The survey results further demonstrate that these behaviors are a particular challenge for young women entering the work force. Moreover, unchecked power imbalances can leave those who serve in subordinate roles vulnerable to a range of negative behaviors.

We cannot know how many careers have been thwarted by workplaces that allow—through tacit acceptance, willful ignorance, or simply neglect—negative behaviors to continue unrestrained. We do know, however, that the results can be devastating to careers and economically harmful to those organizations that leave themselves vulnerable to disengaged and distracted employees, rampant turnover, and possible lawsuits.

Every law firm has an obligation to provide a culture in which people can do their jobs in a safe and respectful environment. The following recommendations offer a road map toward achieving that result.

[NOTE: Recommendations have been incorporated into and expanded upon in Chapter 8.]

Conclusion

The survey yielded several striking findings. First—and no surprise when the survey is viewed in comparison to other organizations, corporations, and industries—is that the majority of the negative behaviors described arose from those in authority who misused their power. Nearly all of the anecdotes reported described events that happened to younger people, where the perpetrator was more senior and, frequently, among the more powerful persons in the firm.

In such circumstances where the source of the negative conduct was a senior partner or firm leader, there was no place for the victim to turn for support or remedial measures. Fear of retaliation and concern about loss of status and opportunity to advance within the firm loomed large.

As noted previously, a few respondents seemed resigned to a profession where humiliation was acceptable and a sink-or-swim culture an appropriate way to train lawyers. Those comments demonstrate how behaviors in the workplace are learned and how culture is perpetuated. It would be difficult to find a book for organization leaders that extols humiliation and bullying as a technique for success in the workplace.

Law firm partners are often placed in leadership roles as a result of their client development and lawyering skills. Talent development and management of people are not necessarily part of that same skill set. Accordingly, firms may choose to consider management courses for all of its leaders, to facilitate skill sets that bring out the best from those who come to work each day, wanting only to serve the firm's clients and live the best values of the legal profession.

We hope that lawyers see in this survey a way to help facilitate a culture of civility, respect, and inclusion.

Notes

Chapter 1

1. "ABC News/Washington Post Poll: Sexual Harassment," langerre-search.com, October 17, 2017, http://www.langerresearch.com/wp-content/uploads/1192a1SexualHarassment.pdf.

2. "New Global Poll: Significant Share of Men Believe Expecting Intimate Interactions, Sex from Employees is OK," care.org, March 8, 2018, https://www.care.org/newsroom/press/press-releases/new-global-poll-significant-share-men-believe-expecting-intimate.

3. Ibid.

4. Barbara Frankel and Stephanie Francis Ward, "Little Agreement between the Sexes on Tackling Harassment, Working Mother/ABA Journal Survey Finds," *ABA Journal*, July 24, 2018, http://www.abajournal.com/news/article/tackling_harassment_survey_women_men.

5. Chai R. Feldblum and Victoria A. Lipnic, U.S. Equal Employment Opportunity Commission, Preface for *Select Task Force on the Study of Harassment in the Workplace*, June 2016, https://www.eeoc.gov/eeoc/task_force/harassment/upload/report.pdf.

6. Ibid., 9.

7. Joanna L. Grossman and Deborah L. Rhode, "Understanding Your Legal Options If You've Been Sexually Harassed," hbr.org, June 22, 2017, https://hbr.org/2017/06/understanding-your-legal-options-if-youve-been-sexually-harassed.

8. 500 Women Scientists Leadership, "When It Comes to Sexual Harassment, Academia Is Fundamentally Broken," blogs.scientificamerican.com,

August 9, 2018, https://blogs.scientificamerican.com/voices/when-it-comes-to-sexual-harassment-academia-is-fundamentally-broken/.

9. Ibid.

10. Margery Eagan, "Why Is Clarence Thomas Still on the Supreme Court?" *Boston Globe*, April 23, 2018, https://www.bostonglobe.com/opinion/2018/04/22/why-clarence-thomas-still-supreme-court/Jbf BaClpmBcPKy16TmhHAL/story.html.

11. Harriet Sinclair, "Video: Brett Kavanaugh's 'Whatever Happens at Georgetown Prep Stays at Georgetown Prep' Comment Comes Back to Haunt Him," Newsweek.com, September 19, 2018, https://www.newsweek.com/brett-kavanaugh-whatever-happens-georgetown-prep-stays-georgetown-prep-1127391.

12. In January, 2019, two republican women were appointed to the Senate Judiciary Committee for the first time in history. See, e.g. Alice Miranda Ollstein, "Blackburn, Ernst Become First Senate Women to Serve On GOP Judiciary," Politico, January 2, 2019, https://www.politico.com/story/2019/01/02/blackburn-ernst-become-first-gop-women-to-serve-on-senate-judiciary-1033118.

13. Deborah Epstein and Lisa A. Goodman, "Discounting Women: Doubting Domestic Violence Survivors' Credibility and Dismissing Their Experiences," *University of Pennsylvania Law Review* 167 (2019):1.

14. Ibid., 2.

15. Vicki Schultz, "Open Statement on Sexual Harassment from Employment Discrimination Law Scholars," *Stanford Law Review Online* 71, no. 17 (2018): 18–43, https://www.stanfordlawreview.org/online/open-statement-on-sexual-harassment-from-employment-discrimination-law-scholars/, at 19. They further cited to research (at 33) demonstrating that "managers who are given unfettered, discretionary authority over subordinates are more likely to abuse it" and that the "problem is exacerbated when those who occupy such positions are 'stars' with high value to the organization."

16. Ibid., 24.

17. David C. Yamada, "Crafting a Legislative Response to Workplace Bullying," *Employee Rights and Employment Policy Journal* 8, no. 2 (2004), at 476.

18. Eve Ensler, "A Letter to White Women Who Support Brett Kavanaugh," Time.com, October 4, 2018, http://time.com/5415254/white-women-brett-kavanaugh-donald-trump/.

19. Chai R. Feldblum and Victoria A. Lipnic, U.S. Equal Employment Opportunity Commission, Select Task Force on the Study of Harassment in the Workplace (June 2016). See #5, at 19.

20. Ibid., 17–18.

21. David C. Yamada, "Crafting a Legislative Response to Workplace Bullying," *Employee Rights and Employment Policy Journal* 8, no. 2 (2004), at 480.

22. Ibid., 481.

23. "How Saying #MeToo Changed Their Lives," *New York Times*, June 28, 2018, https://www.nytimes.com/interactive/2018/06/28/arts/metoo-movement-stories.html.

24. "Penn State Scandal Fast Facts," cnn.com, March 28, 2018, https://www.cnn.com/2013/10/28/us/penn-state-scandal-fast-facts/index.html.

Chapter 2

25. Amy Brittain and Irin Carmon, "Charlie Rose's Misconduct Was Widespread at CBS and Three Managers Were Warned, Investigation Finds," *Boston Globe*, May 3, 2018, https://www.bostonglobe.com/news/nation/2018/05/03/charlie-rose-misconduct-was-widespread-cbs-and-three-managers-were-warned-investigation-finds/MAuQcszq7d81MAPpedpE1I/story.html.

26. Ronan Farrow, "As Leslie Moonves Negotiates His Exit from CBS, Six Women Raise New Assault and Harassment Claims," newyorker.com, September 9, 2018, https://www.newyorker.com/news/news-desk/as-leslie-moonves-negotiates-his-exit-from-cbs-women-raise-new-assault-and-harassment-claims.

27. James B. Stewart, Rachel Abrams, and Ellen Gabler, "'If Bobbie Talks, I'm Finished': How Les Moonves Tried to Silence an Accuser," *New York Times*, November 28, 2018, https://www.nytimes.com/2018/11/28/business/les-moonves-bobbie-phillips-marv-dauer-cbs-severance.html.

28. Rachel Abrams and Edmund Lee, "Les Moonves Obstructed Investigation into Misconduct Claims, Report Says," *New York Times*, December 4, 2018, https://www.nytimes.com/2018/12/04/business/media/les-moonves-cbs-report.html.

29. Mary Childs, "How Les Moonves' Zero Severance Could Be a Turning Point in Harassment Suits," Barron's, December 21, 2018, https://www.barrons.com/articles/how-les-moonves-severance-could-change-the-math-of-sexual-harassment-suits-51545440338.

30. "NBC News Workplace Investigation," https://static01.nyt.com/files/2018/business/NBC_News_Workplace_Investigation.pdf.

31. Ramin Setoodeh and Elizabeth Wagmeister, "Matt Lauer Accused of Sexual Harassment by Multiple Women (EXCLUSIVE),"

Variety, November 29, 2017, https://variety.com/2017/biz/news/matt-lauer-accused-sexual-harassment-multiple-women-1202625959/.

32. Yuki Noguchi, "Fox News Turmoil Highlights Workplace Culture's Role in Sexual Harassment," npr.org, April 19, 2017, https://www.npr.org/2017/04/19/524751613/fox-news-turmoil-highlights-workplace-cultures-role-in-sexual-harassment.

33. Susan Antilla, "How Wall Street Keeps Outrageous Gender Bias Quiet 20 Years After the Boom-Boom Room," thestreet.com, June 4, 2016, https://www.thestreet.com/story/13590242/1/how-wall-street-keeps-outrageous-gender-bias-quiet-20-years-after-the-boom-boom-room.html.

34. Wendi S. Lazar, Executive Editor, ABA Commission on Women in the Profession, *Zero Tolerance: Best Practices for Combating Sex-Based Harassment in the Legal Profession* (Chicago: American Bar Association, 2018), 4.

35. Christian Berthelsen and Laura J. Keller, "BofA Settles Gender-Bias Lawsuit with Ex-Managing Director," Bloomberg, September 21, 2016, https://www.bloomberg.com/news/articles/2016-09-21/bofa-managing-director-s-gender-bias-suit-withdrawn-from-court.

36. Matthew Goldstein, "Morgan Stanley Settles Sex-Discrimination Case for $54 Million," thestreet.com, July 12, 2004, https://www.thestreet.com/story/10170443/1/morgan-stanley-settles-sex-discrimination-case-for-54-million.html.

37. Dune Lawrence and Max Abelson, "Sue Goldman Sachs, You Have to Be Willing to Hang On—For a Long, Long Time," Bloomberg, May 3, 2018, https://www.bloombergquint.com/business/to-sue-goldman-sachs-you-have-to-be-willing-to-hang-onfor-a-long-long-time#gs.siQAKfk.

38. Ibid.

39. Alison Coil, "Why Men Don't Believe in the Data on Gender Bias in Science," wired.com, August 25, 2017, https://www.wired.com/story/why-men-dont-believe-the-data-on-gender-bias-in-science/.

40. Ibid.

41. Alice H. Wu, "Gender Stereotyping in Academia: Evidence from Economic Job Marker Rumors Forum," August 2017, https://drive.google.com/file/d/0BwjFN4HbBrDBbnFqZzdLWThDb0U/view.

42. Ibid., 25.

43. Ibid., 26.

44. Ibid.

45. Ibid. A *New York Times* article about the significance of this study observed: "The underrepresentation of women in top university economics departments is already well documented, but it has been difficult to evaluate

claims about workplace culture because objectionable conversations rarely occur in the open. Whispered asides at the water cooler are hard to observe, much less measure"; Justin Wolfers, "Evidence of a Toxic Environment for Women in Economics," *New York Times*, August 18, 2017, https://www .nytimes.com/2017/08/18/upshot/evidence-of-a-toxic-environment-for-women-in-economics.html.

46. Kathryn Clancy, Katharine Lee, Erica M. Rodgers, and Christina Richey, "Double Jeopardy in Astronomy and Planetary Science: Women of Color Face Greater Risks of Gendered and Racial Harassment," *Journal of Geophysical Research: Planets* 122, no. 7 (2017): 1619–20.

47. Paula A. Johnson, Sheila E. Widnall, and Frazier F. Benya, eds., *Sexual Harassment of Women: Climate, Culture, and Consequences in Academic Sciences, Engineering, and Medicine* (Washington DC: National Academies Press, 2018), 68. https://www.nap.edu/catalog/24994/sexual-harassment-of-women-climate-culture-and-consequences-in-academic.

48. Daisuke Wakabayashi and Katie Benner, "How Google Protected Andy Rubin, the 'Father of Android,'" *New York Times*, October 25, 2018, https:// www.nytimes.com/2018/10/25/technology/google-sexual-harassment-andy-rubin.html.

49. Ibid.

50. Jillian D'Onfro, "Google Walkouts Showed What the New Tech Resistance Looks Like, with Lots of Cues From Union Organizing," CNBC.com, November 3, 2018, https://www.cnbc.com/2018/11/03/google-employee-protests-as-part-of-new-tech-resistance.html.

51. See, e.g., Terry D. Stratton, Margaret A. McLaughlin, Florence M. Witte, Sue E. Fosson, and Lois Margaret Nora, "Does Students' Exposure to Gender Discrimination and Sexual Harassment in Medical School Affect Specialty Choice and Residency Program Selection?" *Academic Medicine* 80, no. 4 (2005); Ying Zhuge, Joyce Kaufman, Diane Simeone, Herbert Chen, and Omaida Velazquez, "Is There Still a Glass Ceiling for Women in Academic Surgery?" *Annals of Surgery* 253, no. 4 (2011).

52. Ibid., 407.

53. Liz Kowalczyk, "How A Crude Photo from a Boston Surgeon Roiled the Medical World," *Boston Globe*, January 12, 2018, https://www.boston-globe.com/metro/2018/01/11/how-crude-photo-from-boston-surgeon-roiled-medical-world/uPJs9uNW8vauKOvmRZDb2N/story.html.

54. Elizabeth Chuck, "#MeToo in Medicine: Women, Harassed in Hospitals and Operating Rooms, Await Reckoning," nbcnews.com, February 20, 2018, https://www.nbcnews.com/storyline/sexual-misconduct/

harassed-hospitals-operating-rooms-women-medicine-await-their-metoo-moment-n846031.

55. Christopher G. Myers and Kathleen M. Sutcliffe, "How Discrimination Against Female Doctors Hurts Patients," *Harvard Business Review* (August 30, 2018), https://hbr.org/2018/08/how-discrimination-against-female-doctors-hurts-patients.

56. Chessy Prout, *I Have the Right To: A High School Survivor's Story of Sexual Assault, Justice, and Hope* (New York: Simon & Schuster Children's Publishing, 2018), 69.

57. Cherise Leclerc, "Phillips Exeter Releases New Report on Sexual Misconduct Allegations," wmur.com, August 24, 2018, https://www.wmur.com/article/phillips-exeter-releases-new-report-on-sexual-misconduct-allegations/22827273.

58. Selim Algar, "Prep School Turned Blind Eye to Sexual Misconduct for Decades: Report," nypost.com, August 24, 2018, https://nypost.com/2018/08/24/prep-school-turned-blind-eye-to-sexual-misconduct-for-decades-report/.

59. Ibid.

60. Amos Kamil, "Prep-School Predators: The Horace Mann School's Secret History of Sexual Abuse," nytimes.com, June 6, 2012, https://www.nytimes.com/2012/06/10/magazine/the-horace-mann-schools-secret-history-of-sexual-abuse.html.

61. "Accusations of Sex Abuse at Boarding School," abcnews.com, August 31, 2018, https://abcnews.go.com/2020/story?id=124035&page=1.

62. Katie J. M. Baker, "Here's The Powerful Letter the Stanford Victim Read to Her Attacker," Buzzfeednews.com, June 3, 2016, https://www.buzzfeednews.com/article/katiejmbaker/heres-the-powerful-letter-the-stanford-victim-read-to-her-ra#.trgR8Q5Xz.

63. Sam Levin, "Stanford Sexual Assault: Read the Full Text of the Judge's Controversial Decision," theguardian.com, June 14, 2016, https://www.theguardian.com/us-news/2016/jun/14/stanford-sexual-assault-read-sentence-judge-aaron-persky. Two years after Judge Persky sentenced Brock Turner, he was removed from his position in a recall election.

64. Christina Cauterucci, "Brock Turner's Father Sums Up Rape Culture in One Brief Statement," slate.com, June 5, 2016, https://slate.com/human-interest/2016/06/brock-turners-dads-defense-proves-why-his-victim-had-to-write-her-letter.html.

65. "Gallery: Larry Nassar's Victims, an 'Army of Survivors,'" *Sports Illustrated*, February 22, 2018, https://www.si.com/more-sports/2018/02/22/larry-nassar-victims-photo-gallery.

66. Will Hobson, "Ex-USA Gymnastics President Steve Penny Indicated on Tampering Charges," *Washington Post*, October 18, 2018, https://www .washingtonpost.com/sports/olympics/ex-usa-gymnastics-president-steve-penny-indicted-on-tampering-charges/2018/10/18/3cde8d54-d287-11e8-8c22-fa2ef74bd6d6_story.html?utm_term=.6d0287d6531a.

67. Dan Murphy, "USA Gymnastics Files for Bankruptcy as Part of 'Reorganization,'" ESPN.com, December 6, 2018, http://www.espn.com/ olympics/story/_/id/25461239/usa-gymnastics-files-chapter-11-bankruptcy-petition.

68. Paula Lavigne and Nicole Noren, "OTL: Michigan State Secrets Extend Far Beyond Larry Nassar Case," espn.com, February 1, 2018, http://www .espn.com/espn/story/_/id/22214566/pattern-denial-inaction-information-suppression-michigan-state-goes-larry-nassar-case-espn.

69. Kim Kozlowski, "What MSU Knew: 14 Were Warned of Nassar Abuse," detroitnews.com, January 18, 2018, https://www.detroitnews.com/story/ tech/2018/01/18/msu-president-told-nassar-complaint-2014/1042071001/.

70. Tracy Connor and Sarah Fitzpatrick, "Gymnastics Scandal: 8 Times Larry Nassar Could Have Been Stopped," nbcnews.com, January 25, 2018, https://www.nbcnews.com/news/us-news/gymnastics-scandal-8-times-larry-nassar-could-have-been-stopped-n841091.

71. Joan McPhee and James P. Dowden, *Report of the Independent Investigation: The Constellation of Factors Underlying Larry Nassar's Abuse of Athletes* (December 10, 2018), 2–3, https://www.nassarinvestigation.com/en.

72. Katie Sharp, "NFL Announces New Domestic Violence Policy," sbnation.com, August 28, 2014, https://www.sbnation.com/nfl/2014/8/28/6079465/ nfl-announces-new-domestic-violence-policy.

73. "NFL Player Arrests," usatoday.com, https://www.usatoday.com/ sports/nfl/arrests/.

74. Deborah Epstein, "I'm Done Helping the NFL Pay Lip Service to Domestic Violence Prevention," *Washington Post*, June 5, 2018, https://www .washingtonpost.com/opinions/im-done-helping-the-nfl-pay-lip-service-to-domestic-violence-prevention/2018/06/05/1b470bec-6448-11e8-99d2-0d678ec08c2f_story.html?utm_term=.abf4f6cfb316.

75. Lyle Moran, "Proving Her Mettle: Olympic Medal-Winning Attorney Fights Sexual Abuse and Discrimination in Athletics," *ABA Journal*, November 2018, http://www.abajournal.com/magazine/article/ olympic_attorney_abuse_discrimination_athletics.

76. *Morrison v. Northern Essex Community College*, 56 Mass. App. Ct. 784, 788 (2002).

77. Max Walters, "Baker McKenzie 'Regrets' Shortcomings in Sexual Misconduct Investigation," lawgazette.co.uk, October 11, 2018, https://www.lawgazette.co.uk/practice/baker-mckenzie-regrets-shortcomings-in-sexual-misconduct-investigation/5067900.article. *See also*: Staci Zaretsky, "Biglaw Firm Under Investigation for Failing to Disclose Partner's Alleged Sexual Assault to Regulators," abovethelaw.com, February 6, 2018, https://abovethelaw.com/2018/02/biglaw-firm-under-investigation-for-failing-to-disclose-partners-alleged-sexual-assault-to-regulators/; "Exclusive: Top Baker McKenzie Partner Sexually Assaulted Associate," rollonfriday.com, February 2018, http://www.rollonfriday.com/TheNews/EuropeNews/tabid/58/Id/5522/fromTab/36/currentIndex/0/Default.aspx.

78. *Weeks v. Baker & McKenzie*, 63 Cal. App. 4th 1128, 74 Cal. Rptr. 2d 510 (First Dist. 1998). *See also*: Mark Hansen, "Partner in Name Only: Lawyer's Suit Claims Age, Sex Discrimination Led to Loss of Choice Assignments," *ABA Journal*, January 1992, https://books.google.com/books?id=B iOs6JxwVe0C&pg=PA26&lpg=PA26&dq=baker+mckenzie+ingrid+beall+l awsuit&source=bl&ots=SFAeykjpC9&sig=Sd9quV_XYdYXWJI9yf-3lWhyj CI&hl=en&sa=X&ved=2ahUKEwizqd6VlfreAhXLwVkKHdypAz4Q6AEw B3oECAEQAQ#v=onepage&q=baker%20mckenzie%20ingrid%20beall%20 lawsuit&f=false.

79. "Exclusive: Dentons Partner Quits After Sex Act Probe Finds Bad Behavior," rollonfriday.com, February 8, 2018, https://www.rollonfriday.com/news-content/exclusive-dentons-partner-quits-after-sex-act-probe-finds-bad-behaviour. *See also*: Kathryn Rubino, "Dentons Partner Out After Investigation into Misconduct," abovethelaw.com, February 9, 2018, https://abovethelaw.com/2018/02/dentons-partner-out-after-investigation-into-misconduct/.

80. *Krunali Parekh v. Dentons US LLP and Alton Delane*. Complaint filed in NY Supreme Court, NY County, Index No. 155465/2018 (filed June 11, 2018).

81. Roy Strom, "Dentons, Ex-Managing Director Defend Against #MeToo Harassment Claim," *American Lawyer*, July 24, 2018, https://www.law.com/americanlawyer/2018/07/24/dentons-managing-director-defend-against-metoo-harassment-claim/.

82. *Francine Friedman Griesing v. Greenberg Traurig, LLP*. Complaint filed in U.S. District Court, S.D.N.Y., No. 12 CV 8734 (filed December 3, 2012).

83. *Wendy Moore v. Jones Day*. Complaint filed in California Superior Court, San Francisco County (filed June 19, 2018).

84. Ibid.

85. Deborah Chang and Sonia Chopra, PhD, "Where Are All the Women Lawyers?" 360advocacy.com, October 29, 2015, https://www.360advocacy .com/wp-content/uploads/2015/10/ChangChopraArticle-1.pdf.

86. *Report of the Florida Bar Special Committee on Gender Bias* (Florida Bar: 2017) https://webprod.floridabar.org/wp-content/uploads/2017/06/ Special-Committee-on-Gender-Bias-Report-2017.pdf.

87. Nicole VanderDoes, "The Judiciary Must Deal with #MeToo— and with What I Know," *ABA Journal*, February 13, 2018, http:// www.abajournal.com/voice/article/the_judiciary_must_deal_with_ metoo_and_with_what_i_know/.

88. Lorelei Laird, "California Judiciary Has Paid Nearly $645K in 6 Years for Gender-Based Misconduct Claims," www.abajournal.com, July 5, 2018, http://www.abajournal.com/news/article/records_show_ california_judicial_branch_has_paid_nearly_645k_in_six_years_o/.

89. Julie K. Brown, "How a Future Trump Cabinet Member Gave a Serial Sex Abuser the Deal of a Lifetime," *Miami Herald*, November 28, 2018, https://www.miamiherald.com/news/local/article220097825.html.

90. Margery Eagan, "Roger Ailes and His Ilk Hurt More Than the Women Who Worked for Them," *Boston Globe*, December 14, 2018, https://www .bostonglobe.com/opinion/2018/12/14/roger-ailes-and-his-ilk-hurt-more- than-women-who-worked-for-them/o4GmWfOSzS990ljpAlQIgL/story .html.

91. Linda Bloodworth Thomason, "'Designing Women' Creator Goes Public with Les Moonves War: Not All Harassment Is Sexual (Guest Column)," *Hollywood Reporter*, September 12, 2018, https://www.hollywoodreporter. com/news/designing-women-creator-les-moonves-not-all-harassment-is- sexual-1142448.

Chapter 3

92. Joanna Weiss, "Why Did #MeToo Only Catch on Now?" *Boston Globe*, March 19, 2018, https://www.bostonglobe.com/ideas/2018/03/19/ why-did-metoo-only-catch-now/rEnMA6Li8O5EQGzSHc3YFL/story. html?event=event12.

93. *Meritor Savings Bank, FSB v. Vinson*, 477 U.S. 57 (1986).

94. *Burlington Industries, Inc. v. Ellerth*, 524 U.S. 742 (1998); *Farragher v. City of Boca Raton*, 524 U.S. 775 (1998).

95. Nancy Gertner, "Losers' Rules," *Yale Law Journal* 122 (October 17, 2012), 110, https://www.yalelawjournal.org/forum/losers-rules.

96. Ibid.

97. Ibid., 115.

98. Yuki Noguchi, "Trainers, Lawyers Say Sexual Harassment Training Fails," NPR.org, November 8, 2017, https://www.npr.org/2017/11/08/562641787/trainers-lawyers-say-sexual-harassment-training-fails.

99. Vicki J. Magley and Joanna L. Grossman, "Do Sexual Harassment Prevention Trainings Really Work?" *Scientific American*, November 10, 2017, https://blogs.scientificamerican.com/observations/do-sexual-harassment-prevention-trainings-really-work/.

100. Chai R. Feldblum and Victoria A. Lipnic, U.S. Equal Employment Opportunity Commission, Select Task Force on the Study of Harassment in the Workplace (June 2016). See #5.

101. J. K. Trotter, "Top Huffington Post Editor Was Investigated for Sexual Harassment," *Gawker*, September 4, 2014, http://gawker.com/top-huffington-post-editor-was-investigated-for-sexual-1626614104.

102. Melanie Ehrenkranz, "Arianna Huffington Ignored Sexual Misconduct at the Huffington Post," Gizmodo, November 14, 2017, https://gizmodo.com/arianna-huffington-ignored-sexual-misconduct-at-the-huf-1820389889.

103. Ibid. The article quoted a source with knowledge of the investigation as stating that "HR protected Arianna and the company more than the employees."

104. Andrew Beaujon, "HuffPost Names New Managing Editor as Jimmy Soni Moves to India," Poynter, May 22, 2014, https://www.poynter.org/news/huffpost-names-new-managing-editor-jimmy-soni-moves-india.

105. J. K. Trotter, "Top Huffington Post Editor Was Investigated for Sexual Harassment." See #101.

106. Ibid.

107. Claire Zillman and Erika Fry, "HR Is Not Your Friend. Here's Why," *Fortune*, February 16, 2018, http://fortune.com/2018/02/16/microsoft-hr-problem-metoo/.

108. *Moussouris v. Microsoft Corp.*, Case No. 2:15-cv-01483-JLR (U.S. Dist. Ct., W.D. Wash.).

109. Deborah Epstein and Lisa A. Goodman, "Discounting Women: Doubting Domestic Violence Survivors' Credibility and Dismissing Their Experiences." See #13, at 43.

Chapter 4

110. Vincent J. Roscigno, "Power, Revisited," *Social Forces* 90, no. 2 (December 2011) 349-74, at 357.

111. Ibid., 358.

112. Ibid., 360.

113. Ibid., 364.

114. Malcolm Gladwell, *The Tipping Point: How Little Things Can Make a Big Difference* (New York: Little Brown and Company, 2000), 234.

115. Robert I. Sutton, "Memo to the CEO: Are You the Source of Workplace Dysfunction?" *McKinsey & Company*, September 2017, https://www.mckinsey.com/featured-insights/leadership/memo-to-the-ceo-are-you-the-source-of-workplace-dysfunction.

116. Jugal K. Patel, Troy Griggs, and Claire Cain Miller, "We Asked 615 Men About How They Conduct Themselves at Work," *New York Times*, December 28, 2018, https://www.nytimes.com/interactive/2017/12/28/upshot/sexual-harassment-survey-600-men.html.

117. Ibid.

118. Ibid.

119. Ibid.

120. Kristen P. Lindgren, Michele R. Parkhill, William H. George, and Christian S. Hendershot, "Gender Differences in Perceptions of Sexual Intent: A Qualitative Review and Integration," *Psychology of Women Quarterly* 32, no. 4 (2008): 436.

121. Rhiana Wegner and Antonia Abbey, "Individual Differences in Men's Misperception of Women's Sexual Intent: Application and Extension of the Confluence Model," *Elsevier Personality and Individual Differences* 94 (May 2016): 16–20.

122. Ibid., 17.

123. Ibid., 19.

124. Ibid., 20.

125. Emma C. Howell, Peter J. Etchells, and Ian S. Penton-Voak, "The Sexual Overperception Bias Is Associated with Sociosexuality," *Personality and Individual Difference* 53, no. 8 (December 2012): 1014.

126. Isabelle Engeler and Priya Raghubir, "Decomposing the Cross-Sex Misprediction Bias of Dating Behavior: Do Men Overestimate or Women Underreport Their Sexual Intentions?" *Journal of Personality and Social Psychology* 114, no. 1 (2017): 104.

127. Jonathan W. Kunstman, "Sexual Overperception: Power, Mating Motives, and Biases in Social Judgment," *Journal of Personality and Social Psychology* 100, no. 2 (February 2011), 10.

128. See e.g., Kristen N. Jozkowski, Zoë D. Peterson, Stephanie A. Sanders, Barbara Dennis, and Michael Reece, "Gender Differences in Heterosexual College Students' Conceptualizations and Indicators of Sexual

Consent: Implications for Contemporary Sexual Assault Prevention Education," *Journal of Sex Research* 51, no. 8 (2014): 904–16.

129. Ibid., 913.

130. Ibid., 914.

131. Ibid., 913.

132. Ibid., 913. For an interesting analysis of the importance of "careful attention to the use of the language of consent when discussing sexual violence prevention" and the need for a "clear distinction between the term and concept underlying the word itself," *see* Melanie Ann Beres, "Rethinking the Concept of Consent for Anti-Sexual Violence Activism and Education," *Feminism & Psychology* 24, no. 3 (2014): 385.

133. Jennifer L. Berdahl, "Harassment Based on Sex: Protecting Social Status in the Context of Gender Hierarchy," *Academy of Management Review* 32, no. 2 (April 2007): 644.

134. Ibid.

135. Jennifer L. Berdahl, "The Sexual Harassment of Uppity Women," *Journal of Applied Psychology* 92, no. 2 (2007): 426.

136. Ibid., 434.

137. Rachel Arnow-Richman, "Of Power and Process: Handling Harassers in an At-Will World," *Yale Law Journal Forum* (June 18, 2018): 90.

138. Beth A. Quinn, "Sexual Harassment and Masculinity: The Power and Meaning of 'Girl Watching,'" *Gender & Society* 16, no. 3 (June 2002): 391–92.

139. Ibid., 399.

140. Ibid., 399.

141. Ibid., 400.

142. Vicki Schultz, "Reconceptualizing Sexual Harassment," *Yale Law Journal* 107 (1998): 1712.

143. Ibid., 1721.

144. Ibid., 1732.

145. Vicki Schultz, "Open Statement on Sexual Harassment from Employment Discrimination Law Scholars," citing to other scholarly works by, among others, Kimberle Crenshaw, Angela P. Harris, and Irene Brown and Joy Misra. See #15, at 29.

146. Dan Cassino, "Sexual Harassment Claims Have Fallen Among Young White Women, but Not Older Women or Black Women," hbr.org, February 21, 2018, https://hbr.org/2018/02/sexual-harassment-claims-have-fallen-among-young-white-women-but-not-older-women-or-black-women.

147. Nicole T. Buchanan and Alayne J. Ormerod, "Racialized Sexual Harassment in the Lives of African American Women," PsycNET, September 25, 2008, http://psycnet.apa.org/record/2002-11059-007, at 116.

148. Ibid.

149. Ibid.

150. Deborah Epstein and Lisa A. Goodman, "Discounting Women: Doubting Domestic Violence Survivors' Credibility and Dismissing Their Experiences." See #13, at 43.

151. Chai R. Feldblum and Victoria A. Lipnic, U.S. Equal Employment Opportunity Commission, Select Task Force on the Study of Harassment in the Workplace (June 2016). See #5, at 14.

152. *See, e.g.,* M.V. Lee Badgett, Holning Lau, Brad Sears, and Deborah Ho, "Bias in the Workplace: Consistent Evidence of Sexual Orientation and Gender Identify Discrimination," *The Williams Institute*, June 2007, https://cloudfront.escholarship.org/dist/prd/content/qt5h3731xr/qt5h3731xr.pdf?t=lnq17l.

153. Vicki Schultz, "Open Statement on Sexual Harassment from Employment Discrimination Law Scholars," referencing a number of studies analyzing the experiences of LGBTQ and transgender individuals in the workplace. See #15, at 26.

154. Vicki Schultz, "Reconceptualizing Sexual Harassment." See #142.

155. Collier Meyerson, "Sexual Assault When You're on the Margins: Can we All Say #MeToo?" *The Nation*, October 19, 2017, https://www.thenation.com/article/sexual-assault-when-youre-on-the-margins-can-we-all-say-metoo/.

156. Heather McLaughlin, Christopher Uggen, and Amy Blackstone, "Sexual Harassment, Workplace Authority, and the Paradox of Power," *American Sociological Review* 77, no. 4 (August 2012): 641.

157. Jan Wynen, "Sexual Harassment: The Nexus Between Gender and Workplace Authority: Evidence from the Australian Public Service," *Australian Journal of Public Administration* 75, no. 3 (September 2016): 355.

Chapter 5

158. J. T. Jost, L. Rudman, I. V. Blair, D. R. Carney, N. Dasgupta, J. Glaser, and C. Hardin, "The Existence of Implicit Bias Is Beyond Reasonable Doubt: A Refutation of Ideological and Methodological Objections and Executive Summary of Ten Studies That No Manager Should Ignore," *Research in Organizational Behavior* 29 (2009): 46.

159. Ibid., 50.

160. Lauren Stiller Rikleen, *Ending the Gauntlet: Removing Barriers to Women's Success in the Law* (Eagan, Minnesota: Thomson/Legalworks, 2006), 293.

161. Joanna Weiss, "Why Did #MeToo Only Catch on Now?" *Boston Globe*, March 19, 2018. See #92.

162. Laura Guillen, "Is the Confidence Gap Between Men and Women a Myth?" *Harvard Business Review*, March 26, 2018, https://hbr.org/2018/03/is-the-confidence-gap-between-men-and-women-a-myth.

163. Ibid.

164. Jennifer L. Berdahl, "The Sexual Harassment of Uppity Women," *Journal of Applied Psychology* 92, no. 2 (2007): 435.

165. Michael Housman and Dylan Minor, "Toxic Workers," *Harvard Business School*, Working Paper 16-057 (2015), 5, https://www.hbs.edu/faculty/Publication%20Files/16-057_d45c0b4f-fa19-49de-8f1b-4b12fe054fea.pdf.

166. Ibid., 23.

167. Ibid.

168. Chai R. Feldblum and Victoria A. Lipnic, U.S. Equal Employment Opportunity Commission, Select Task Force on the Study of Harassment in the Workplace (June 2016). See #5, at 24–25.

169. Jena McGregor, "How too Much Focus on 'Superstar' Workers Enables Harassment," *Washington Post*, December 19, 2018, https://www.washingtonpost.com/news/on-leadership/wp/2017/12/19/the-metoo-movement-is-a-warning-sign-about-the-star-system-at-many-companies/?utm_term=.7a3239ae6f40.

170. Emilio J. Castilla, "Gender, Race, and Meritocracy in Organizational Careers," *American Journal of Sociology* 113, no. 6 (May 2008), 1516.

171. Ibid., 1485.

172. Karen S. Lyness and Madeline E. Heilman, "When Fit Is Fundamental: Performance Evaluations and Promotions of Upper-Level Female and Male Managers," *Journal of Applied Psychology* 91, no. 4 (2006): 782.

173. Ibid., 783.

174. Ibid., 784.

175. Examples of the structural barriers that exist in the legal profession were described in detail by this author in *Ending the Gauntlet: Removing Barriers to Women's Success in the Law* (Eagan, Minnesota: Thomson/Legalworks, 2006).

176. Nicole M. Stephens and Cynthia S. Levine, "Opting Out or Denying Discrimination? How the Framework of Free Choice in American Society

Influences Perceptions of Gender Inequality," *Association for Psychological Science* 22, no. 10 (2011): 1233.

177. Ibid.

178. Ibid., 1235.

Chapter 6

179. Anna-Maria Marshall, "Idle Rights: Employees' Rights to Consciousness and the Construction of Sexual Harassment Policies," *Law & Society Review* 39, no. 1 (2005): 99.

180. Ibid., 100.

181. Ibid., 114–15.

182. Deborah Epstein and Lisa A. Goodman, "Discounting Women: Doubting Domestic Violence Survivors' Credibility and Dismissing Their Experiences." See #13, at 55–56.

183. Jonathan Brock, Billie Pirner Garde, and Marcia Narine Weldon, "What Exactly Is Zero Tolerance on Sexual Harassment?" *Boston Globe*, January 2, 2018, https://www.bostonglobe.com/opinion/2018/01/02/what-exactly-zero-tolerance-sexual-harassment/3mKqMjzMDll3UZqgWoXu7N/story.html.

184. Chai R. Feldblum and Victoria A. Lipnic, U.S. Equal Employment Opportunity Commission, Select Task Force on the Study of Harassment in the Workplace (June 2016). See #5, at 15.

185. Maura Dolan, "9th Circuit Judge Alex Kozinski Steps Down After Accusations of Sexual Misconduct," *Los Angeles Times*, December 18, 2017, http://www.latimes.com/politics/la-pol-ca-judge-alex-kozinski-20171218-story.html.

186. Dahlia Lithwick, "For 20 Years He Made Us All Victims and Accomplices," slate.com, December 13, 2017, http://www.slate.com/articles/news_and_politics/jurisprudence/2017/12/judge_alex_kozinski_made_us_all_victims_and_accomplices.html.

187. Lilia M. Cortina and Vicki J. Magley, "Raising Voice, Risking Retaliation: Events Following Interpersonal Mistreatment in the Workplace," *Journal of Occupational Health Psychology* 8, no. 4 (2003): 249.

188. Ibid., 260–61.

189. Ibid., 262.

190. Ibid.

191. Simine Vazire, "What Reporting Sexual Harassment Taught Me," slate.com, July 9, 2018, https://slate.com/technology/2018/07/what-reporting-sexual-harassment-taught-me.html.

192. 500 Women Scientists Leadership, "When It Comes to Sexual Harassment, Academia Is Fundamentally Broken," blogs.scientificamerican .com, August 9, 2018. See #8.

193. Chai R. Feldblum and Victoria A. Lipnic, U.S. Equal Employment Opportunity Commission, Select Task Force on the Study of Harassment in the Workplace (June 2016). See #5.

194. Sabrina I. Pacifici, "Powerful Women Talk About Power (and Powerlessness)," *New York Magazine*, October 2018, https://www .thecut.com/2018/10/women-and-power-introduction.html?_ga=2.13273265 .704594373.1544388552-2001917653.1544388552.

Chapter 7

195. Mark Shanahan, "Playwright Robert Brustein Angers Some with 'Witch Hunt' Reference on Facebook," *Boston Globe*, January 10, 2018, https://www.bostonglobe.com/lifestyle/names/2018/01/10/playwright-robert-brustein-angers-some-with-witch-hunt-reference-facebook/G1ULD-vri2v4q6ov5o2NL3L/story.html#comments.

196. Heather Mac Donald, "The Negative Impact of the #MeToo Movement," Imprimis, April 2018, https://imprimis.hillsdale.edu/ the-negative-impact-of-the-metoo-movement/.

197. Candace Bertotti and David Maxfield, "Most People Are Supportive of #MeToo. But Will Workplaces Actually Change?" *Harvard Business Review,* July 10, 2018, https://hbr.org/2018/07/most-people-are-supportive-of-metoo-but-will-workplaces-actually-change.

198. Claire Cain Miller, "Unintended Consequences of Sexual Harassment Scandals," *New York Times*, October 9, 2017, https://www.nytimes .com/2017/10/09/upshot/as-sexual-harassment-scandals-spook-men-it-can-backfire-for-women.html.

199. Ibid.

200. Vivia Chen, "The Backlash Is Building," *American Lawyer* (November 2018).

201. Katherine Tarbox, "Is #MeToo Backlash hurting Women's Opportunities in Finance?" hbr.org, March 12, 2018, https://hbr.org/2018/03/ is-metoo-backlash-hurting-womens-opportunities-in-finance.

202. Sandra F. Sperino and Suja A. Thomas, *Unequal: How America's Courts Undermine Discrimination Law* (New York: Oxford University Press, 2017).

203. Ibid., 143, 145.

204. Heather Mac Donald, "The Negative Impact of the #MeToo Movement." See #196.

205. Melvyn Krauss, "Why More Women Are Winning at Symphonies' Musical chairs," *Denver Post*, July 28, 2016, https://www.denverpost.com/2016/07/28/why-more-women-are-winning-at-symphonies-musical-chairs/.

206. Heather Mac Donald, "The Negative Impact of the #MeToo Movement." See #196.

Chapter 8

207. "Why Diversity Matters," Catalyst Information Center, July 2013, https://www.catalyst.org/system/files/why_diversity_matters_catalyst_0.pdf.

208. Chai R. Feldblum and Victoria A. Lipnic, U.S. Equal Employment Opportunity Commission, Select Task Force on the Study of Harassment in the Workplace (June 2016). See #5, at 31.

209. Candace Bertotti and David Maxfield, "Most People Are Supportive of #MeToo. But Will Workplaces Actually Change?" See #197.

210. Paula A. Johnson, Sheila E. Widnall, and Frazier F. Benya, eds., *Sexual Harassment of Women: Climate, Culture, and Consequences in Academic Sciences, Engineering, and Medicine.* See #47.

211. Wendi S. Lazar, Executive Editor, ABA Commission on Women in the Profession, *Zero Tolerance: Best Practices for Combating Sex-Based Harassment in the Legal Profession*, at 53. See #34.

212. Chai R. Feldblum and Victoria A. Lipnic, U.S. Equal Employment Opportunity Commission, Select Task Force on the Study of Harassment in the Workplace, June 2016. See #5, at 31.

213. Ibid., 32.

214. Candace Bertotti and David Maxfield, "Most People Are Supportive of #MeToo. But Will Workplaces Actually Change?" See #197.

215. Dina Gerdeman, "Sexual Harassment: What Employers Should Do Now," *Harvard Business School*, April 11, 2018, https://hbswk.hbs.edu/item/sexual-harassment-what-employers-should-do-next.

216. Vicki Schultz, "Open Statement on Sexual Harassment from Employment Discrimination Law Scholars." See #15, at 32–33.

217. Robert I. Sutton, "Memo to the CEO: Are You the Source of Workplace Dysfunction?" See #115.

218. Stephanie Scharf, "Report of a National Survey of Women's Initiatives: The Strategy, Structure and Scope of Women's Initiatives in Law Firms"

(The NAWL Foundation, November 2012), https://www.nawl.org/p/cm/ld/fid=82.

219. Joanna L. Grossman and Deborah L. Rhode, "Understanding Your Legal Options If You've Been Sexually Harassed," hbr.org, June 22, 2017. See #7.

220. Chai R. Feldblum and Victoria A. Lipnic, U.S. Equal Employment Opportunity Commission, Select Task Force on the Study of Harassment in the Workplace, June 2016. See #5, at 34–35.

221. Dina Gerdeman, "Sexual Harassment: What Employers Should Do Now." See #215.

222. Vicki Schultz, "Open Statement on Sexual Harassment from Employment Discrimination Law Scholars." Critically, this article also called (at 31) for harassment policies and training to be "linked to larger plans to eliminate race, race/sex, and other forms of intersectional discrimination and to facilitate full and equal inclusion of women and men of all races into all jobs at every level throughout the organization, especially top positions." See #15, at 25.

223. Rachel Arnow-Richman, "Of Power and Process: Handling Harassers in an At-Will World," *Yale Law Journal Forum* (June 18, 2018): 101.

224. Wendi S. Lazar, Executive Editor, ABA Commission on Women in the Profession, *Zero Tolerance: Best Practices for Combating Sex-Based Harassment in the Legal Profession*, at 43. See #34.

225. Dina Gerdeman, "Sexual Harassment: What Employers Should Do Now." See #215.

226. J. T. Jost, L. Rudman, I. V. Blair, et al., "The Existence of Implicit Bias Is Beyond Reasonable Doubt," 62. See #158.

227. Nabila Ahmed, "Wall Street Is Adding a New 'Weinstein Clause' Before Making Deals," Bloomberg, August 1, 2018, https://www.bloomberg.com/news/articles/2018-08-01/-weinstein-clause-creeps-into-deals-as-wary-buyers-seek-cover.

228. Vicki Schultz, "Open Statement on Sexual Harassment from Employment Discrimination Law Scholars." See #15, at 22, 31.

229. Wendi S. Lazar, Executive Editor, ABA Commission on Women in the Profession, *Zero Tolerance: Best Practices for Combating Sex-Based Harassment in the Legal Profession*, at 51–52. See #34.

230. Chai R. Feldblum and Victoria A. Lipnic, U.S. Equal Employment Opportunity Commission, Select Task Force on the Study of Harassment in the Workplace, June 2016. See #5, at 39.

231. Beth K. Whittenbury, *A Manager's Guide to Preventing Liability for Sexual Harassment in the Workplace* (CreateSpace Independent Publishing Platform, 2013).

232. Katie J. M. Baker, "What Do We Do with These Men?" *New York Times*, April 27, 2018, https://www.nytimes.com/2018/04/27/opinion/sunday/metoo-comebacks-charlie-rose.html?module=inline.

233. Chai R. Feldblum and Victoria A. Lipnic, U.S. Equal Employment Opportunity Commission, Select Task Force on the Study of Harassment in the Workplace, June 2016. See #5, at 38.

234. "What to Do with the 'Bad Men' of the #MeToo Movement," *New York Times*, May 2, 2018, https://www.nytimes.com/2018/05/02/opinion/bad-men-metoo-movement.html.

235. Ibid.

236. Ibid.

237. Ibid.

238. Ibid.

239. Wendi S. Lazar, Executive Editor, ABA Commission on Women in the Profession, *Zero Tolerance: Best Practices for Combating Sex-Based Harassment in the Legal Profession*, at 58. See #34.

240. Chai R. Feldblum and Victoria A. Lipnic, U.S. Equal Employment Opportunity Commission, Select Task Force on the Study of Harassment in the Workplace, June 2016. See #5, at 38.

241. Katie Johnston, "How Business Schools Are Teaching Students About Workplace Harassment," *Boston Globe*, May 3, 2018, https://www.bostonglobe.com/business/2018/05/03/tackling-workplace-sexual-harassment-before-starts/GHPOwWkvhqfaAsmGhQTdvJ/story.html.

242. Susan Bisom-Rapp, "Sex Harassment Training Must Change: The Case for Legal Incentives for Transformative Education and Prevention," *Stanford Law Review Online* 71 (2018): 64.

243. Jonathan W. Kunstman, "Sexual Overperception: Power, Mating Motives, and Biases in Social Judgment," *Journal of Personality and Social Psychology* 100, no. 2 (February 2011), 11.

244. Karen S. Lyness and Madeline E. Heilman, "When Fit Is Fundamental: Performance Evaluations and Promotions of Upper-Level Female and Male Managers," *Journal of Applied Psychology* 91, no. 4 (2006): 784.

245. Deborah Epstein and Lisa A. Goodman, "Discounting Women: Doubting Domestic Violence Survivors' Credibility and Dismissing Their Experiences." See #13, at 59–60.

246. Chai R. Feldblum and Victoria A. Lipnic, U.S. Equal Employment Opportunity Commission, Select Task Force on the Study of Harassment in the Workplace, June 2016. See #5, at 52.

247. Candace Bertotti and David Maxfield, "Most People Are Supportive of #MeToo. But Will Workplaces Actually Change?" See #197.

248. Chai R. Feldblum and Victoria A. Lipnic, U.S. Equal Employment Opportunity Commission, Select Task Force on the Study of Harassment in the Workplace, June 2016. See #5, at 25–30.

249. Brad Wolverton, "Penn State's Culture of Reverence Led to 'Total Disregard' for Children's Safety," *Chronicle of Higher Education*, July 12, 2012, https://www.chronicle.com/article/Penn-States-Culture-of/132853.

250. Dina Gerdeman, "Sexual Harassment: What Employers Should Do Now." See #215.

251. Wendi S. Lazar, Executive Editor, ABA Commission on Women in the Profession, *Zero Tolerance: Best Practices for Combating Sex-Based Harassment in the Legal Profession*, at 60. See #34.

252. Chai R. Feldblum and Victoria A. Lipnic, U.S. Equal Employment Opportunity Commission, Select Task Force on the Study of Harassment in the Workplace, June 2016. See #5, at 41.

253. Ibid., 16–17.

254. *Recommended Practices for Anti-Retaliation Programs*, Occupational Safety and Health Administration (2017), https://www.osha.gov/Publications/OSHA3905.pdf.

255. Ibid.

256. *See, e.g.*, Lauren Stiller Rikleen, *You Raised Us—Now Work with Us: Millennials, Career Success, and Building Strong Workplace Teams* (Chicago: American Bar Association, 2014).

257. Chai R. Feldblum and Victoria A. Lipnic, U.S. Equal Employment Opportunity Commission, Select Task Force on the Study of Harassment in the Workplace, June 2016. See #5, at 42.

258. Jennifer Schuessler, "The Prosecutor Who Stared Down Bill Cosby," *New York Times*, April 29, 2018, https://www.nytimes.com/2018/04/29/arts/television/cosby-kristen-feden-prosecutor.html.

259. Dina Gerdeman, "Sexual Harassment: What Employers Should Do Now." See #215.

260. Chai R. Feldblum and Victoria A. Lipnic, U.S. Equal Employment Opportunity Commission, Select Task Force on the Study of Harassment in the Workplace, June 2016. See #5, at 16.

261. Vicki Schultz, "Open Statement on Sexual Harassment from Employment Discrimination Law Scholars." See #15, at 47.

262. Ian Ayres and Cait Unkovic, "Information Escrows," *Michigan Law Review* 111, no. 2 (2012): 147. This article details a variety of ways in which

information escrows may be created, used, and safeguarded. It further analyzes, in the employment context, the employer's concerns about maintaining a strong affirmative defense to a lawsuit by demonstrating effective reporting mechanisms.

263. Wendi S. Lazar, Executive Editor, ABA Commission on Women in the Profession, *Zero Tolerance: Best Practices for Combating Sex-Based Harassment in the Legal Profession*, at 60. See #34.

264. *See, e.g.*, Joanna L. Grossman and Deborah L. Rhode, "Understanding Your Legal Options If You've Been Sexually Harassed," hbr.org, June 22, 2017. See #7.

265. Anna-Maria Marshall, "Idle Rights: Employees' Rights to Consciousness and the Construction of Sexual Harassment Policies," *Law & Society Review* 39, no. 1 (2005): 118.

266. FindLaw, "Sexual Harassment: What If It Happened at Your Firm?" January 10, 2018, https://careers.findlaw.com/legal-career-assessment/ sexual-harassment-what-if-it-happened-at-your-firm.html.

267. Heather McLaughlin, Christopher Uggen, and Amy Blackstone, "Sexual Harassment, Workplace Authority, and the Paradox of Power," *American Sociological Review* 77, no. 4 (August 2012): 641.

268. Dina Gerdeman, "Sexual Harassment: What Employers Should Do Now." See #215.

269. James L. Detert, "Cultivating Everyday Courage," *Harvard Business Review*, November–December 2018, https://www.hbr.org/2018/11/ cultivating-everyday-courage.

270. Ryan K. Jacobson and Asia A. Eaton, "How Organizational Policies Influence Bystander Likelihood of Reporting Moderate and Severe Sexual Harassment at Work," *Employee Responsibility and Rights Journal* 30, no. 1 (March 2018): 48–49.

271. Chai R. Feldblum and Victoria A. Lipnic, U.S. Equal Employment Opportunity Commission, Select Task Force on the Study of Harassment in the Workplace, June 2016. See #5, at 57.

272. Brigid Schulte, "To Combat Harassment, More Companies Should Try Bystander Training," HBR.org, October 31, 2018, https://hbr .org/2018/10/to-combat-harassment-more-companies-should-try-bystander-training.

273. Erin Mulvaney, "Men Are Worried, but EEOC Panel Finds Little Evidence to Support #MeToo Backlash Fears," *National Law Journal*,

October 31, 2018, https://www.law.com/2018/10/31/men-are-worried-but-eeoc-panel-finds-little-evidence-to-support-metoo-backlash-fears/?slret urn=20181109110741.

274. Joan C. Williams and Suzanne Lebsock, "Now What?" *Harvard Business Review*, https://hbr.org/cover-story/2018/01/now-what.

275. Claire Cain Miller, "Unintended Consequences of Sexual Harassment Scandals," *New York Times*, October 9, 2017. See #198.

Chapter 9

276. Sermon of Rabbi Danny Burkeman, delivered September 19, 2018, Temple Shir Tikva, Wayland, Massachusetts. Rabbi Burkeman's referred to Coach Urban Meyer's apology, which can be found at http://www.espn.com/college-football/story/_/id/24450171/urban-meyer-press-conference-ohio-state-buckeyes-sets-wrong-tone; Harvey Weinstein's statement can be found at https://www.nytimes.com/interactive/2017/10/05/us/statement-from-harvey-weinstein.html; Charlie Rose's statement can be found at https://www.vox.com/identities/2017/11/20/16682728/charlie-rose-apology-sexual-harassment. Rabbi Burkeman notes that, with respect to Rabbi Maimonides' comments on the elements of an apology, three of the stages are outlined in Hilchot Teshuva 1:1 and the fourth is added in Hilchot Teshuva 2:9. These texts are available in Hebrew and English on www.sefaria.org.

277. Robert I. Sutton, "Memo to the CEO: Are You the Source of Workplace Dysfunction?" See #115.

278. Nancy Gertner, "Losers' Rules," *Yale Law Journal* 122 (October 17, 2012). See #95, at 123.

279. Mary Beard, *Women & Power* (New York: Liveright Publishing Corporation, 2017), 16–17.

280. Ibid., 37.

281. Ibid., 38.

282. Ibid., 40.

283. Ibid., 52.

284. Ibid., 52.

285. Linda Bray Chanow and Lauren Stiller Rikleen, *Power in Law: Lessons from the 2011 Women's Power Summit on Law and Leadership* (January 2012), https://law.utexas.edu/cwil/2011-womens-power-summit/images/Summit_White_Paper-FINAL.pdf, at 9.

286. Robert I. Sutton, "Memo to the CEO: Are You the Source of Workplace Dysfunction?" See #115.

287. Paula A. Johnson, Sheila E. Widnall, and Frazier F. Benya, eds, *Sexual Harassment of Women: Climate, Culture, and Consequences in Academic Sciences, Engineering, and Medicine.* See #47, at 133–34.

288. Cynthia Grant Bowman, "Women in the Legal Profession from the 1920s to the 1970s: What Can We Learn from Their Experience About Law and Social Change?" *Cornell Law Faculty Publications*, Paper 12.

289. Jodi Kantor and Megan Twohey, "A Year of Reckoning," *New York Times*, October 6, 2018, https://www.nytimes.com/2018/10/06/sunday-review/me-too-weinstein-a-year-later.html.

Appendix

290. Lauren Stiller Rikleen, *"Survey of Workplace Conduct and Behaviors in Law Firms,"* Women's Bar Association of Massachusetts (2018), https://wbawbf.org/sites/default/files/WBA%20Survey%20of%20Workplace%20Conduct%20and%20Behaviors%20in%20Law%20Firms%20FINAL.pdf.

Index